Stall Points

Stall Points

Most Companies Stop Growing—
Yours Doesn't Have To

Matthew S. Olson and Derek van Bever

Yale University Press

New Haven & London

Set in Garamond and Stone Sans types by The Composing Room of Michigan, Inc.
Printed in the United States of America.

Library of Congress Cataloging-in-Publication Data
Olson, Matthew S., 1951–
    Stall points : most companies stop growing—yours doesn't have to / Matthew S.
Olson, Derek van Bever.
        p.   cm.
    Includes bibliographical references and index.
    ISBN 978-0-300-13687-6 (clothbound : alk. paper)
    1. Corporations—Growth.   2. Strategic planning.   3. Business planning.
I. Van Bever, Derek, 1957–   II. Title.
    HD2746.O47 2008
    658.4′012—dc22

                                                                    2008006073

A catalogue record for this book is available from the British Library.
The paper in this book meets the guidelines for permanence and durability of the
Committee on Production Guidelines for Book Longevity of the Council on Library
Resources.

10 9 8 7 6 5 4 3 2 1

To George Bodway of Hewlett-Packard and to his fellow members of the Corporate Executive Board—past, present, and future

Contents

Preface

Anyone setting out to write a book on growth is well advised to fortify for the journey by reading Pankaj Ghemawat's "Growth Boosters," a review of growth literature published in the July 2004 issue of the *Harvard Business Review*. In warming up to review recent publications from the leading consultancies, Ghemawat shares research he conducted through *Books in Print* on the market for new books on growth. His major finding? Regardless of the economic cycle, irrespective of overall publishing trends in the business book market, the literature on growth continues to, well, grow. He advises would-be authors to measure themselves against the highest standards of novelty, validity, and utility before adding their voices to the conversation. We kept this "Ghemawat standard" in mind as we set forth to write this book.

At the Corporate Executive Board, we have added steadily to the literature on growth across our twenty-five years of service to the world's leading executives, along the way guiding our members to best-practice standards in performance. For readers to whom we are new, the Corporate Executive Board is the premier network for leaders of the world's largest public and private organizations to improve their performance and that of their organizations. Serving over 80 percent of the Fortune 500, and with a third of our members headquartered outside the United States, we build membership programs around specific executive constituencies, such as heads of human resources, chief financial officers, and chief information officers, and then we conduct shared-cost research into the urgent concerns facing these executives. The history of our company can in many ways be viewed as a continuous inquiry into the challenges of growth and the best practices for overcoming them: each new executive constituency we serve brings its own perspective to the table.

For the members of our Corporate Strategy Board—several hundred heads of strategy, planning, and development at leading corporations worldwide—the quest to understand the keys to profitable growth has been especially vigorous, and it was in this membership that the book you are reading was conceived.

Stall Points is organized into three sections:

The growth experience of large firms. Relying on a comprehensive quantitative analysis of the growth experience of more than five hundred companies that have numbered among the Fortune 100 across the past fifty years, we explore how common it is for companies to stall in their growth and what the short-and long-term consequences of those stalls are. This analysis contains sobering news: it is common to stall, it is hard to see a stall coming, and it is extremely hard to recover from a stall. In fact, companies that do not recover quickly face long odds at returning to a sustainable growth track. Ever.

The root causes of growth stalls. We complement the quantitative analysis with detailed case analysis of a subset of the Fortune 100 to determine why growth stalls occur. Although we identified forty-two individual root causes in our analysis, the good news for executives is that these causes cluster: four categories account for just over half of all stalls we cataloged. Further, the vast majority of stalls are controllable—related to some strategy choice or organization design decision made by senior management. We describe each of the root causes of stalls in this section and provide a self-test for each, so that the reader may self-diagnose the degree to which any of these "red flags" are at work in his or her organization.

Avoiding (or recovering from) growth stalls. The controllability of stall points that we describe above leads us to the central implication of our work for executives: you must continually articulate and stress-test the assumptions underlying your strategy because it is the assumptions that you believe the most deeply or that you have held as true for the longest time that are likely to prove your undoing. You may think you are currently doing this, but the odds are that you are not, and it is an oversight that you suffer at your peril. We present in this section a set of practices in use in leading corporations to articulate key assumptions with precision, to open them to the organization for scrutiny, and to monitor them continuously to spot changes in the external environment that might render them obsolete. Our final chapter presents guidance to readers who fear that their organization might be in the midst of a stall, based on our analysis of the strategies of organizations we have called "restarters."

Stall Points is written with four audiences in mind. The first is general managers and executive management of companies, who carry a fiduciary responsibility for charting a course to growth for their organizations. Our hope is that you will find in the cases and practices we include here some actionable, proven approaches for challenging—and improving—current revenue plans and assumptions.

Second, we intend this book as a reference for the chief strategist, charged more generally with stewardship for growth across the longer term. (Indeed, one of our principal takeaways from early presentations of this material is the benefit to be gained by positioning the strategic planning function as the "conscience" for revenue beyond the tactical planning horizon.) For both purposes, we have included as much richness from our research files on the case-study companies as seemed advisable in a book whose overall length we have tried to contain.

Third, we intend this book for boards of directors and the governance community generally. We believe that the board is uniquely placed to challenge management assumptions underlying strategy and to ensure that the results of that challenge are being acted on, but we also believe that this role has been increasingly forfeit in recent years. The cause of this inattention, of course, has been one of epic distraction amid the "shot from the woods" of corporate governance reform. Ironically, however, the forces for board independence that have arisen as a result have served to reduce the intimacy of the typical board with company and industry issues. We believe in a limited role for the board in strategy-making; indeed, in our view, it is not the responsibility of the board to make strategy, it is the responsibility of the board to ensure that management *has* a strategy and that resources are being allocated effectively to support that strategy. And we believe that oversight performance here must improve. Testing of the assumptions underlying firm strategy is risk management in its purest— and potentially most helpful—form.

Last, we intend this book for students of business. We have taught aspects of this work at Harvard Business School, at the graduate business programs of George Washington University and Georgetown University, and to roomfuls of institutional analysts and investors, and we have seen firsthand how helpful it is to frame this exciting terrain in a way that invites and supports purposeful discussion and learning.

We dedicate this book to George Bodway, former manager of strategic planning for Hewlett-Packard, and to his fellow members of the Corporate Executive Board past and present, who have taught us across the years that at the heart of any worthy inquiry lies a worthy question. *Stall Points* explores just such a question.

A Letter to Growth Leaders: Applying the Lessons of Stall Points to Your Organization

To Growth Leaders:

Despite the ocean of academic literature and consulting advice on the subject, growth strategy continues to be one of the least understood management disciplines. As hard as it is to craft compelling strategy alternatives, it is often even harder to diagnose with precision the deep sources of weakness in your current strategy.

Perhaps the cruelest aspect of the growth challenge is that, by the time you spot those deep sources of weakness, it's too late—you've hit the stall point. If an organization you've led has experienced such a growth stall, what may have been most surprising was its suddenness. Most organizations actually *accelerate* into a stall, with growth going negative just as if the props had been knocked out from under their corporate strategy. Few on the senior team typically see the stall coming: core performance metrics often fail to register that trouble is on the horizon. And unless the team can diagnose the causes and regain the growth track quickly—turning the company around within several years of the stall—the odds are against their ever returning to healthy top-line growth. The average company, when measured against the S&P 500 index, loses 74 percent of its market capitalization in the decade surrounding that growth stall, and the chief executive and senior team turn over more than half the time.

Gauging Your Stall Risk

To estimate the risk you currently run of a stall, take the following self-test. As you reflect on strategy conversations in your organization, do any of the following statements sound familiar?

A CHECKLIST OF STRATEGY ASSERTIONS (CHECK AS MANY BOXES AS APPLY)

☐ "Our customers will continue to value our premium-priced innovations."
☐ "Our customers are willing to pay higher prices for our great service."
☐ "Our brand has power—it protects us from new competitors."
☐ "We accept lower market share for high margins."
☐ "Our quality enables us to sustain a price position in the market that is 'good enough but not best.'"
☐ "We are planning some major acquisitions that will ramp up our growth."
☐ "Our core market is getting saturated—we need to step out into greenfield opportunities."
☐ "The businesses in our portfolio might be viewed as too broad, but they are complementary—when one business is in a down cycle, others tend to be up."
☐ "It's okay to take a growth time-out to fix core operations."
☐ "Our senior team is very effective—we've all grown up and worked together for years."

How many boxes did you check? Three? Four? Five or more? It wouldn't be surprising if you did. The strategy assertions listed above are fairly common. They can serve as the foundation of a powerful, well-tooled business system, and in fact the assertions we present here are particularly prevalent in the strategies of market leaders. What also unites the statements in the list is that they represent a specific type of strategy assertion—a *strategic assumption,* an observation about markets or competitors or technologies that arises from direct observation, is then enshrined in the strategic plan, gets translated into operational guidance, and eventually hardens into accepted orthodoxy.

But although these statements are common and have their origins in the real world, they are no less dangerous for that. The strategic assumptions listed here have figured in the growth stalls of companies as varied as 3M, Apple, Banc One, Caterpillar, Daimler-Benz, Levi Strauss, Toys "R" Us, and Volvo. So although having the above assumptions somewhere in your strategic plan does not ensure that your growth will stall, it does indicate that you are exposed to a risk that has brought down exemplary organizations in the past.

Why Most Companies Stop Growing

So which are they, these assumptions—strategy foundation or unhedged risk? The problem is that they can be both. What typically happens is that, across time, an assumption migrates from one to the other, from an accurate depiction of the world to a dangerously misguided or obsolete perspective. In fact, the situation is slightly more dire than this. Our analysis of hundreds of stall points in leading companies has led us to the fundamental conclusion that the assumptions a management team holds most deeply—has known so long or so well that they are no longer actively debated—pose the greatest danger to growth. In other words, it's not what you know that isn't so that will stop your growth run—more than likely, it's what you know that's *no longer* so.

For a variety of reasons, questioning assumptions is not something that most top teams do, or do well. The senior executive team does not effectively stress-test the assumptions on which strategy is based to ensure that those assumptions continue to reflect external market realities and customer preferences. Part of the explanation is the nature of the senior executive mandate: the CEO and his or her executive team are paid to develop a vision and then execute that vision—with resolve. Another is human nature: introspection and self-doubt don't figure highly in the personality profile of the executives at the top of great enterprises. And a final part is process: there are few "safe" rooms for a CEO to express midnight anxieties. And as for the senior line: if we're being honest, the "Assumptions and Risks" section in virtually all strategic plan templates is generally treated as a pro forma exercise rather than as an occasion to "go deep."

What You Can Do about It

The good news for the reader of this book is that we now know enough to guide you in the questions you should ask—the places that you should feel vulnerable—to avoid the fate that has befallen your predecessors. The Stall Points Initiative profiled here is a thoroughly researched and quantitatively grounded analysis into the causes of top-line growth stalls in large organizations and of the specific practices currently being used to avoid these stalls. Our database is the growth experience of the Fortune 100 across the past half-century of commercial history, but we believe that the insights from our analysis apply to a much broader set of high-growth, high-ambition firms.

A Five-Step Plan for Using This Book

This book contains guidance for all the constituents involved in setting and monitoring growth strategy: the CEO, the senior line, the strategy staff, and the board of directors. In directing your team how to use this book, we suggest that you prioritize the following five steps:

1. The chief executive and the strategy team should read the entire book, paying particular attention to part I, "The Growth Experience of Large Firms," and part III, "Avoiding (or Recovering from) Growth Stalls." Chapters 12 and 13 contain six practices that you should evaluate for potential implementation in your organization.
2. Senior line and staff should read at least parts II and III of the book to build their literacy as to why companies stall and how leading companies avoid, or recover from, stalls.
3. Have all members of the senior team take the self-test entitled "'Red Flag' Warnings of an Impending Stall" (appendix 5). We have built a confidential survey tool into the Web site associated with this book to make this easy to accomplish (www.stallpoints.executiveboard.com). Charge your head of strategy or an external facilitator with analyzing the results to identify areas of agreement (and disagreement) and to lead a group discussion targeted on these areas.
4. Following this conversation, identify the practices you wish to adopt in order to identify and track strategic assumptions on an ongoing basis. Our Web site houses not only additional information on the practices profiled in the book but also an ongoing conversation on your peers' reactions and plans.
5. If you and your team are in the midst of grappling with a growth stall, you will want to review the guidance we provide in the postscript, "If You're in Freefall." We make five recommendations to guide restart strategy drawn from our observations of organizations that have successfully restarted growth.

Every element of the Stall Points Initiative—this book, the exercises it contains, the Web site and tools the site links to, and the executive network that stands behind it—is designed for the reader's use. Our hope is that these resources constitute a powerful asset for performance improvement for leadership teams that are willing to invest the work and time required to get better at this critical activity.

If at any time we might help your organization apply the insights contained in this book, please feel free to call on us.

FOR THE CORPORATE EXECUTIVE BOARD

Matthew S. Olson
Derek van Bever

Part I The Growth Experience

of Large Firms

Chapter 1 What Are the Limits to Growth?

When we are asked to address a group of executives or business school students on the subject of corporate growth, we typically start the conversation by posing a simple question: Is there any absolute limit (theoretical or empirical) to how large a company can grow? And we depict the choice at the center of this thought experiment with an illustration (fig. 1.1). Two curves—both proceeding from the origin at a forty-five-degree angle, but the curve on the left tapers off and flattens whereas its counterpart on the right continues its northeastward march. Which would you choose?

In the rooms we've polled, it's generally a close call. The voting typically shades toward the "no limits" side of the question, but not by much—maybe sixty to forty or so. The "pro-limits" group support their view with reference to the array of ills that flesh is heir to: the increasing complexity that comes with size, the managerial challenge of growing an ever larger denominator, and the like. The "no limits" camp runs to the principle in the wording of the question—that there is no law, no theoretical requirement, that growth tail off and that the combined effects of globalization of markets, improving management

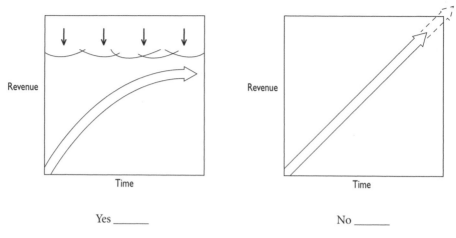

Fig. 1.1 Which side are you on?

science, and the rise of information technology continue to provide ample running room for large corporations to grow.

Proponents on either side of the debate can marshal impressive academic authority. In his classic study *The Visible Hand,* the economic historian Alfred Chandler provided a foundation under the bullish side of the argument, celebrating the power of such forces as divisionalization and vertical integration to enable corporations to achieve a size and scope never before seen in the world economy. Members of the cautionary camp cite the reasoning of Edith Penrose, who argued in *The Theory of the Growth of the Firm* that company growth must slow of necessity as managerial demand outstrips internal (and external) supply. More recently, Clayton Christensen of Harvard Business School, among others, has argued that resource allocation systems at large corporations simply cannot direct resources efficiently to the (initially) small markets that define tomorrow's high-growth opportunities.[1]

What makes the question most provocative, perhaps, is that there is truth on both sides. It's entirely natural to assume that there are limits to growth—both as to the absolute size that an organization can attain as well as to the rate of growth that it can sustain as it gets larger. Our analysis of the growth experience of large firms across the past century does suggest, however, that we are getting progressively better at engineering longer and higher runs of growth—even in our largest enterprises.

THE ORIGINS OF THE STALL POINTS INITIATIVE

The question is certainly not academic for the executives setting strategy at our largest corporations. Starting about a decade ago, we were given a glimpse into the internal deliberations over this issue in one of the modern era's iconic growth companies, Hewlett-Packard.

In the spring of 1996, we were meeting in Palo Alto with George Bodway, then the manager of corporate planning for Hewlett-Packard. We were there to interview him for a separate research project, and during our time together he showed us an interesting analysis he'd done a couple of months earlier.

As part of a longer-range look for planning purposes, Bodway had plotted a growth path for Hewlett-Packard to see just how big the company would become if it kept up its historical rate of growth. Kind of a pleasant, dreamy exercise for the strategist. And, as students of modern business history are aware, HP's growth performance is extraordinarily distinguished. Forty years of remarkably consistent 20 percent compound annual growth across the modern era, breaking into the Fortune 50 in 1987, climbing to Fortune 14 by 1997. Bodway's extrapolation suggested that, at its historical trend line, HP would be Fortune 10 by the turn of the century, Fortune 5 a few years later, and Fortune 1 by 2010.

Bodway spotted a problem, however, when he plotted the growth rates of the Fortune 1, 5, and 10 companies across time—3.3 percent, 4.6 percent, and 7.8 percent, respectively. And here comes HP, growing at a 19.5 percent annual clip and with no intention of slowing down. An irresistible force meeting a seemingly immovable object. Clearly a problem for a company that has taken no small pride over the years in its ability to invent and grow.

Once alerted to this impending collision, Corporate Planning at HP decided to tackle head-on the issue of barriers to large corporate growth. Beginning in the summer of 1996, they assembled what they called the HP Growth Initiative, a diverse group of academics, corporations, and research partners, to study various aspects of the problem. For our part, the Corporate Executive Board was invited to establish the fact set—the historical analysis of how often and why large companies stall. Our project had two parts, each a formidable undertaking. The first was a longitudinal analysis of the growth history of every company that has ever been featured in the Fortune 50, from the inception of the index in 1955 to the present day, to understand how prevalent growth stalls are in large companies and what impact stalls have on market capitalization, employment, net income growth, and future growth prospects. The second was a deep dive into a set of fifty companies representative of the overall sample to understand *why* companies stall. A team of analysts at our firm conducted exhaustive secondary research on each of these companies—journal articles, books, case studies, analyst reports—as well as personal interviews with company representatives and outside experts. We filled a six-drawer file cabinet with dossiers on the fifty companies and then analyzed each case to determine the root causes of company stalls and, as important, their contemporary perspectives on growth. So, for each company, we asked whether management saw the stall coming, what the consequences of the stall were, and what, if anything, management did to attempt to overcome it.

This, then, was the original Stall Points Initiative, prepared at the direction of the HP working group and shared with that group and, after that, with member companies of the Corporate Executive Board. The findings were sobering to all the participants—no one more so than the HP management team (with a name like "Stall Points," it's pretty clear that the study will deliver some hard messages!). To bring our story up to the moment, HP, of course, experienced a much different decade than the one that George Bodway envisioned on that early exhibit: the divestiture of Agilent in 1999, a growth stall in 2001, the page 1 drama of the Carly Fiorina years. As of this writing, the company is recovering rather handsomely, having responded to the Dell challenge with a wholesale renovation of the business model in its personal systems group, but all eyes are on revenue growth. The company sits at Fortune 14, posting positive revenue growth of 7 percent to 8 percent per year, and closing in on the $100 billion revenue mark.

THE RISE OF THE CLASS OF 2015

What has caused us to update the analysis and to share this work with a broader audience is our belief that the lessons we have learned about stall points in corporate growth are important for a broadening set of leadership teams to understand and to act on. Two clear trends that have been developing across the past decade create urgency for these firms in the present hour—and in the years ahead.

One of the most challenging aspects of the Stall Points analysis is our finding that the historical record strongly suggests the existence of a "danger zone" for stalls—an absolute level, measured in revenues, by which most large firms have stalled in their growth. (This "danger zone" is described more fully in chapter 2.) The danger zone has risen steadily across the past fifty years, at about the rate of overall GNP growth, and is at approximately $40 billion today.

What gives this finding particular relevance is that an unprecedented number of firms will be approaching this danger zone in the coming years. We call this phenomenon "the rise of the Class of 2015"—a swelling in the ranks of large corporations that has been developing across the past several decades and that will become unmistakable across the coming decade. A consequence of this trend toward corporate giantism—an unprecedented number of firms aiming to reach unprecedented size—is that a large number of executive teams are today architecting their way into the stall danger zone.

The increasing concentration of wealth and size at the top of industry league tables has been well remarked in the literature on growth. In an excellent analysis entitled "Strategy in an Era of Global Giants," Lowell Bryan and Michele Zanini of McKinsey and Company mark the rise across the past several decades of what they call the "mega-institution."[2] The specific subjects of their study are the 150 global companies with the largest market capitalization at the end of 2004. As a group, and as individual enterprises, these megainstitutions have come to command an ever-larger share of markets and market capitalization, and, in the extreme, to redefine our understanding of just how large a company can grow. In 2004, the *average* megainstitution had $79 billion in market capitalization, $48 billion in revenue, net income of over $4.4 billion, and more than a hundred thousand employees. Even in this field of titans, the largest of the large have reached almost unbelievable scale compared to historical precedent: Wal-Mart, with 1.7 million employees and $286 billion in revenue (2004 figures); Exxon Mobil, with $25 billion in net income in the same year; General Electric with a 2004 market capitalization approaching $400 billion.

Beyond the unprecedented growth in size of the occupants at the top of the league tables, we expect the ranks of megafirms making up the Class of 2015 to grow substantially across the coming decade. To size this phenomenon, we calculated how many firms today are at the size that it took to be in the Fortune 100 when the index was created, in 1955. That is, if you could be in the top one hundred in 1955 with $300 million in revenue (as was American Standard, the original occupant of the Fortune 100 slot), what would that translate to today ($1.8 billion), and how many companies are at that size or greater? We then modeled this growth rate out an additional decade, to 2015.[3] In short, the population of megafirms has multiplied almost thirtyfold (from 100 to 2,808) in the past fifty years and will double again across the next decade, to 6,728, in

2015. By far the fastest growth in this population will be outside the United States: the number of non-U.S. firms rises from 1,800 in 2004 to 5,200 in 2015. More than 6,700 firms, all barreling headlong toward the danger zone for stalls we have described above. Does a trap, or snare, await the leadership teams of these firms as they execute against their high ambitions?

THE INCREASING CHALLENGE OF TOP-LINE GROWTH

The challenge of growth is, of course, not just on the agenda of this population of aspiring high-fliers. The stated growth goals of management teams across the large corporate economy reflect a desire to return to the lush growth rates of the late 1990s. This ambition is proving ever more elusive, however. Our analysis of the growth rates of companies with $1 billion in revenue and above reveals that aggregate growth rates of companies in the first five years of the present century are only just over half those of the five years prior, in the late 1990s. In this population, average annual growth rates were 9.2 percent from 1995 to 2000, falling to 4.9 percent in the years 2000–2005. This decline is especially severe for companies in the $10 billion+ revenue category, posting annual growth rates from 2000 to 2005 of only 4.3 percent, compared to 8 percent from 1995 to 2000. This low single-digit growth reality stands in marked contrast to the much-voiced desire for renewed growth by market and industry leaders.

Part of what may be going on here is that we are reaching the end of the road of the formula for producing income growth that has characterized the recent past. To spot this, we examined the substantial delinking of income growth rates from revenue growth rates that has been under way since the mid-1990s, with the former now accelerating away from the latter (fig. 1.2). The exhibit tracks the year-over-year growth, in five-year periods from 1955 to 2005, of income and revenue for the universe of very large (Fortune 100–sized) firms. We also divide this time stretch into three eras. The first, which extends across the first thirty years of this period and is, we would argue, the normative state, we've called the Era of Congruent Growth Rates. In this era, revenue growth and income growth roughly track with each other. The second period, from 1985 to 2000, we've dubbed the Era of Corporate Restructuring. In this period, income growth pulls away from revenue growth, separated by a full five points by 2000. The final period, to the present day, we call the Era of Delinked Bottom-Line Growth, with income growth exceeding revenue growth by fully ten percentage points.

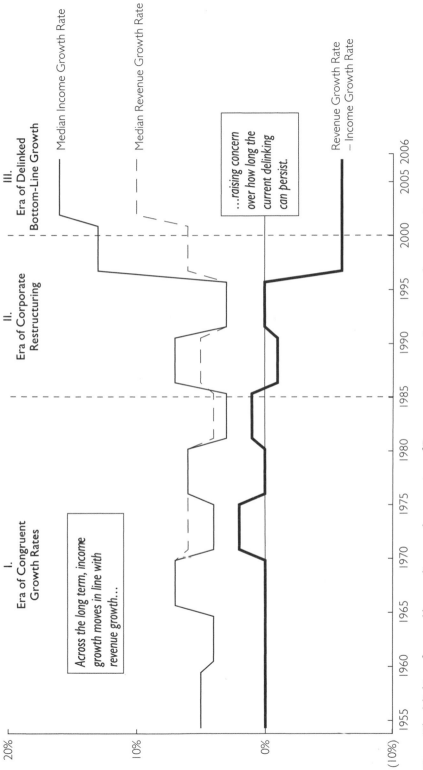

Fig. 1.2 The delinking of top- and bottom-line growth: comparison of Fortune 100 revenue vs. income growth, 1955–2006

The reaction of the typical corporate executive or general manager when shown this chart is anything but alarm. After all, coaxing greater and greater returns from a dollar of revenue is practically the core requirement of a business leader today. But the longer view represented across fifty years brings today's challenge into focus. The early 1990s period of corporate restructuring and business process reengineering appears to have set up an income growth ramp that top-line growth has not been able to match. With large firm income growing more than twice as fast as revenue, the crux question becomes, "How long can this unprecedented delinking persist?"

EXTENDING THE GROWTH RUN

The "growth expectancy" of the corporation is commonly presented as an S-curve—an adolescence of varying length spent searching for a viable formula around which to organize, followed by (for the fortunate) a decades-long rush of growth as the correct formula catches in the marketplace.

Less well recognized—perhaps because of its subtlety, perhaps the difficulty of organizing discussion around an emerging uncomfortable truth—a "stall point," a distinct downward inflection in the growth rate that, for most companies, is a one-time event with lasting consequences. That moment one would isolate, from some future vantage, as the end of the era of high growth and the beginning of a more certain period of maturity and stability. This period is also marked by lower valuation as the market adjusts to the expectation of a future state for the company in which income growth must increasingly shoulder the market valuation burden over revenue growth.[4]

What is perhaps most remarkable about this pattern is not that it is so often repeated, but that the final movements—the stall and its consequences—are, from time to time, delayed by companies and leadership teams able to extend the growth run long past expectation. This accomplishment, because it is rare, commands an audience all its own in the financial community and serves as an almost irresistible attractant to talent.

DEFINING THE LIMITS TO GROWTH

So what exactly causes very large companies to reach the end of their growth runs? When companies suffer these major, multiyear inflection points in their growth histories that we have labeled "stalls," is it due to exterior market conditions, regulatory constraints, or some sort of mysterious, internal organizational dynamic? The question is hardly a stale one, either for the executive teams at modern megafirms such as Hewlett-Packard or Microsoft or Wal-Mart, or for society as a whole, with an impending wave of corporate giantism breaking over the world's economies across the coming decade.

It has been hard for even the most empirical thinkers to avoid resorting to analogies to human growth and energies when considering this question. More than a century ago, Alfred Marshall, in his *Principles of Economics,* compared the life cycle of a company to that of a person growing in strength into maturity, and then inevitably declining, until replaced by younger, more vigorous competitors.[5] Here, the classic S-curve of corporate growth prevails, with the small company struggling, then finally hitting on its growth formula, accelerating up through the middle market and into the ranks of large corporations, and eventually flattening its growth curve into expected maturity.

Just as intuitively obvious is the line of thinking that very large firms must reach apogee when they have effectively saturated their markets. There is the unsophisticated take on this ("How many more Wal-Marts can America support?"), as well as more complex arguments about the global saturation of demand for many categories of "middle-class" products and services.[6]

From another angle, theorists in the fields of population ecology and industrial organization have grappled with the question of decline, usually from the point of view that it is simply unavoidable, governed by the fairly immutable laws of organizational life cycle theory.[7] As Henry Mintzberg, a penetrating observer who looks at the issue from the dual perspectives of organizational theory and corporate strategy, has written, "Should we not be encouraging the demise of large spent organizations, so that they can be replaced in a natural cycle of renewal by younger, smaller, less constrained and more vibrant ones?"[8] Henry Kravis could hardly have put it better.

Despite the academic interest in the issue, relatively few applied studies have been done. And those that have been done have tended to look at the shorter-term volatility of corporate growth performance. Illustrative here is a 2005 study by McKinsey and Company that looked at large corporate "topple rates"—the probability that a company in the top quintile of revenue growth performance in its industry would fall out of it within five years. Not surprisingly, they found that this rate had tripled since the mid-1970s and that the culprit was a confluence of forces they dubbed "hypercompetition."[9]

Let's examine the empirical record as to the limits of growth and pull our focus up to the sweep of the century just past.

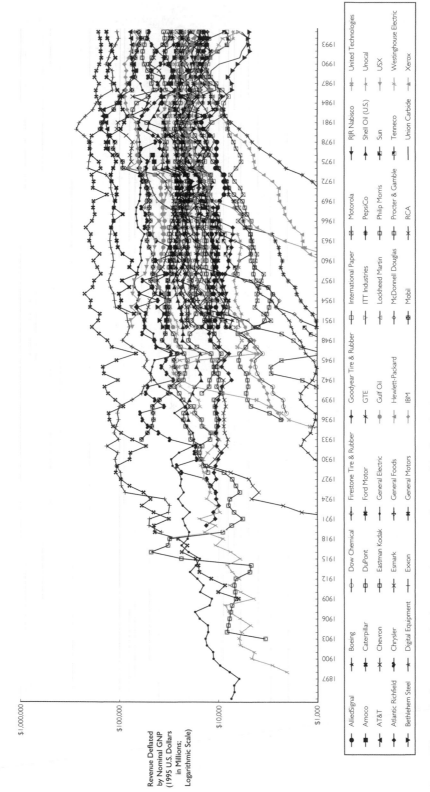

Fig. 1.3 What are the barriers to unbroken growth? Revenue history of the forty-five largest U.S. corporations, 1895–1995

IS THERE AN UPPER BOUND TO GROWTH?

First, as to absolute size, the collective empirical experience of the large corporate sector suggests that there is indeed some outer boundary that we are pressing against—some upper limit to growth that we are redefining across time but that contains our ambitions at any moment.

This upper limit is illustrated most clearly in an analysis that served as the jumping-off point for the initiative that gave birth to this book (fig. 1.3). Prepared by analysts in the strategy department of Hewlett-Packard, the exhibit portrays the top-line growth experience of the forty-five largest U.S. corporations across the twentieth century. We've blown it up to wall-chart size in our offices, but even at the scale we've reproduced it here you can clearly grasp the two perspectives it offers. If you focus on the distinct lines in the exhibit, you can follow the growth experience of individual titans: General Electric on a growth tear at the end of the nineteenth century; Westinghouse bursting onto the scene shortly thereafter; RCA on vertical ascent in the early 1920s. If, on the other hand, you step back and squint, to look at the growth experience of the companies as a whole, you see a more meaningful pattern—what we've come to call the "cloud layer" in the picture. Whatever growth trajectory individual companies are on, their trajectories flatten, or stall, as they approach the top of the league tables, and then converge back into the pack. As if their growth ambitions have been held back or contained by some hidden hand exerting downward force.

Second, the flattening of growth rate with size that the cloud layer image suggests is not true just for this set of companies—the largest of the large corporations—it is broadly true of the large corporate economy as a whole. To test this proposition, we conducted an analysis of the growth rate across the past decade of sixteen hundred publicly traded companies with revenues greater than $1 billion and plotted this against their size at the end of the period (fig. 1.4). At the lower end of the size spectrum—companies with 2006 revenue of approximately $1 billion—you see a wide range of growth rates—from negative 20 percent to 160 percent. As you move from left to right, you see a narrowing and flattening of real revenue growth rates, to an average of 6 percent for companies $100 billion and above. Why is this result so common, so predictable?

These exhibits represent two perspectives on growth in the large corporate sector: one a movie, if you will, of the growth experience of a small set of the largest firms in the American economy across a century; the other a snapshot of

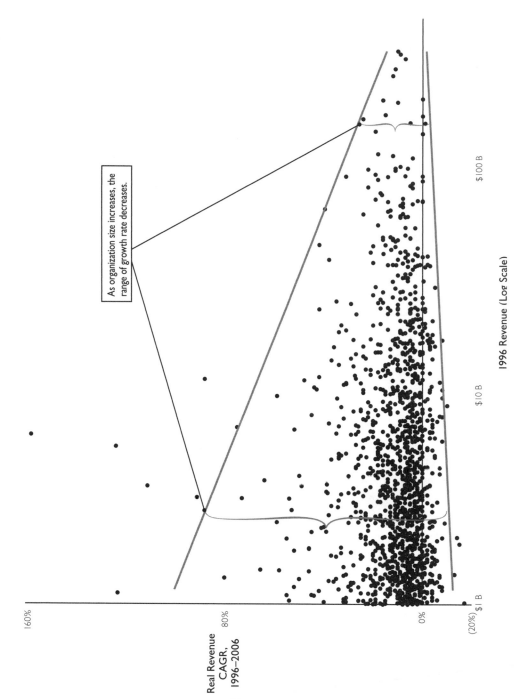

Real Revenue
CAGR,
1996–2006

As organization size increases, the
range of growth rate decreases.

160%

80%

0%

(20%) $1 B

$10 B

$100 B

1996 Revenue (Log Scale)

Fig. 1.4 Intuitively correct—size matters to growth rate: revenue growth rate vs. size, 1,600 publicly traded companies

the relation between size and growth for a much broader set of firms, across a briefer and more recent time frame. And yet neither view offers insight into the core questions on the mind of senior executives: How common is it for a company to stall in its growth? Is it inevitable? When does it happen? Why does it happen? Can I avoid a stall or delay it or recover from it?

These are the questions we attempt to answer in this book, and we've devoted an extraordinary amount of effort into understanding the dynamics of growth in the large corporate sector. What we've learned is that the growth runs of large firms do typically meet turning points across history and that these turning points, or stalls, carry real consequences for the prospects of these companies and their leaders—in the moment and across time. Learning what *particular* factors—in market situations or in organizational dynamics or in particular managerial decisions—were centrally important to these inflections, and from these experiences learning how to spot these causes in time to extend a growth run, is the ambition of this book.

Chapter 2 Stall Points in Companies' Growth Runs

As we noted in the preceding chapter, we secured our seat at the table of the HP Growth Initiative by undertaking a large assignment: to review the growth history of companies in the large corporate sector and identify the incidence and consequences of growth stalls, as well as their causes, in this population. For the population we have selected for study—all Fortune 100–sized companies across the past half century—that is a large task indeed. More than five hundred companies across fifty years—twenty-five thousand years of company experience to mine for insight. How does the analyst decide where to focus?

Given the immensity of the task, we developed a methodology that allowed us to identify and focus in on the most significant periods in the histories of these companies—the major turning points, rather than two- or three-year turns in fortune. We provide a complete explanation of our methodology in appendix 2. The element of our methodology that is important for the general reader to understand is the useful construct of the "stall point."

Stall points represent secular, multiyear turning points in a company's fortune—significant downturns in corporate revenue growth.

Two terms in the foregoing sentence merit clarification: by "significant," we intend differentiation from short-term, or cyclical, downturns and from subtle, or slight, changes in growth rates; by "downturn," we intend slower—though not necessarily negative—growth. Any given stall point is, of course, overly precise; its utility lies in helping us identify the period in corporate history most worthy of detailed examination. As we explain below, the stall points we identify represent the year of greatest difference, or delta, in growth rate; they are not necessarily the year that management began to act on their growth challenges, nor are they typically the beginning (or end) of the reversal in company fortunes. Probably the best way to think about the stall point is that it marks the year when someone close to the company (an executive, perhaps, or an outside observer or analyst) could no longer miss that trouble of some sort was brewing. This makes stall points remarkably useful places to locate our inquiry.

THE SEARCH FOR STALL DELTAS

We identified the revenue stall points for a company by comparing the ten-year growth rate before and after each year of company history in the period under study. The difference between the two—between the growth rates of those ten-year blocks—was what we termed the "stall delta" for that year. At the tail ends of the study period, we shortened preceding or subsequent ten-year periods as needed to broaden the range of years for analysis (for example, comparing the ten years between 1991 and 2001 to the five years from 2001 to 2006). The years in which the deltas reach maximum values—the fixed points in time where slowing growth rates are most acute—define the stall points for a particular company.

To illustrate our methodology, we reproduce a twenty-year trace of history for the Goodrich Corporation (fig. 2 1). From its founding in Akron, Ohio, in 1870, by Benjamin Franklin Goodrich, the company's history has been marked by innovation, with polyvinyl chloride (PVC), synthetic rubber, and tubeless tires among the landmark early discoveries of the company's labs. The company ranked forty-four in the Fortune 100 for 1955, at $630 million in revenue, and broke through the $1 billion mark a dozen years later, in 1967.

The company's more recent history has been significantly choppier, including a complete refocus of the firm away from its signature tire business, which it exited in 1988. When across the last fifty years, from 1955 to the present day, can Goodrich be said to have stalled? The time slice of history that we reproduce here contains the answer. To address this question, we examined the

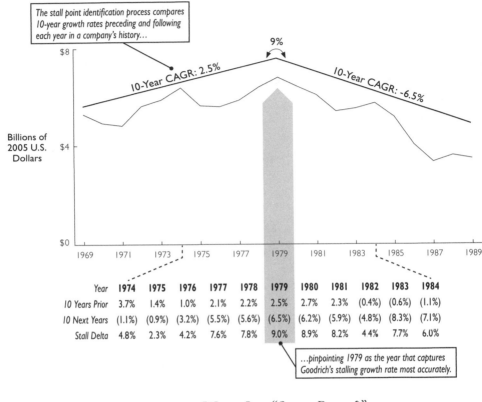

The stall point identification process compares 10-year growth rates preceding and following each year in a company's history...

9%

$8

10-Year CAGR: 2.5%

10-Year CAGR: -6.5%

Billions of 2005 U.S. Dollars

$4

$0

| 1969 | 1971 | 1973 | 1975 | 1977 | 1979 | 1981 | 1983 | 1985 | 1987 | 1989 |

Year	1974	1975	1976	1977	1978	1979	1980	1981	1982	1983	1984
10 Years Prior	3.7%	1.4%	1.0%	2.1%	2.2%	2.5%	2.7%	2.3%	(0.4%)	(0.6%)	(1.1%)
10 Next Years	(1.1%)	(0.9%)	(3.2%)	(5.5%)	(5.6%)	(6.5%)	(6.2%)	(5.9%)	(4.8%)	(8.3%)	(7.1%)
Stall Delta	4.8%	2.3%	4.2%	7.6%	7.8%	9.0%	8.9%	8.2%	4.4%	7.7%	6.0%

...pinpointing 1979 as the year that captures Goodrich's stalling growth rate most accurately.

─────WHAT IS A "STALL POINT?"─────

A "stall point" is the moment in time that best represents a turning point, or significant downturn, in corporate revenue growth.

Fig. 2.1 Where's the stall point? Analysis of BFGoodrich revenue growth, 1969–1989

differential in the growth rate for the decade before and after each year in the study period. So, for example, if we zero in on 1974, the first column below the graphic, we can see that the growth rate for the ten years before 1974 was 3.7 percent, while the growth rate for the ten years beyond was (1.1 percent), creating a differential, or delta, of 4.8 percent. Scanning across that bottom row, the year of greatest absolute delta was 1979, the year that captures Goodrich's stalling growth rate most accurately.

Using this methodology, we repeated the above analysis for each of the more

---

WHY REVENUE GROWTH?

Readers of this book who judge their performance by metrics other than revenue growth may be wondering why we chose revenue and not profits, value, or some other measure to focus our analysis of historical growth and stall patterns. It is a fair question, and one that we considered at length.

Our choice of revenue rests on two premises. The first is that revenue growth more than any other metric is the primary driver of long-term company performance. This is not to say that revenue growth without profits is desirable but to suggest that high growth through margin management alone is not sustainable. The second reason is more mundane: it's hard to "engineer," or manipulate, the top line across time. By contrast, market value and profit measures are much more variable. Deflating market capitalization by an underlying index can eliminate some, but not all, of this variability; and as for profit, the combined effect of one-time charges, changes in accounting rules, and the inevitable short-term manipulations make for numerous peaks and valleys.

Because the focus of our study was broad—hundreds of firms across dozens of industries—and long—stretching across more than fifty years—we focused on revenue performance to guide us to the most meaningful turning points in corporate growth history.

---

than five hundred companies we included in the sample, for the fifty years of modern commercial history that we analyzed. We were able to divide companies by whether or not they had suffered a stall, as well as how much warning insiders and outsiders had that a stall was coming. In the balance of this chapter, we review the four major lessons to arise from this analysis: The Near Certainty of a Stall; Stall Points Rising across Time; The (External) Invisibility of an Impending Stall; and The Myth of "Soft Landings."

THE NEAR CERTAINTY OF A STALL

Perhaps the easiest observation to make from our analysis of the growth experience of Fortune 100 companies across time is that most large companies stall. It

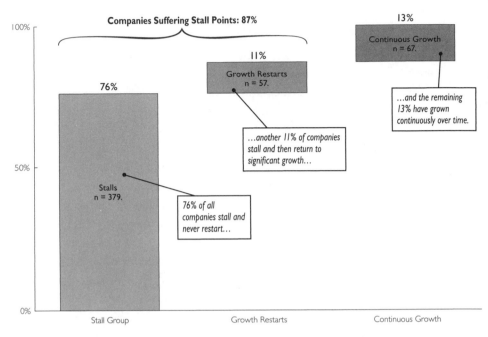

Fig. 2.2 Stacked odds: growth experience of Fortune 100–sized company sample

is a commonplace to note that "trees don't grow to the sky," but what is slightly more interesting is the range of sizes at which companies stall: companies can stall at any size, though the vast majority of stalls occur in the $1 to $10 billion revenue range. So stalls can and do happen to almost everyone. And for most companies, it is not an issue of getting too big. Most stalls occur well before companies reach megainstitution size. (For a complete list of companies in the study universe, and their stall disposition, see appendix 1.)

To understand the prevalence of stalls, we've divided the company universe into three groups: Stall Group companies; Growth Restarts; and Continuous Growth companies (fig. 2.2). As we indicate above, the vast majority (87 percent) of the Fortune 100 and Global 100 companies we studied fall into the Growth Stalls category, suffering one or more stall points across the period under study. The remaining 13 percent of companies have been able to grow steadily across the period (which we define as maintaining greater than 6 percent real growth or avoiding a material decline of 4 percent or more). These are typically companies in their first growth run, such as Best Buy, or companies riding a particular industry wave, such as Microsoft or Dell. The Continuous Growth companies in our sample have compiled a highly respectable growth history across our research period, growing real revenues at a compounded annual rate of 11.6 percent and market capitalization at 14 percent.[1]

Restarting growth after a stall proves surprisingly hard to do. Most stalling companies never return to significant growth (which we defined as achieving at least a 6 percent real growth rate in the period following the stall to the present day). Only 11 percent of the companies we studied were able to achieve this level of recovery. This group contains an interesting mix of companies—Johnson and Johnson, McKesson, and Tyson Foods, among others.

STALL POINTS RISING ACROSS TIME

Our aggregate analysis of stall points from 1955 to the present suggests that external barriers to large firm growth are steadily lifting across time (fig. 2.3). Across the past half century, the danger zone for large firm stalls has risen con-

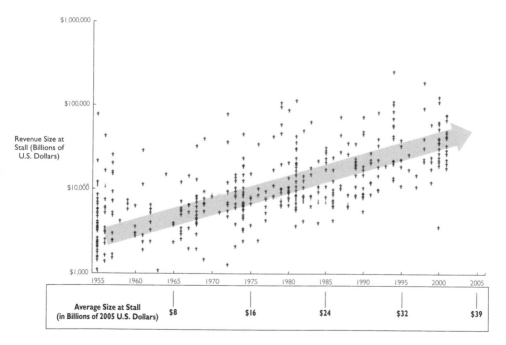

Fig. 2.3 Stall "danger zone" rising across time: company size at stall, 1955–2005

sistently at approximately 4 percent per annum. Likely candidates to explain this rising danger zone are the continuing globalization of markets, the application of new information technologies, and the development of increasingly sophisticated managerial best practices. Together, these factors appear to have raised the danger zone for median size at stall from less than $10 billion (current dollars) in 1965 to almost $40 billion today. These factors are likely to continue to allow leadership teams of large firms more room for top-line growth runs into the future.

THE (EXTERNAL) INVISIBILITY
OF AN IMPENDING STALL

Our third major finding concerns how difficult it is to see a stall coming—at least from the outside. As part of our analysis, we studied the time period just in advance of revenue stalls to see if an external analyst could discern some clue that a stall was imminent—some pattern in revenue or margin growth rates that would be a leading indicator.

At least from the outside, the answer is "no"—there are no clear leading indicators of a stall (fig. 2.4). This finding is especially troubling to the securities analysis community, which would like to imagine that there is some "tell," or signal, that a downturn is coming. For 45 percent of the stall companies studied, however, revenue growth rates actually *accelerated* into their stalls. Only 42 percent experienced *decreasing* revenue growth rates before their stall year. The acceleration in revenue growth often takes the form of "buying revenue" through merger and acquisition activity just before the stall, a pattern that has held across time. Following RCA's appointment of Robert Sarnoff, son of the legendary general, as chief executive in 1966, RCA went on a "mini-binge," acquiring Random House that year and Hertz the next. Three-year growth rates before and after the company's 1967 stall were 9.2 percent and (2.2 percent), respectively. More recently, Philip Morris's management followed the same playbook, acquiring General Foods and Kraft in the years directly preceding the company's 1994 stall, with three-year pre- and post-stall growth rates of 16.7 percent and (3.1 percent), respectively.

Compounding the difficulty of stall prediction, changes in margin health before the stall point provide little reliable guidance, either. Compressing margins (an indicator of "buying" future growth) were only slightly more prevalent than expanding margins at companies in the year immediately preceding their stalls. Raytheon, which stalled at $5 billion in 1981, turned in impressive margin

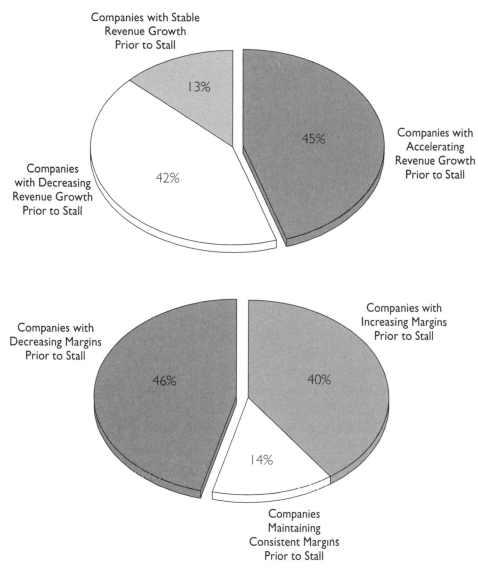

Fig. 2.4 Stalling companies give little warning: revenue and margin performance surrounding stall

expansion in the years before the stall, climbing steadily from 2.8 percent net margins in 1971 to 5.5 percent in 1979. Top-line growth turned negative the following year.

The evidence suggests that financial model approaches to predicting impending revenue problems seriously miss the deeper drivers of stalls—both in the competitive environment and in management actions.

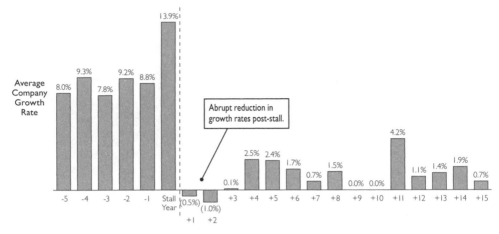

Fig. 2.5 The myth of growth rate "soft landings": revenue growth experience of stalling companies in years surrounding stall

THE MYTH OF "SOFT LANDINGS"

Perhaps the most significant finding in our "stall search" was the indication that, when stalls come, they are equally surprising to management—to insiders with privileged information. At any rate, they come on fast (fig. 2.5).

It's tempting to imagine that a company traces a growth track the way a glider floats on currents of air and that when the winds begin to subside, management, like a glider pilot, can guide the enterprise in for a soft landing. Certainly the classic S-curve model of corporate growth that we mentioned in chapter 1 suggests this pattern of gradual slowing. The reality, however, is that companies behave more like rocks than gliders. Our analysis of revenue growth rates in the years preceding and following stall points gives little comfort to management teams hoping for gradual descents into slow revenue growth maturity. Our research indicates that soft landings are rare in nature and that most stalls exhibit a fairly steep, sudden drop-off in revenue growth performance. For the more than four hundred firms in our sample that suffered stalls, revenue growth in the five years preceding the stall hovered somewhere between 8 percent and 10 percent. In the year before the stall, the average company increased growth to just shy of 14 percent. And then, the precipice. Growth in the two years after the stall turned negative and across the following decade was a dismal 0.7 percent.

The very jaggedness of this pattern is significant because it leads us directly to a central finding. It is reasonable to infer from this examination of the abruptness of stalls that they are a surprise to the external analyst poring over published financials and company statements in search of clues to future performance. We believe that stalls are as often a surprise to management—at least in their ferocity and longevity. At a minimum, the steep revenue growth rate decline following a stall suggests that there were moving parts management just wasn't aware of. The data bear witness to the difficulty of the fundamental managerial balancing act of simultaneously minding the long-term and short-term growth horizons of the firm. When we shared this finding with George Stalk of the Boston Consulting Group, he was quick to spot the red flag whipping back and forth for management in this finding: as he observed, and we illustrate through case examples in later chapters, the world tends to come at you quicker than you think, and you have to be faster at responding than you might have imagined.[2]

Chapter 3 The Costs of a Stall

Rounding out this first part of our analysis, we now turn from the prevalence of stalls to their consequences, which are severe. We examined the costs of a stall in two timeframes: In the moment, how severely was the company punished, in terms of the impact on market capitalization and employee turnover; and across time, how debilitating are the effects of a stall in terms of the prospects of eventual recovery? How hard is it to "get back up again"? This chapter does not contain good news.

DELAYED BUT CERTAIN PENALTY

As we have discovered, stalls are quite common, but the market punishment that awaits the stalling company is no less severe for that. A simple graphic illustrates our largest finding here: although the markets may be slow to react to a stall, the market impact on the company is devastating (fig. 3.1).

To quantify the impact of a stall on shareholder value, we compared the decline in market capitalization from three years before the stall to

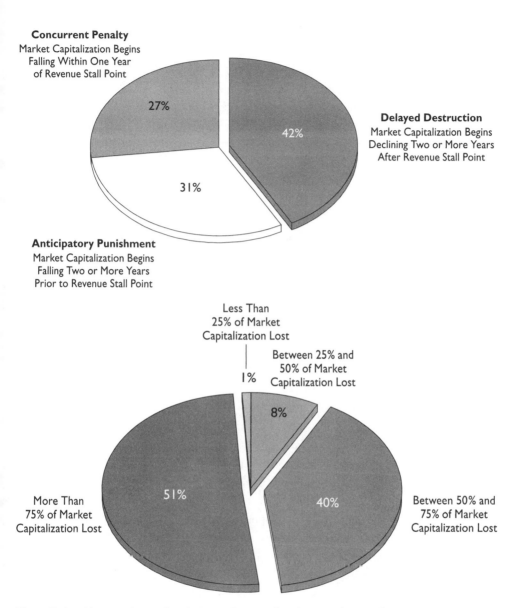

Concurrent Penalty
Market Capitalization Begins
Falling Within One Year
of Revenue Stall Point

27%

Delayed Destruction
Market Capitalization Begins
Declining Two or More Years
After Revenue Stall Point

42%

31%

Anticipatory Punishment
Market Capitalization Begins
Falling Two or More Years
Prior to Revenue Stall Point

Less Than
25% of Market
Capitalization Lost

Between 25% and
50% of Market
Capitalization Lost

1%

8%

More Than
75% of Market
Capitalization Lost

51%

40%

Between 50% and
75% of Market
Capitalization Lost

Fig. 3.1 Delayed but certain penalty: timing and extent of market capitalization destruction in years surrounding stall

ten years following the stall—from peak to trough, as it were—relative to the S&P 500 index's performance. Valuation consequences are severe: few firms escaped with declines of less than 25 percent, and the population as a whole suffered a median drop in value of just under 75 percent. Nine of ten stalling firms in our sample lost at least half of their market value in the years surrounding their downward growth rate inflection, while over half lost more than 75 percent of their value. Interestingly, two-thirds of stalling firms saw their major valuation declines commence a year or more after their top-line stall, suggesting that efficient market theory (current price accurately reflects all available information) has its limits. Our hypothesis is that analysts are willing to look the other way in the short term, appeased by continuing earnings performance.

THE NEED FOR SPEED IN RECOVERING FROM STALLS

Although the odds of a Fortune 100–sized company suffering a meaningful revenue stall are high, a significant percentage of these firms eventually succeed in reigniting meaningful top-line growth runs. But here's the kicker: almost all the companies that are successful at this recover quickly—stumble, and not stall. George Bodway of Hewlett-Packard captured this sentiment perfectly when he observed, "All companies stumble, but the great companies recover— and they all recover fast."[1]

The best way to see this need for speed is to examine the exhibit with which we close out this chapter and the review of the quantitative analysis that we conducted (fig. 3.2). This exhibit returns to where we started this section, the experience of Fortune 100 companies since 1955. As we saw in chapter 2, almost all large companies stall, 87 percent, with only 13 percent able to maintain continuous growth, generally those still in their first growth run. Of the stalling companies, 46 percent stall to moderate to high real growth rates in the decade following the stall, so they settle in to a minimum of 2 percent real growth or higher across the decade. The remaining 54 percent of companies stall to slow or negative growth—so below 2 percent per year across that decade. And this is the critical watch period. Look over at the last of the three bars in the exhibit. Once stalled to slow growth, a company has only a 7 percent chance—a one-in-fourteen shot—at recovering to moderate to high growth—that is, to more than 2 percent real growth per year. Ever. The much more common fate for companies in this category is captured by the bottom two slices in the bar: 26 percent of firms are relegated to slow or negative growth, and the vast majority, 67 percent, disappear from the radar entirely—acquired, bankrupt, or taken private.

This is the hard truth of a top-line growth stall—and the fate to be avoided for as long as possible. For readers who are managing a business that is still in a run of healthy growth, it's worth a tremendous amount of focus to prevent a

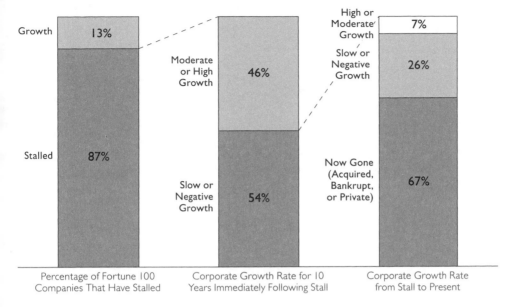

High	More Than 6% Above GNP
Moderate	From 2 to 6% Above GNP
Slow	From 2% Below to 2% Above GNP
Negative	From 6 to 2% Below GNP
Highly Negative	More Than 6% Below GNP

Fig. 3.2 The need for speed in recovering from stalls: incidence and timing of recovery from revenue stalls in Fortune 100–sized companies

stall because the odds are stacked against you in terms of restarting growth. That said, recovery is possible: 7 percent of companies that stall to slow or negative growth are able to pull themselves back to high or moderate growth. An ounce of prevention really is worth a pound of cure.

So here's the news so far. Most large companies stall. The market cap implications are devastating. It's very difficult to recover growth after a stall. What should the executive or business manager do? To avoid or anticipate a stall, what signs should company managers look for? That is the subject of the next part of this analysis.

Part II Root Causes
of Growth Stalls

Chapter 4 Why Companies Stall

In part I of this analysis we have explored the incidence of growth stalls in large firms, documenting their prevalence, their duration, and their consequences. We have drawn conclusions from a comprehensive dataset of the growth experience of more than five hundred Fortune 100–sized firms across the past fifty years.

We now turn to the examination of why companies stall. Our inquiry into what causes large firms to fall off their growth curves was guided by the fact that, unlike many theorists, we had relatively precise historical guidance into when, across the past half century, individual Fortune 100–sized firms experienced true inflection points in their growth fortunes. Guided by these specific stall points, we chose a sample of fifty companies (allocated across industrial sectors to reflect the universe of "stallers" accurately as a whole) for in-depth analysis of what happened to them in the years surrounding their apogees (see appendix 3). We believe that this Gang of Fifty is representative of the population as a whole, with proportional representation across sectors as well as across the fifty years of history captured in the analysis.

For each company, we concentrated our analysis on the pre- and post-stall years, assembling analyst reports, financial filings, business press coverage, officer memoirs, and, in many cases, interviews with key executives. (Even though the subject was sensitive, these interviews were refreshingly candid; whatever the time frame of the stall, company executives were eager to share the insights that their firms had gleaned from the experience and that they now teach to a new generation of management.) These and other sources formed the raw material for spirited, extended debates among our team of analysts, focused on each of the fifty chosen "stalls."

Respecting the complexity of each situation but still desiring consensus around specific causes, we allowed for the identification of up to three decisive stall factors, inductively chosen, from the host of potential market issues, geopolitical situations, technological changes, management activities, and organizational design elements to which their revenue slowdowns could be attributed. After applying the same bottom-up methodology to each of the fifty companies, we then aggregated these root causes into logical groupings, forming a comprehensive taxonomy of stall factors covering revenue slowdowns for Fortune 100-sized companies across the past half century. We call the resulting root cause tree our "thicket" of root causes (fig. 4.1).

This exhibit is the most important illustration in this book for the business leader to be able to interpret. On first viewing the thicket, it is hard to avoid the conclusion that a company can falter in many ways. It also brings home the point that for very large companies the task of sustaining growth is extremely difficult—it's almost as if you must do everything right in order to avoid a stall. We think, however, that the news of this analysis is better than that. Looking at the exhibit as a whole you can see that the root causes of stalls are not so varied or complex that we can't see patterns. In fact, the primary stall factors are knowable and preventable.

To understand this exhibit, let's begin by working from the bottom of the chart up: we have identified forty-two discrete root causes, some grouped into categories and represented by a single top-line category on the thicket (for example, the root causes Antitrust and Government Subsidized Overcapacity are summed up to the top-line Regulatory Actions, to the far left) and some that simply appear as top-line categories, such as Economic Downturn, just to the right. (See appendix 4 for a complete list of root cause definitions.) Across the top line of the thicket, we present a percentage representing the incidence of root causes represented by the particular category, summing to 100 percent from left to right across the chart. Thus, Regulatory Actions represent 7 percent of the root cause factors we identified, and so on. These root causes sum to

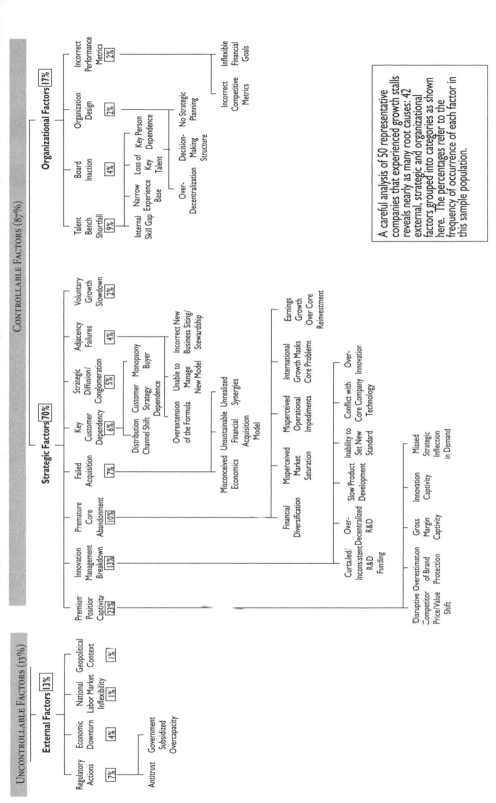

Fig. 4.1 "Thicket" of root causes of revenue stalls

three major categories: External (or Uncontrollable) Factors; Strategic Factors; and Organizational Factors, with summary percentages for each.

Now that we've analyzed the thicket from the bottom up, let's mine it for insight by examining it from the top down.

THE DOMINANCE OF CONTROLLABLE FACTORS

The major finding of our analysis—one that should give both pause and hope to leaders of growing enterprises—is that the vast majority of stall factors, some 87 percent, are controllable, related to a strategy choice or organization design decision. Further, even within this broad controllable category, an eighty-twenty logic is at work, allowing us to concentrate our attention on the small set of most critical stall contributors. In fact, just four top-line causes collectively account for more than half of all stalls:

Top Four Stall Categories

- Premium Position Captivity: failure to shift tactics in response to the advent of a low-cost competitor or changing customer preferences (23 percent)
- Innovation Management Breakdown: failure to achieve desired or required returns on investments in new products and services (13 percent)
- Premature Core Abandonment: failure to exploit growth opportunities in the core franchise or to adjust the business model to meet new competitive requirements (10 percent)
- Talent Bench Shortfall: lack of adequate leaders and staff with the skills and capabilities required for successful strategy execution (9 percent)

In the chapters that follow, we move from left to right across the root cause tree, explaining and illustrating each category and helping the reader diagnose whether each area should be a cause for concern in his or her organization. We devote special attention to the four categories listed above, dedicating a chapter to each (chapters 6, 7, 8, and 10, respectively).

Before we begin our march across the thicket, we would like to focus on the lesson at the heart of this analysis—and the great opportunity facing today's executive teams to avoid the mistakes of their predecessors.

THE ROLE OF SHARED STRATEGIC
ASSUMPTIONS IN CREATING STALLS

Our analysis of why so many of today's leading corporations have stalled in their growth provides a significant advantage to the executive teams of growing companies who seek to follow in their footsteps but to avoid their fates. Working our way to the heart of fig. 4.1: most large companies have stalled, most of these stalls can be attributed to controllable factors, and the vast majority of these factors relate back to a strategy choice or decision by the executive team. What unites the admittedly diverse stall factors under the Strategic Factors banner of our thicket is that these were failures of executive team direction—or instances of executive team inaction. They were not external, uncontrollable constraints imposed on the senior management team at gargantuan firms at the limits of their markets. All were issues being openly discussed in their respective organizations in the years surrounding their revenue stalls, and all were challenges quite plausibly within the management team's power to respond with a more effective strategy initiative. Yet the stubborn patterns of ineffective response suggest a deeper problem.

If the overwhelming majority of factors underlying growth stalls are controllable by senior leadership and the bulk of these are repeated patterns of strategy mistakes, why don't executive teams break out of these apparently recurring behaviors and pursue alternative responses? With gifted leaders and access to counsel from the most sophisticated strategy consultancies in the world, why do senior executive teams at tremendously successful organizations fail to adapt their strategies *correctly* and *adequately* when revenue trajectories begin to flag?

After hundreds of hours of in-depth examination of the internal debates, posited actions, and confessionals of senior executives at case study firms undergoing stalls, we are convinced that much of the answer lies in the insights of organizational psychologists into the related phenomena of shared "mental models" and the underlying assumption sets that support them.

The mental model concept was established in psychology by Princeton University cognitive science professor Philip Johnson-Laird in his book *Mental Models* (1983). The concept has been applied before to management science, notably by MIT professors Peter Senge and Daniel Kim, who have emphasized the utility of shared mental models of the world in helping senior management teams make decision-making more efficient when faced with a flood of information and complex causal relationships (fig. 4.2).[1] These models serve at a subconscious level as frameworks for intuitive judgment and as proxies for rig-

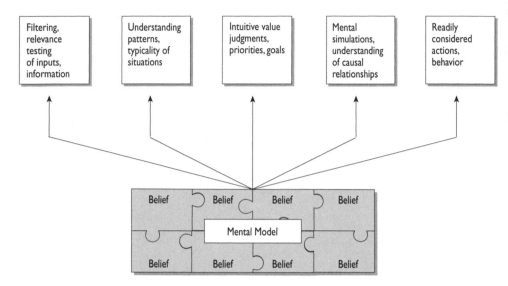

Fig. 4.2 Thought processes governed by mental models

orous analysis. Filtering information, recognizing patterns, making value judgments, forging chains of causality—all these thought processes rely on the models we have developed and through which we interpret the world.

The formation of these shared mental models is extraordinarily strong in successful organizations, where the positive feedback to the validity of the shared mental model has been in place for some time (and usually corresponds to the career tenures of the senior team). The problem arises when the set of *strategic assumptions* on which the model is based begins to deteriorate (fig. 4.3). The mental models of management teams are constructed of sets of assumptions about markets, competitors, and technologies that help speed decision-making under conditions of ambiguity. When these underlying assumptions behind company strategy begin to erode, however, the shared mental model of the senior team can first gradually, then suddenly, depart from reality.

Once undermined, the mental models of the senior team lead to a peculiar isolation and resistance to new external market and strategy realities. What had formerly been the shared *and valid* vision of the senior team turns into a screen that distorts the team's view of the best way forward. As Constantinos Markides of the London Business School has observed, "Mental models can be good because they allow us to process information and make decisions quickly. How-

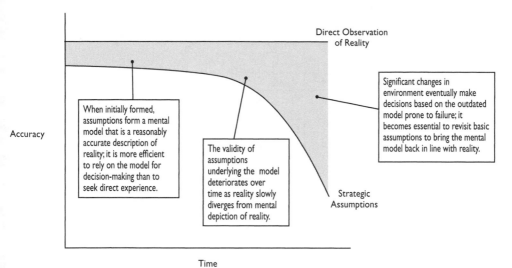

Fig. 4.3 The accuracy of strategic assumptions decays across time

ever, very strong mental models can hinder active thinking and the adoption of new ideas because they act as filters that screen incoming information. . . . It is therefore essential that we routinely question our mental models."[2]

In a different realm, this tendency to cling to obsolete or incorrect mental models has been characterized as "groupthink." Coined by the political scientist Irving Janis in his landmark study, *Victims of Groupthink* (1972), the term refers to "a deterioration of mental efficiency, reality testing and moral judgment that results from in-group pressures . . . when the members' striving for unanimity override their motivation to realistically appraise alternative courses of action."[3] What was true of infamous U.S. public policy fiascoes, the subject of his book—the Bay of Pigs invasion, say, or the failure to anticipate the Japanese attack on Pearl Harbor—is no less true in the corporate setting. Indeed, the problem is likely to be even more pronounced in an organization that has enjoyed a long run of success and in which the group's judgments and intuition have been rewarded. Under these conditions, any highly cohesive group of decision-makers placed in a high-stress situation is likely to fall prey to the symptoms of groupthink: closed-mindedness, pressure toward uniformity, overestimation of its own capability, and limited consideration of alternatives and dissonant information. The balancing act for an executive team wishing to avoid this syndrome is to achieve the benefits of group cohesiveness while con-

Company	Year of Inflection	Flawed Assumption Underlying Inflection
3M	1973	Core markets will always value the company's premium-priced innovations
Altria	1994	Achieving higher profit margins justifies ceding market share
American Express	1988	Credit cards are not a substitute for the company's premium charge cards
Apple Computer	1988	Achieving higher profit margins justifies ceding market share
AutoNation	1999	Convenience and selection can sustain a "good enough" price position
BankAmerica	1981	Retail banking profitability will continue in long-term decline
Bank One	1998	Brand power outweighs cost-efficiencies in the industry rollup race
BFGoodrich	1979	Foreign tire companies will not meet U.S. price/performance demands
Caterpillar	1975	The parts and service network will protect a price premium despite rivals' advances
Citicorp	1998	Business-unit autonomy will not inhibit effective risk management
ConAgra	1989	It is possible to resume growth after a temporary slowdown taken to boost margins
Daimler-Benz	1988	Customers are willing to pay premium prices for "engineering perfection"
Dana	1979	Independent market strategy is less important than integration with key customer production
Digital	1989	PCs will never meet the performance demands of minicomputer customers
Disney	1972	Revenue growth from syndication of existing products enables substantial cuts in core animation talent
Eastman Kodak	1973	Low-end rivals will never meet mainstream customers' requirements
GTE	1966	Major acquisitions are the best method to enable future company growth
Hitachi	1994	Low-end rivals will never meet mainstream customers' requirements

Fig. 4.4 Flawed assumptions underlying selected growth inflections

tinually revisiting the underpinnings of that cohesiveness—the shared assumptions that underlie strategy.

FLAWED ASSUMPTIONS BEHIND
COMPANY STALLS

Behind each revenue stall we studied, we found that the shared assumptions of the senior executive team about their strategic position were dangerously incorrect (fig. 4.4). During these companies' growth runs, their assumptions

Company	Year of Inflection	Flawed Assumption Underlying Inflection
H. J. Heinz	1974	Cost cutting to support the earnings growth ramp can be maintained indefinitely
IBM	1968	Minicomputers will never meet the demands of core mainframe customers
Kmart	1967	The company has achieved saturation in the discount retail market
Levi Strauss & Co.	1977	Brand power provides safety against new competitors and distributors
Matsushita	1992	Market requirements for product quality supersede those for timeliness
Philips Electronics	1978	Country managers should continue to hold sway over product divisions
RCA	1967	The age of big breakthroughs in consumer electronics has passed
Reebok	1988	Athletic footwear will always sell based on fashion over performance
Rubbermaid	1990	Product proliferation will neither confuse customers nor drive up costs
Sears	1969	Nonproduct competitive advantages will protect the company's pricing premiums
Tenneco	1981	A diversified portfolio will never face a broad downturn and a cash deficit simultaneously
Toshiba	1994	It is possible to manage resource allocation among highly dissimilar businesses
Toys R Us	1992	Broad product selection can sustain a premium price position
Unisys	1987	Market requirements for product quality supersede those for timeliness
United Technologies	1981	Corporate center capabilities can more than compensate for multibusiness strategic complexity
Volvo	1995	The luxury automobile category will always support s high cost structure
Xerox	1972	The low end of the market is severable; sales force strengths will protect pricing premiums

about competitors, customers, and sources of advantage had been dependable and useful, but somehow, across the years preceding their stalls, they had weakened, gone unquestioned, and no longer formed the basis of effective strategy. Common patterns abound: the conviction of Altria and Apple senior management to hold to high-margin positioning in the face of market share erosion; the related belief on the part of management of Toys "R" Us and AutoNation that selection and convenience trump price in their respective sectors; and the reliance of BancOne and Levi's on brand power to provide safety against new competitors and distribution channels.

Examined individually, the root causes of growth stalls may seem dizzyingly complex in their variety. But, just as the stall factors themselves largely fall into a number of useful, stable groupings, so too do the underlying strategic assumptions that lead to stalls. Across the next run of chapters, we will define and illustrate each factor that causes revenue stalls, describe its major variants, and provide a set of diagnostic "self-test" questions for the reader to gauge its current seriousness for his or her organization.

Chapter 5 External (Uncontrollable) Factors

The intuitive thinking around corporate size and growth would suggest that external, "uncontrollable" factors—market saturation, government regulation, business cycle constraints, or geopolitical disruptions—would account for a substantial portion of the root causes of growth slowdowns for such giant organizations. Interestingly, however, only a small minority of stall factors link back to such contextual issues in our catalog of the primary constraints to continued growth. (And even here, as we are constantly reminded by general managers in our membership, there is hope: the events we document may be uncontrollable, but our corporate responses are not. So, to the "glass is half-full" crowd, 100 percent of stalls are controllable!)

The first issue we note above—market saturation—in fact never arose as a primary stall factor, despite the reflexive concern of many that today's large corporations are running out of elbow room in their core markets. Indeed, from a macroeconomic perspective, research would suggest that concentration levels across industry have been declining since the 1960s. Even in the most oligopolistic of markets, the market share of the most dominant players seldom exceeds 10 percent to 15 percent, so the possibility of expanding share is generally a competitive given.[1]

Nonetheless, we did identify instances in the case studies we reviewed of root causes that were both significant and external to the firm—beyond the control of management. Although from an overall perspective these exogenous constraints accounted for only 13 percent of our allocation of stall factors, they are worth examining because when they do present, they are memorable for the speed and magnitude of their impact. On the left-hand side of the thicket of stall factors (see fig. 4.1), we disaggregate this set of external, uncontrollable factors into four principal variations: Regulatory Actions; Economic Downturn; National Labor Market Inflexibility; and Geopolitical Context.

REGULATORY ACTIONS

Some of the significant stalls associated with regulatory intercession in our sample are shown here (fig. 5.1). For business historians, the cases represented here are familiar. DuPont and Dow, stalling in 1951 and 1953, respectively, were forced to give up oligopolistic positions built in the war years. For DuPont, there was an additional challenge in 1957 when a Clayton Act ruling against the firm forced it to disgorge its holding of sixty-three million shares in General Motors, a relationship that had existed for more than forty years, beginning with an investment in the fledgling automobile company in 1914 by Pierre S. du Pont, who later became GM's president.

Xerox's and IBM's 1970s-era stalls involved aggressive antitrust actions alleging predatory behavior. As remedy, Xerox was required to license its xerography patents to competitors, including IBM and Kodak. Amid allegations of predatory pricing and monopolistic behavior, IBM was compelled to divest its service bureau arm with its accompanying $100 million in contracts. Fearing government reaction, IBM management delayed the company's entry into the increasingly important minicomputer segment, ushering in a rare, five-year hiatus in the company's otherwise steady, decades-long growth track.

Most of the regulatory actions we noted in our review of case companies took place in the earlier years of our study period, associated with a more activist era in (at least U.S.) antitrust actions. From this historical perspective, more recent cases, such as Microsoft's five-year battle with U.S. antitrust authorities from 1999 to 2004 and its subsequent four-year engagement with the European Commission, are the exception, not the rule.

A more current concern for executives of leading corporations is perhaps not

Company	Stall Point	Government Action	Impact on Strategy
DuPont	1951	• Antitrust decisions (1945–1954) force dissolution of international chemical oligopoly • Supreme Court ruling requires DuPont to sever ties with General Motors (1957)	• Dissolution of patent-pooling arrangements with foreign chemical firms and the sale of its 23 percent stake in GM remove two key drivers of both top- and bottom-line growth for DuPont
Dow	1953	• To support war effort, government requires Dow to share its proprietary processes for manufacture of magnesium and synthetic rubber; Dow's R&D forced to shift from basic science to military engineering	• Dow is left without a key competitive advantage in two core product areas • The R&D shutdown puts the company 10 years behind, according to company executives
RCA	1967	• 1958 antitrust investigation targets RCA's patent pooling and licensing arrangements	• RCA agrees to a consent decree breaking up its patent pool to avoid civil antitrust action by Zenith; the settlement effectively limits RCA's profit potential from color television sales
IBM	1968	• 1970 antitrust suit alleges predatory pricing, monopolistic behavior	• Suit forces the divestiture of IBM's service bureau, with its $100 million in contracts • Fearing government reaction, the company fails to enter the increasingly important minicomputer segment
Xerox	1972	• FTC action alleges monopoly behavior, unlawful aggressiveness toward other industry players	• The company is forced to license its xerography patents to competitors including IBM and Kodak
ITT	1976	• 1971 antitrust suit over purchase of Hartford Insurance; case settled with FTC amid tremendous controversy	• The company is allowed to keep The Hartford in its portfolio, but future acquisitions are limited to companies with less than $100 million in assets

Fig. 5.1 Selected stall points influenced by antitrust actions

trial in the antitrust courts but rather trial in the courts of public opinion, where ongoing inquiry takes place into what we might refer to as a company's "permission to grow." Executive teams of companies at the top of industry league tables—Wal-Mart, General Electric, BP, and others—are increasingly sensitive to local and societal perceptions of their motives and impact and increasingly in need of at least the tacit approval of these key external constituencies to advance their growth agendas. We have documented impressive advances in practices for managing reputation and risk to reputation, and we believe that the increased transparency into company actions enabled by the Web will place this issue on an increasing number of strategic agendas.[2]

ECONOMIC DOWNTURN

Next among the stall factors beyond the direct control of executive teams is the straightforward factor of powerful, overwhelming economic downturn. With the sustained run of economic growth of the past decade and a half behind us, disrupted only minimally by mild, technical recessions, it is perhaps easier to understand why relatively few companies suffer sustained, serious revenue growth inflections from business cycle downturns in recent business history. That said, for large enterprises substantially exposed to sectors highly sensitive to downturns, the effects can persist long enough to inflect a revenue trajectory for years.

Caterpillar's revenue stall in the early 1980s is instructive as to how an external event such as a substantial but time-bounded economic downturn can aggravate other, lesser competitive challenges, producing a much longer inflection of revenue growth. For thirty-five years following World War II, Caterpillar enjoyed a return on equity of 18 percent or better, as both Europe and the United States went through huge infrastructure investment processes, with Caterpillar holding a dominant market share of earth-moving equipment of at least 50 percent across worldwide markets. The synchronized downturns of both developed and underdeveloped economy infrastructure investments in the late 1970s and early 1980s (triggered primarily by a collapse in oil field investments worldwide and heavy debt burdens in developing countries) not only pushed demand for Cat's products down strongly but opened a worldwide opportunity for Caterpillar's emerging Japanese competitor, Komatsu, to build market share with heavy equipment that was less expensive and rapidly increasing in quality.[3]

Without the external force of collapsing demand, Caterpillar management would likely have fought its way through to streamlined new manufacturing processes, new labor agreements with the United Auto Workers, and a renewed cost-competitiveness with Komatsu faster and with less disruption to its top-line growth line. As it was, the firm was forced simultaneously to balance earnings growth maintenance, manufacturing process reform, labor strike management, product line renovation, and marketing organization restructuring through a period of sagging demand. As one observer noted, "A company caught between a skeptical, stubborn union and a smart, tough competitor has a dilemma on its hands—no easy way to move, no obvious course for forcing this Rubik's Cube into line."[4]

After an extremely rocky decade in the 1980s, Caterpillar recovered, posting particularly strong performance across the past five years. The company's innovations in manufacturing process have been admired and studied for the past two decades, but even time-bounded external economic factors can have long-term consequences for growth trajectories if they strike at inopportune moments of difficulty from other directions.

NATIONAL LABOR MARKET INFLEXIBILITY

Another contextual factor with historical resonances (and a modern echo in the dilemma of the United States's Big Three auto manufacturers) is a factor we've named National Labor Market Inflexibility—the inability of a company to adjust the size or activities of its workforce in response to new market conditions. Again, the appearance of this as a decisive factor in a company's long-term revenue growth history was rare, but for large, labor-intensive firms in unionized industries (and supportive national government settings), it has occasionally proved terrifically important. The case of Volvo in the late 1980s is illustrative.

Volvo served the Swedish economy almost as a national champion across the post–World War II period. Under CEO Gunnar Engellau, the company was built into a successful niche manufacturer of autos and trucks, stressing reliability and safety over styling in a variety of export markets. Some of this positioning was due to growing workforce management constraints that had begun in the late 1960s and continued through the 1970s. Operating under a series of socialist governments, Volvo's labor cost disadvantage slowly climbed until, by 1980, the company operated with hourly wages 25 percent higher than those in the United States, and an estimated 800 percent higher than new competitors arising in Asia's newly industrializing economies. Hourly labor costs alone were only part of the story. Paid absenteeism averaged 20 percent, and idled production employees were still paid 85 percent of their wages.

Executive management struggled mightily against these unfavorable cost conditions, but to little avail. CEO Pehr Gyllenhammar, who joined the firm from Skandia in 1971, sought to diversify production. In 1973, Volvo announced that it would become the first non-American car manufacturer to build a car manufacturing plant in the United States. (The company built the plant but did not begin production, owing to a downturn in the economy in that period.) Unable to manage either capacity or labor costs, Volvo management took actions that severely limited the company's competitiveness, first lengthening car model life cycles out to almost fifteen years (in an industry with prevailing four- to six-year model lifetimes) and raising prices on midlevel models to levels 20 percent or more above luxury model prices in key export markets such as the United States.[5]

These actions took place as Japanese automakers introduced new luxury brands such as Infiniti and Acura targeted precisely at Volvo's key market segments in the American export market. CEO Gyllenhammar initiated a diversification initiative across the late 1970s and early 1980s. It wasn't until the mid- to late 1990s that Volvo, fueled with cash from the divestiture of its nonauto businesses and somewhat more competitive labor costs, began to rebuild its position in its core auto business.

GEOPOLITICAL CONTEXT

Moving to the right across our categorization of external factors, we hit a stall factor even more unfamiliar to modern ears, Geopolitical Context: external geopolitical events such as outbreak of war, impact of a new pricing cartel, or other "shots from the woods" from the larger realm of international affairs. Although a contemporary reader would be unaccustomed to granting much mind share to such external shocks, given the apparent consensus across the international scene in favor of only mildly constrained trade and direct investment activities, such governmental interventions on occasion still have the power to knock large corporations' growth plans off their projections for a significant, multiyear period.

The case of Alcoa in the early 1990s is illustrative. Throughout the postwar era, Alcoa's revenues and profits followed a fairly predictable roller-coaster pattern of mini-booms and busts, driven on the demand side by cycles in the auto, appliance, and beverage can businesses and on the supply side by step-function increases in production capacity that predictably followed demand surges with overcapacity price busts. Despite these ups and downs, Alcoa grew steadily across the 1960s, 1970s, and 1980s at a nearly double-digit rate, smoothed across the decades.

This pattern was broken in the early 1990s by the unforeseen consequences of the breakup of the Soviet Union. Alcoa had just finished a brief flirtation with diversification away from aluminum and into a range of unrelated engineered materials—ceramics, plastics, and composites—that ended when the board selected the recently arrived Paul O'Neill to replace Charles Parry as chairman and chief executive in 1987. Again, as in the past, a set of demand factors peaked to create a revenue and profit boom across 1988, 1989, and 1990. The wild card element of Soviet government action began in this period, however, as the Soviet Union, under extreme foreign currency distress, began to dump its internal aluminum production into the then-booming international commodity markets. Across a three-year period, Russian exports surged more than fivefold, collapsing world prices by more than 30 percent to the lowest inflation-adjusted level ever recorded. Alcoa's profits crumbled nearly 80 percent across the period as price premiums were slashed to hold revenue declines to the 5 percent range.

Of course, Alcoa's climb out of its stall was as unexpected as its collapse, when major producers worldwide combined forces with Russia to form an OPEC-style producers' accord to more closely match production with demand growth. The lesson remains: though rare, government intercessions in oligopolistic markets can disrupt even seasoned industry competitors accustomed to the ebb and flow of economic cycles.

In summary, across these diverse types of contextual stall factors that can beset very large firms, relatively few of these external forces produce lasting, long-term inflections in revenue growth. That said, when they do occur, if they coincide with deep, existing issues of competitiveness, they can be the triggering event for a stall, if not the most serious, underlying driver of the problem.

EXTERNAL (UNCONTROLLABLE)
FACTORS DEFINED

External factors beyond the direct control of the executive teams figure in a surprisingly small share of large company revenue stalls across the study period—only 13 percent for the case companies analyzed. These "uncontrollable" factors present in four ways: Regulatory Actions; Economic Downturns; National Labor Market Inflexibility; and Geopolitical Context. In the cases we studied, these external forces typically served as tipping points for long-term revenue growth inflections, aggravating existing competitive problems. A contemporary issue that is growing in importance on the strategic agenda of leading firms is the monitoring (and management) of reputation risk, specifically of ongoing "permission to grow"—the implicit permission granted by communities, local and otherwise, for a company to pursue its growth agenda.

Self-Test Questions for
Executive Leadership

1. Do we actively identify and manage gaps between our stakeholders' expectations and perceptions of our operations, policies, products, and markets?
2. Do we track opinions of our key stakeholders on issues related to our growth regularly (every twelve to eighteen months)?
3. Do we adequately incorporate the accomplishment of mid- and long-term public opinion strategy goals into our operational growth plans?
4. Do we explore alternative business models or alterations to the existing business model that might lower public resistance to our expansion plans?
5. Do we plan scenarios for low-probability but high-impact events, such as government intercessions, in our growth markets?

Interpreting the Results

Negative answers to two or more of these questions suggest that an executive team should thoroughly review the company's risk management activities with an eye toward achieving a more explicit understanding of the links between corporate reputation and mid- and long-term growth plans and options. For those seeking further direction, a diagnostic aid is available on our Web site, www.stallpoints.executiveboard.com.

Strategic Factors

Chapter 6 Premium Position Captivity

Without a close second, the largest, most consistent category of factors responsible for serious revenue stalls is that which we have labeled Premium Position Captivity, the inability of a firm to respond correctly to a challenge posed by a new low-cost competitor, or to a significant shift in customer valuation of product features. Nearly a fourth of the stall factors recorded in our sample cases were forms of this endemic—and fundamentally strategic—problem. This challenge is becoming increasingly familiar to students of business, as we become accustomed to seeing giant incumbent firms in a variety of industries suddenly placed in serious distress by so-called disruptive competitors, typically armed with a lower price made possible by a significantly lower-cost business model.

Across the fifty-year period of our analysis, Premium Position Captivity has remained the most consistent generator of serious revenue stalls among large firms, renewed periodically by distinct waves of business model innovation ranging from the rise of new retailing models in the 1960s to low-cost manufacturing in the 1970s and 1980s to the appearance of technology-driven disruptors in the 1990s and through to the present.

CAUGHT BETWEEN THE BASELINE AND THE NET

Our historical trace of corporate performance would suggest that Premium Position Captivity is accelerating dramatically as a strategic stall factor: the incidence of company stalls in this category doubled across the decade of the 1990s. Apart from the rise of low-cost business models, an explanatory factor here might well be what McKinsey and Company has dubbed "the vanishing middle market": the decline of middle-tier products and services in a range of industries, as volume (and value) flow to both low-end and (very) high-end market tiers. For just the five-year period from 1999 to 2004, a McKinsey analysis found that the growth rate of revenues for middle-tier products fell behind industry averages by nearly 6 percent, whereas low-end and high-end categories outstripped averages by 4 to 9 percent.[1]

Incumbent firms, having grown to Fortune 100 size on scale economies and iterations of products for the "thick" part of the market (the "vanishing middle," in McKinsey's terms), find themselves fenced off from exploiting low-end market growth by their cost base and unable to generate sufficient volume from high-end niches to keep their growth rates up to past standards. The combination of mass market unit sales volumes and pricing premiums from incremental product enhancements proves impossible to sustain.

The management responses to these challenges that produced subsequent multiyear stagnations of revenue growth come in five variations that reappear across time in our sample of company histories: Disruptive Competitor Price/Value Shift; Overestimation of Brand Protection; Gross Margin Captivity; Innovation Captivity; and Missed Strategic Inflection in Demand.

DISRUPTIVE COMPETITOR PRICE/VALUE SHIFT

The first behavior is, of course, the "nonresponse" response to a new, disruptive competitor entering the market with a lower-priced and (at least as perceived) lower-quality product (fig. 6.1). Some of the classic cases of nonresponse are reviewed here. In the early 1970s, Eastman Kodak was confronted by a welter of new competitors in both film and camera equipment that had the effect of introducing a new, low-price tier into the company's domestic markets for these

Company	Original Positioning	New Competitor(s)	Case Summary
Eastman Kodak	Superior quality, innovative photographic products for amateurs; standard-setting film, print paper, chemicals and cameras	Film: Fuji, Polaroid, DuPont Cameras: Canon, Polaroid, Pentax, Olympus	• Advent of new competitors in the 1970s introduces a new low-price tier into domestic film and camera markets • Kodak's initial response is to cut back prices marginally while continuing premium pricing based on a quality differential • Competitors continue to make inroads across the following decades; Kodak (finally) enters the discount film market in 1994 with its Funtime™ label
Daimler-Benz	High-end luxury automobiles, produced with world-class German engineering; price premium is intended to reinforce the Mercedes "mystique"	Lexus, Infiniti	• Japanese carmakers introduce lower-cost premium brands in the late 1980s • Daimler-Benz continues cost-plus pricing, believing that low-price competitors will never develop a rival brand image • Lexus sales surpass Mercedes sales in the United States in 1991; BMW sales surpass Mercedes in Germany in 1992 • Daimler-Benz posts a first-ever full-year loss in 1993; new Mercedes chief adopts market-driven target pricing
Caterpillar	Highest quality, most durable construction equipment; company proud of its ability to "perfect" products rather than innovate	Komatsu	• Komatsu grows rapidly with inexpensive, innovative earthmovers that directly challenge Caterpillar • Early actions are largely symbolic: Cat tries to rally its workforce against Komatsu, but maintains its premium positioning • Between 1981 and 1986, Cat loses seven share points in the United States, almost entirely to Komatsu • Company pursues strategies to lower production costs throughout the 1980s

Fig. 6.1 Representative stalls due to premium position captivity

Company	Original Positioning	New Competitor(s)	Case Summary
Sears	General merchandiser of broad array of consumer durables; routinely rated by consumers as one of America's highest-quality companies	Kmart (and later Wal-Mart, Target)	• Kmart and the discount retail segment (in its entirety) emerge in the 1960s • Sears upgrades its merchandise, expanding its line to include higher priced (higher margin) products • This new positioning confuses customers, so Sears slashes prices to maintain loyalty • Kmart steals share from Sears throughout the 1970s and 1980s • Sears finally adopts "everyday low prices" in 1988, but is simply unable to compete with Kmart on price

Fig. 6.1 Continued

products. Kodak management responded with a half-hearted price rollback but continued its policy of premium pricing based on the assumed power of its quality advantage. Kodak finally entered the discount film and camera segments in the mid-1990s, but not before suffering a halving of its market share in cameras and losing a third of its share in its core film business. Cruelly enough, this challenge was followed close on the heels by an even more fundamental challenge to the Kodak franchise and business model, and the generations of Kodak executive management since that time have been earnestly and publicly searching for firm footing under the company's growth strategy as it crosses the chasm between film and digital formats and markets.

Just as Kodak was challenged in responding to new, largely foreign entrants to its home markets, the management of Sears was struggling mightily in the late 1960s and early 1970s with unaccustomed challenges to its supremacy. It is an antique observation now to note just how completely Sears once dominated the domestic retail scene: by 1972, Sears operated nine hundred "big format" stores and twenty-six hundred catalog and retail outlets. Its sales accounted for 1 percent of U.S. gross national product. Two-thirds of Americans shopped at a Sears within any three-month period, and more than half of U.S. households held a Sears credit card.

Across the 1960s, trouble emerged for Sears in the form of discount retailers, such as Kmart (Sam Walton opened his first Wal-Mart in 1962), and "category

killers," such as Herman's Sporting Goods, offering lower-cost or broader selection than the traditional Sears formula could deliver. The 1970s was a decade
of free fall for "The Big Store," as the magnitude of the unfolding challenge became clearer to Sears management. Their first instinct, attempted in the early
years of the decade, was to move up market, adding upscale merchandise and
fashionable clothing (and higher prices!) to its stores. These higher prices and
premium goods confused customers, who defected in droves. Management
then changed course, implementing a price-cutting strategy that lured customers back but eroded all retail profits. The company moved sideways across
the 1980s, entering and then exiting the financial services business, and has
since stabilized and consolidated its retailing position, merging with rival
Kmart in 2005, but at a vestige of its former dominance.

In the early 1980s, Caterpillar was confronted with inexpensive, innovative
earthmovers from the Japanese producer Komatsu that directly challenged
Caterpillar's market leadership. As the company bled market share to Komatsu
across the first half of that decade, Caterpillar management exhibited the classic premium position response of assuming that the market share lost to the
lower-cost–lower-quality position would stabilize, allowing the premium-
priced bulk of the market to continue undisturbed. By 1986, Cat had lost seven
share points in the United States, almost entirely to Komatsu, in a decade in
which its revenue growth would slide to the low single digits and it would be
forced to shift its focus to strategies aimed at lowering production costs.

OVERESTIMATION OF BRAND PROTECTION

The second common behavior for premium-positioned firms under attack is to
fall back on the presumed shelter of brand equity. From American Express to
Coca-Cola to Heinz to Campbell Soup and others faced with presumably
lower-quality competition, the assumption of companies that have made
decades-long investments in their brands is that this brand equity can be cashed
in as protection of a pricing premium. Borden's original positioning as the most
dependable quality dairy producer faded as consumers increased their faith in
regional brands and private labels; with no real quality advantage, Borden
stumbled, assuming its brand equity to be worth "about a buck a gallon."[2]

No less a brand-management paragon than Procter and Gamble discovered
the limits to this proposition. It found itself stalled in the early 1990s, besieged
in a range of product categories by the rise of lower-priced house brands. Across
late 1992 and early 1993, the company saw across-the-board market share ero-

sion in a sobering range of products (some of the company's iconic brands participated in this dollar share retreat, including Ivory, Tide, Mr. Clean, Bounce, Cascade, Crest, Duncan Hines, and Pampers). P&G's CEO at the time, Ed Artzt, was resolute and straightforward about the unforced nature of the error, commenting in the *Wall Street Journal:* "We let too many non-value-added costs creep into the system and passed them on to the consumer. It was a disease of good times. And, in the process, we eroded some of the loyalty to our brands because the quality and performance added to our brands weren't always enough to justify in consumers' minds the difference in price."[3]

Artzt initiated a major value pricing campaign, discontinuing many trade discounts and incentives in the process, and closed thirty of the company's 147 manufacturing plants, removing three management layers and reducing headcount by 13,000, or 12 percent. His successor as chief executive, John Pepper, continued these initiatives, further pruning the company's stable of brands and launching a major initiative, Organization 2005, focused on globalizing brand management.

P&G's is one of the "stealthier" stalls we encountered in our analysis—the company's deflated market cap grew more than 30 percent from 1991 to 1999, on the back of steadily increasing earnings, and the company has posted healthy year-on-year revenue growth rates across the early years of the present century.

GROSS MARGIN CAPTIVITY

A third factor delaying effective response to a premium position threat is the barrier formed by years of performance metric systems designed around generous margins. Gross margin captivity occurs as the organization finds itself constrained by its own management system metrics (fig. 6.2). In this exhibit we capture examples of organizations having difficulty managing the balance between profitability and market share, as well as misgauging market requirements for product quality and speed. Compaq and Philip Morris (now Altria) shared stalls in the early 1990s brought on by a resistance to yielding on gross margins in the face of gathering competition. Companies such as these, with business models built around 40 percent margins, can find themselves delaying a response until, with a sudden spasm, the organization finds it must discard its former metrics and model in an attempt to confront the new reality of its situation.

	Company	Historic Metric(s)	How Metric Became Outmoded	Company Reaction
Companies mismanaging balance between profitability and market share	Compaq	40% gross margin	Gathering reputation of "clone" manufacturers for quality and value; emergence of the $1,000 personal computer	New management shifts metrics to unit cost and product development cycle time following drastic price cuts ("The Compaq Shock")
	Philip Morris	Gross margin	The price advantage of discount cigarettes prompts smokers to forgo loyalty to the Marlboro brand	Management shifts attention to rebuilding market share lost to discount segment; this shift in strategy prompts "Marlboro Friday" price cuts
Companies misgauging market requirements for product quality and speed	Caterpillar	Ten-year new product development cycle	Nimble, low-cost rival Komatsu steals formerly loyal Cat customers with a stream of innovative earthmovers	Cat reduces product development cycle to six years by the late 1980s— and to three years today
	Daimler-Benz	Ten-year new product development cycle	New, lower-cost rivals and traditional competitors introduce a new generation of innovative luxury cars far faster than Benz	The rapid introduction of the new C-class and the expansion into minivans, sports utility vehicles are emblematic of the firm's commitment to new products

Fig. 6.2 Representative examples of gross margin captivity

INNOVATION CAPTIVITY

A fourth behavior is to simply bull ahead and attempt to out-innovate the new, lower-cost competitor. More often than not, the business models built up around premium positions are designed for serial, incremental innovation in order to create a cycle of incremental premium price positions. Innovation captivity practically guarantees that the response to lower-cost competition is another round of product enhancement, rather than the immensely more difficult strategy of rethinking the cost basis of the business in order to lower price.

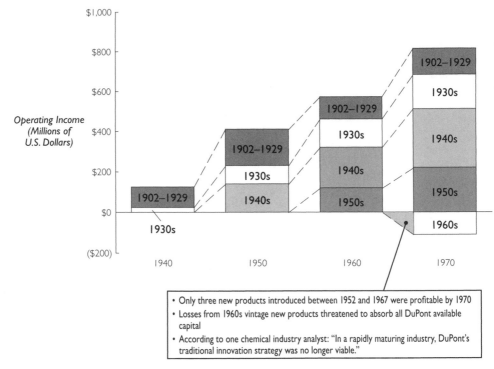

Fig. 6.3 Rise (and fall) of returns from product innovation: DuPont operating income by product vintage, 1940–1970

But for companies whose business models and cultures have been purposefully designed to create ever more products, the answer is less simple. Illustrative here on a massive scale is the story of DuPont across the four decades following World War II (fig. 6.3). Across the 1950s and 1960s, earnings from products developed and introduced in the prior decade continued to contribute strongly to DuPont's operating income. That positive cycle of innovation investment was broken by 1970, when products introduced in the preceding decade for the first time began to dilute operating income.

As DuPont's experience in the 1970s exemplifies, wholly admirable companies with ferociously strong cultures of innovation, and business models dependent on those innovations, find it very hard to respond to market slowdowns with anything other than *more innovation*. Limited by their histories and evolution as new product and service developers, strategy choices other than innovation can simply be off the table for the senior executive team. And the cost structures built up to support innovation can make it difficult to contemplate any strategy choices dependent on lower margins or reduced costs.

MISSED STRATEGIC INFLECTION IN DEMAND

Last, there is a management behavior strongly in the ascendant in more recent stalls (those after 1990) that we have labeled Missed Strategic Inflection in Demand. Here, the organization and its multiple, sophisticated market sensing activities simply fail to recognize the importance of a growing new behavior or customer preference in its core markets. The firm's "premium bet" increasingly finds itself placed on a product or service attribute in decline as disruptive entrants emphasizing different, underrecognized features gain ground.

A huge part of the problem for management teams in these situations is the gap between (typically) ongoing success and nascent, dissonant market intelligence about the new core market behavior. Illustrative here is the history of Levi Strauss across the 1990s as its apparent revenue growth success through the midpoint of the decade masked two critical changes in customer behavior that hollowed out the ground underneath the business by decade's end (fig. 6.4). Across the early 1990s, Levi's enjoyed strongly growing revenues even as it lost relationships with distributors such as the Gap and as both designers and retailers themselves introduced jeans products at the high and low ends of the market. The rise of house brands and of super-premium designer jeans looked manageable—or ignorable—as long as revenue growth continued healthy. By the time revenue growth began to flag, Levi's market share had been halved and the company found itself with an expensive retailing strategy and a product line out of step with both the high and low ends of the denim jeans market.

The market data of these phenomena, as they played out across the decade, were not hidden from Levi's executives; sorting out the message from the "noise" was the challenge, since current success warped correct interpretation of developing market intelligence. The Levi's story illustrates how difficult it is to respond to a premium captive position in the absence of a burning platform—if your sales are continuing to rise, how do you focus concern? At decade's end, Gordon Shank, then chief marketing officer, admitted ruefully, "We didn't read the signs that all was not well. Or we were in denial."[4]

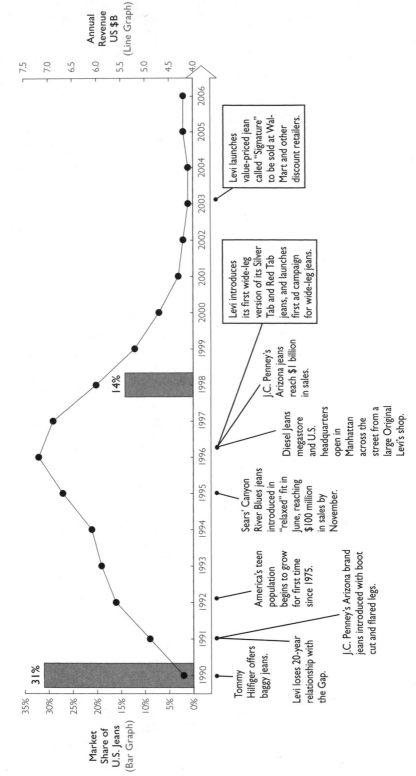

Fig. 6.4 Levi's misses customer value shift: timeline of LS&Co performance vs. competitive landmarks, 1990–2006

THE FIXATION ON TRADITIONAL RIVALRIES

Whatever the particular behaviors that cause individual large firms to stay hostage to their premium positions "on defense," they nearly all share a common trait "on offense": a fixation on traditional rivalries and competitors. Much of this has to do with the market situations in which they have grown to their present scale; as dominant organizations, they typically are oligopolists, trading market share and temporary advantages back and forth among a small set of known competitors. The firm's competitive metrics and competitor intelligence activities have been honed, often for decades, by the known rigors of its oligopolistic situation. A new disruptive competitor, operating with a different business model, can simply be off the radar.

Our research files are rife with examples attesting to fixation with known, traditional rivals that crosses history and industry boundaries (fig. 6.5). Gillette was focused on the moves of Warner-Lambert as it acquired Schick and distribution rights to Wilkinson in the early 1970s, taking attention away from the disposable razor low-end threat of BIC. Later in the decade, Xerox obsessed on IBM's and Eastman Kodak's threat to its high-end copier business, ignoring the gathering low-end threat of Ricoh and Canon. Reebok's strategy centered on LA Gear's threat to its fashion footwear positioning in the late 1980s, missing the meteoric rise of Nike's hybrid athlete/performance-as-fashion positioning. In all these cases, the new competitors were acknowledged, but the focus of the executive team was conditioned by prior competitive history.

DISDAIN, DENIAL, AND RATIONALIZATION

We can't close this chapter without commenting on the incredible difficulty that management teams have in crediting the threat posed by low-end or disruptive rivals—the incredulity of market leaders at having their dominance challenged by (seemingly) unworthy upstarts. Behind the company stories we have shared in this chapter is a deeper paralysis that gripped many market leaders who stalled across this time period. Kodak unseated by Fuji cameras and film not overnight but across fourteen long years in which Kodak management scarcely deigned to acknowledge Fuji's existence. Sears refusing to take Kmart seriously for the seventeen years that it took to unseat them from the number one ranking. The long, slow slide of Caterpillar.

You would have expected to find a history of furious efforts to combat these new threats in the companies we studied (fig. 6.6). Instead, you find the three-

Company	Traditional Rival(s)	Competitive Preoccupation	New Entrant(s)
Caterpillar	IBH, J.I. Case, Deere	In the early 1980s, acquisitions by German rival IBH and Case, as well as new products introduced by Deere challenge Caterpillar's product superiority and dealer network	Komatsu
Daimler-Benz	BMW	BMW's new model introductions propel BMW's German sales past Mercedes' for the first time ever in 1992	Lexus, Infiniti
Digital	IBM	IBM's 1987 launch of the AS400 line of minicomputers is the first legitimate challenge to DEC's dominance	Apple, Sun, PC manufacturers
Eastman Kodak	DuPont, 3M	U.S. chemical rivals expand into private label, branded film segments in early 1970s	Fuji
Gillette	Schick, Wilkinson	Warner-Lambert acquires Schick; Colgate buys distribution rights to Wilkinson in early 1970s	BIC
H.F. Ahmanson	Wells Fargo, Bank of America	Wells and Bank of America challenge Ahmanson's position in the affluent market segment in the early 1990s	Countrywide Mortgage
Reebok	LA Gear	LA Gear's fashionable footwear challenges the core of Reebok's positioning in the late 1980s	Nike
Xerox	IBM, Eastman Kodak	IBM and Kodak develop products to target Xerox's traditional mid- to high-end market position in the early 1970s	Ricoh, Canon

Fig. 6.5 Selected examples of preoccupation with traditional rivals

part psychology of paralysis: disdain, denial, and rationalization.[5] The quotations surely speak for themselves: Kodak sniffing at what it termed "other manufacturers." The quotation from Caterpillar's chairman, an equal mix of denial and self-deception. The bravado of Sears's planning director: "Take our sales and divide them by four, and we're still bigger than the next guy." These com-

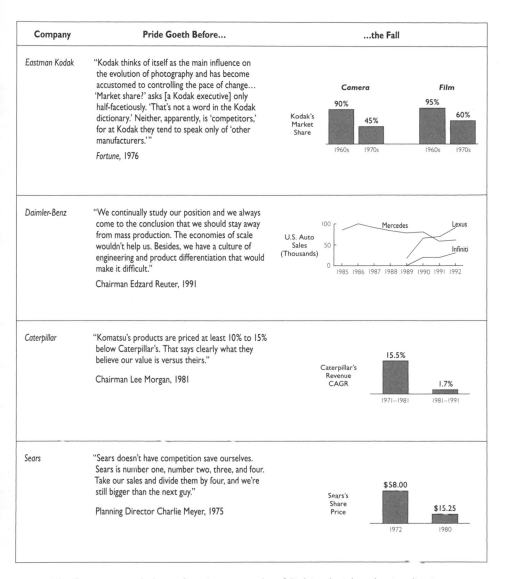

Company	Pride Goeth Before...	...the Fall
Eastman Kodak	"Kodak thinks of itself as the main influence on the evolution of photography and has become accustomed to controlling the pace of change... 'Market share?' asks [a Kodak executive] only half-facetiously. 'That's not a word in the Kodak dictionary.' Neither, apparently, is 'competitors,' for at Kodak they tend to speak only of 'other manufacturers.'" *Fortune,* 1976	
Daimler-Benz	"We continually study our position and we always come to the conclusion that we should stay away from mass production. The economies of scale wouldn't help us. Besides, we have a culture of engineering and product differentiation that would make it difficult." Chairman Edzard Reuter, 1991	
Caterpillar	"Komatsu's products are priced at least 10% to 15% below Caterpillar's. That says clearly what they believe our value is versus theirs." Chairman Lee Morgan, 1981	
Sears	"Sears doesn't have competition save ourselves. Sears is number one, number two, three, and four. Take our sales and divide them by four, and we're still bigger than the next guy." Planning Director Charlie Meyer, 1975	

Fig. 6.6 The three-part psychology of paralysis: examples of disdain, denial, and rationalization

panies were all highly successful incumbent firms whose revenue growth runs were interrupted by unlikely, disruptive competitors. And their strategic responses have been constrained by assumptions that slowly—and then completely—lost their validity. There are no indications that these behaviors will not endure and reappear in corporate history with some frequency.

STRATEGIC ASSUMPTIONS BEHIND PREMIUM POSITION CAPTIVITY

Behind the actions (and inactions) of executive teams at firms trapped in a premium captive posture lies a set of assumptions about customers, competitors, and markets. These beliefs supported the shared worldview of the team and the specific strategies that allowed the firm to enjoy its growth run preceding its revenue stall. And like all assumptions—whether the stall in question happened in 1955 or 2005—they were valid beliefs until, at some point, they weren't. The typology of strategic assumptions behind stalls due to premium position captivity deserves some unpacking. The resulting list of beliefs can serve as a starting point and outline for executive teams who wish to gauge the robustness of their assumption sets.

False Assumptions about Customers

- Core customers will be unwilling to trade away some level of product performance for lower price.
- Pricing premiums earned through incremental product enhancements will stand up to pricing challenges from "lower-performance" products and services.
- Customers will always continue to value and pay for incremental improvements in product performance; there is little risk of overshooting market needs.

False Assumptions about Competitors

- Low-end players will never be able to meet core customers' performance demands or match the company's rate of improvement in product or service features.
- Advantages in brand equity, sales force size and sophistication, and distribution networks will thwart inroads by low-end rivals.

False Assumptions about Market Evolution

- The low end of the market is severable; losses of market share due to erosion at the bottom of the market can be limited and isolated from mainstream market segments.
- The competitive focus should remain on traditional rivals and their product and marketing initiatives; competitive benchmarking should be concentrated on at-scale rivals.

PREMIUM POSITION CAPTIVITY DEFINED

The single largest stall factor identified in our case study analysis was Premium Position Captivity, the inability of a firm to respond effectively to a challenge posed by a new low-cost competitor or to a significant shift in customer valuation of product features. Five subvariants of this behavior were present in our case studies: Disruptive Competitor Price/Value Shift; Overestimation of Brand Protection; Gross Margin Captivity; Innovation Captivity; and Missed Strategic Inflection in Demand. In all instances, the core problem is the inability of a premium-positioned company to migrate its business model effectively to a new, lower-cost basis.

Self-Test for Executive Leadership

1. Do we have a structured approach to test for shifts in key customer groups' valuations of our product and service attributes?
2. Do we refresh this information (on shifts in customer valuation) frequently enough? (At least annually, if not more frequently)
3. Do we track the dollar and volume of total market share held by new entrants whose business models differ from our own?
4. Have we proven ourselves capable of self-cannibalizing our existing product and revenue streams with lower-cost products and services?
5. Do we systematically (and honestly) test our core customers' willingness to pay a premium for superior performance and/or brand reputation?

Interpreting the Results

Negative responses to two or more of these questions suggest the need to reexamine current market research practices, particularly those investments focused on core customer groups. The test you should apply is "Can we catch (very) early shifts in preference away from premium performance or brand power?" Negative responses here also suggest an opportunity for contingency planning as to how, in case of need, your organization could modify your current business model (including its current margins and cost basis) to respond to a low-cost entrant in less than eighteen months. For additional information on challenges related to such business model transformation, please visit our Web site, www.stallpoints.executiveboard.com.

Chapter 7 Innovation
Management Breakdown

Many of us associate the longevity of major corporations with individual histories of new product introductions: car manufacturers, obviously, with the world trained to expect important innovation on an annual basis; consumer goods companies, with "new, improved" features anticipated even more frequently; and technology firms, with expectations of accelerating innovation and price performance that have hardened into "law." Moore's Law (describing the inverse relation between integrated circuit performance and cost) is, after all, a management decision and not a dictate of nature. In point of fact, it is fair to say that most very large corporations rely on business models that have evolved in order to generate sequential rounds of product innovation. That said, when things go wrong here—in the heart of these organizations' most important business process—extremely serious, multiyear revenue growth problems result.

Across fifty years of contemporary business history, revenue stalls with innovation management problems behind them were the second most common category of growth crisis. More than half of the organizational stall histories we examined had innovation management factors at play. As witnesses to the growth plans and priorities of many major contemporary firms, what makes this most troubling to us is the stated reliance of many of these organizations on product or service innovation as a central, weight-bearing component of their expected revenue growth ramps going forward.[1] It's the quasi-magical plug, or *ingredient X,* used to close the gap between gains from pricing, acquisitions, and market share and the top of the multiyear growth bar into the future.

PROBLEMS OF PROCESS MANAGEMENT—
NOT PRODUCT FAILURES

For the revenue growth stalls we attributed to innovation management, what we saw emphatically were not problems with individual or even sporadic new product launch failures; a "New Coke" may occasionally belly-flop, but the resulting problems are typically temporary growth stumbles rather than long-term turning points in a company's growth fortunes. By contrast, the secular revenue growth stalls we identified were attributable to serious inefficiencies or dysfunctions in activities somewhere along the activity chain of product innovation leading from basic research and development to product commercialization.

While we think of established, enduring, innovation-led companies as relatively robust organizations, with their time-proven ability to regenerate growth, what strikes one immediately when looking across the stall factors that we identified is how precarious the business process of innovation management really is (fig. 7.1).

When we investigated the case studies, we saw, for instance, stalls whose origins lay in design choices about where and how basic R&D functions were located. Famously, Xerox PARC (Palo Alto Research Center) in the 1970s was located across the country from headquarters, too isolated for productive interaction with the sales and marketing leadership of the firm to commercialize breakthroughs in personal computing.[2] We saw decisions about funding levels at a variety of organizations create time-delay breaks in innovation processes that were difficult retroactively to catch back up to needed revenue growth. At some of the most respected innovation companies—Apple, for instance—we saw development cycle times slowed by a commitment to overengineering, with knock-on revenue growth consequences in fast-moving market situations. In product commercialization, new business organization, and the internecine struggles to set new technology standards, we saw cases of multiyear—and in some cases terminal—revenue growth consequences.

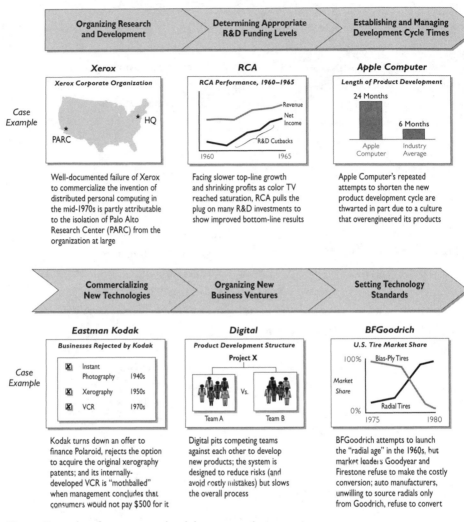

Fig. 7.1 Examples of management breakdown across the innovation process

Despite the complexity, what joins these diverse factors is that they are the result of conscious managerial decisions, not of problems thrown up by technology development or hard science. They highlight the fragility of a stream of activities across multiple functions that can be inadvertently disturbed by perfectly logical decisions taken for other company objectives but that, with time lags, can blow back with lasting revenue growth consequences.

In our review of company stalls due to Innovation Management Breakdown, we identified six root cause manifestations of the problem: Curtailed/Inconsistent R&D Funding; Over-Decentralized R&D; Slow Product Development; Inability to Set New Standard; Conflict with Core Company Technology; and Over-Innovation.

CURTAILED/INCONSISTENT R&D FUNDING

Not surprisingly, the most prevalent subfactor under innovation management breakdown is that which deals with the level and consistency of the R&D budget. It's a historically curious phenomenon, however, in that most stalls with this factor behind them are limited to the period before the last decade. And in fact, as research by Booz Allen and Hamilton has shown, R&D funding as a percentage of sales at very large companies has been growing quite healthily since at least 1999. (Booz's survey of the top one thousand public companies reveals that R&D funding averaged 6.5 percent of sales in this population from 1999 to 2002, a rate that accelerated to an average of 11 percent from 2002 to 2004.) At least at the time of this writing, *the absolute level* of R&D spending in these firms is perhaps not the primary cause for concern.[3]

This is not true historically, however. At ten companies we studied, multi-year breaks in R&D investments came back, with a time lag, in the form of emptied innovation pipelines and flagging revenue growth trajectories. RCA, for example, deliberately shriveled funding in television technology as color TV sales flattened in the mid-1960s in order to maintain strong growth in earnings. The same logic prevailed at Heinz through the late 1980s and early 1990s, as CEO Tony O'Reilly focused like a laser on managing earnings through cuts in marketing and R&D, eventually trailing off revenue growth by the mid-1990s. In commenting on the costs of this devotion to the bottom line for Heinz and several of its industry peers, O'Reilly's successor as CEO, Bill Johnson, confessed: "We weren't supporting our brands, and we weren't being innovative at all. . . . In terms of cost cutting, the mistake for the industry, in retrospect, is that it did not take the cost out of the system. It took the cost out of the product."[4]

Ford, Disney, Coke and others played the same underinvestment game with consequences for their revenue stalls, often guided by financial metrics in performance systems that were blind to the costs of disinvestment in the future product line. Executive teams leading today's largest firms may have taken (at least temporarily) the worry over the absolute level of R&D investment off the table. Into the future, the distinction made by Heinz CEO Johnson between taking costs out of the *product* instead of out of the *system* is probably the salient historical lesson.

OVER-DECENTRALIZED R&D

For firms shifting their R&D activities substantially out to their business units, there are strong cautionary tales in our cases. The logic behind moving the majority of R&D activity out to business units is clear—the closer to markets and individual business unit strategy, the higher the return on investment should be. The problem seems to occur when the decentralization logic is combined with an explicit (or implicit) metric that drives the organization toward a high share of new revenue growth from new product introductions. The result can be an overallocation of resources to ever-smaller incremental product opportunities at the expense of sustained R&D investment in larger, future product platforms.

A stand-out example here is 3M and its revenue stall in the mid-1970s, following decades of robust top-line growth. From its founding in 1902, the company had followed a clear formula for success: developing innovative solutions in industrial applications that supported a premium position and then leap-frogging to the next opportunity as the market matured. This strategy, which observers termed "the corporate millipede" ("make a little, sell a little, make a little more"), produced by the early 1970s a product portfolio of more than sixty thousand products (most with sales under $100 million), with over 25 percent of total corporate sales coming from products less than five years old.

The growth potential inherent in this niche-jumping strategy began to erode in the 1970s, as the firm approached $5 billion in revenue. As the recession of the early 1980s loomed, 3M management made the decision to hold R&D expenditures below historic averages of just over 6 percent of annual sales in order to boost earnings. In this, they succeeded dramatically, raising earnings growth substantially into the double-digit range. Simultaneously, management pushed the bulk of the R&D budget out and down below the sector level, to the company's forty-two individual divisions (typically organized around individual product lines).

At the same time, total growth was slowing as divisions focused on ever-smaller niche segment opportunities. From 1979 to 1982, the company saw its annual growth rate fall from 17 percent down to just over 1 percent, with sales per employee creeping downward simultaneously. With the bulk of R&D controlled by product-centric business units, major new product development activity was replaced by incremental product line extensions, eventually slowing revenue growth dramatically. As former CEO Allen F. Jacobson observed of that era, "Historically, our drive for profit and our preference for developing premium-priced products aimed at market niches meant that we were not comfortable competing only on price. As a result, we never fully developed our manufacturing competencies. And when competitors followed us, we would refuse to confront them—it was always easier to innovate our way into a new niche."[5]

Of course, 3M did pull the nose of the ship up again across the course of the 1980s under the leadership of president Lewis Lehr, repatriating a significant percentage of R&D resources up out of the company's divisions into four larger sectors. This gave the company the critical mass it needed to push larger-scale innovation, even as lower-cost competitors continued to encroach on previous niche markets, such as magnetic tape. It is a story that continues to the present, as subsequent leaders have carried on the fight to move the center of gravity of 3M's innovation process up out of divisions and toward larger-scale opportunities.

SLOW PRODUCT DEVELOPMENT

A third subcategory of innovation management linked to eventual revenue stalls is slow product development—internal engineering, prototyping, and testing processes that, though a source of pride to the company, are dramatically out of step with the pace of external developments in the market. Quite often, slow product development co-presents with other stall factors. For example, at Caterpillar, the company's ten-year development cycles and "cult of perfection" were rooted in its premium position strategy. At Apple in the late 1980s, sustaining innovation in the core PC business lagged because of reduced R&D budgets overall, with much of the remaining funding channeled into developing "the next big thing." The core business suffered, and competitors began to close the gap to their superior technology.

Stalls at Boeing and Motorola highlight the challenge of synchronizing the pace of engineering and development to the speed of market change. Boeing's 777 airliner is generally assumed to be a product success, but delays in its development allowed Airbus to seize the initiative and market share that Boeing has only recently reclaimed. Similarly, Motorola has become almost notorious for periodic advancements in cell phone technology that, because of the mismatch between its internal product cycle development speed and external cell phone market developments, prevent it from translating engineering enhancements into longer-lasting commercial advantage.[6]

We've come to refer to Motorola internally as "the stutter-stepper of American industry" for its uncanny ability to pioneer new businesses and then to migrate to new, high-growth opportunities just in time to recover its growth track. This tends to create a jagged pattern in the company's year-on-year growth rate but also points up the company's unusual ability to restart growth on demand.

INABILITY TO SET NEW STANDARD

A fourth subcategory of innovation breakdown involves companies that have succeeded in the technical task of creating a game-changing new product or service technology but then fail to get the breakthrough established as a new industry standard. Readers will likely associate the failure to set a new standard with the technology sector. For example, Apple's 1989 stall followed offers in the mid-1980s to license its Mac operating system, making it available to a wider audience. It would be a mistake, however, to assume that this phenomenon is limited to computing and personal electronics.

Having failed to set the industry standard with the tubeless tire, Goodrich hoped that introducing a BFGoodrich radial tire to the American market in the late 1960s and early 1970s might offer a second chance. The technology was pioneered in Europe by Michelin, a company with a limited presence in North America. Radial tires provided better performance and led to greater fuel efficiency; the disadvantage to the producer was the cost to retool production plants and the opportunity cost of no longer producing replacement bias/belted tires.

Goodrich management entered negotiations with Michelin for a joint venture but broke off the talks when Michelin would not allow Goodrich to control the venture. Goodrich converted much of its production capacity to radials, and Ford expressed interest in using the tires on a number of vehicles, including the then-popular Mustang. Engineers across the industry came to acknowledge radials as the superior technology. Yet, in the late 1960s, Goodyear, the number one U.S. tire manufacturer, denounced radial technology and launched a campaign emphasizing the less-than-smooth ride at low speeds as well as the need for special tuning. Goodrich, a relatively small supplier, failed to promote the radial tire aggressively enough on its own. The company soon retrenched, and the bias/belted tire remained the standard until 1973, when rising gasoline costs caused demand for better fuel efficiency to become a top consideration. By that time, Michelin had strengthened its position in North America and bested both Goodrich and Goodyear. Goodrich executives at that point agreed to invest in—but not advance—the company's position in tires, deciding that it would have to take a back seat to the faster-growing chemicals business.

Developing or gaining access to standard-setting technology is difficult, but the strategic choices involved in whether to open access to that technology, as well as how to beat competitors with stronger market power, proved in Goodrich's case to be the more difficult—and expensive—challenge. (As a grace note to this entire episode, the company exited the tire business a decade ago, licensing the BFGoodrich brand name to longtime rival Michelin.)

CONFLICT WITH CORE COMPANY TECHNOLOGY

Of increasing relevance to contemporary companies is a set of company stalls that had at their center the problem of exploiting a new, superior technology to which they had easy access or had generated themselves in their own research shops but that was in direct competition with an existing, dominant technology in their core business. The example of digital photography comes easily to mind at Eastman Kodak, where the new technology was acknowledged and explored in the early 1990s but where the self-disruption challenge simply couldn't be managed.

A case from longer ago—but perhaps even more dramatic—is the example of Siemens from the mid-1970s to the mid-1980s, with its handling of fax technology. By the close of the 1970s, Siemens was the dominant player in telex communications (remember telex?), with over 50 percent of the world's installed subscriber base. Earlier in the decade, Siemens's corporate R&D shop had developed the core technologies behind fax transmission, and in 1971 the technology was transferred to the then robustly growing telex division (fig. 7.2). The *logical* home for the new technology was in the long-range telecommunications unit, alongside the dominant telex unit. At the same time, the *worst* home for the fax was alongside telex, which was by far the more compelling magnet for investment and was itself beginning to face into a difficult future. Because of this siting decision, the business development opportunity behind fax technology was ignored, ostensibly for quality reasons, even as a set of Japanese companies led by Fujitsu began to invest heavily in the technology because of its ability to transmit images, not just characters. Across the ensuing

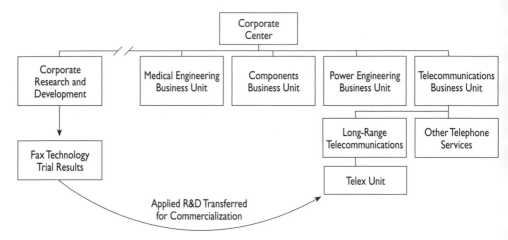

Fig. 7.2 The siting decision for new fax business incubation: Siemens organizational structure circa 1971

eight years, the quality curve of the technology steepened, eventually equaling telex transmission quality. By 1979, the game was lost: Siemens never resumed the manufacture of fax machines, choosing instead to license the technology and source the units for the German market, even as the telex business began its terminal decline. In reflecting on corporate parenting lessons learned, the vice president of corporate strategy at Siemens stated: "In 1971, we gave the fax technology to our telex department, but they did not seriously pursue the opportunity. . . . It was important for the Japanese companies to improve the technology—that's why they dominate the market today. If Siemens had given the fax opportunity to a separate new division rather than telex, we would have been more successful in the fax market."[7]

OVER-INNOVATION

Perhaps the most frustrating source of stalls for innovation-driven organizations are those related to what we have labeled "over-innovation"—major organizations where successive, iterative cycles of product innovation begin slowly to yield more new costs than new revenues. Much current literature has focused on the issue, typically from the perspective of the costs incurred from complexity in the business system as SKUs (stock-keeping units) proliferate. The recommendations here typically go toward cost management through product line simplification.

A revealing recent example of this is the case of Rubbermaid. The company enjoyed great growth across the 1980s, averaging 19 percent annual growth across the decade. It was even *Fortune* magazine's most admired company in 1993. But just as those issues of *Fortune* were hitting the newsstands, Rubbermaid was beginning to falter. Top-line growth for the first five years of the 1990s averaged only 9 percent, and earnings crashed in 1995.

As much as anything, Rubbermaid had been hostage to its formula, placing product proliferation at the center of its competitive strategy. In the words of then-CEO Wolfgang Schmitt, "Our objective is to bury competitors with such a profusion of products that they can't copy us."[8] By 1995, the company's product line extended to more than five thousand SKUs, sourced from a supplier base that exceeded ten thousand vendors, with over 30 percent of its sales from products introduced within the past five years. Within its product line color palette were 426 colors, including eighteen "distinct" shades of black!

In 1994, Rubbermaid experienced a doubling of the price for resin—its principal raw material—and a group of low-end competitors, including Tucker and Sterilite, entered its core housewares market. Rubbermaid management, naturally enough, attempted to pass on the resin cost increase to customers, a decision not wholeheartedly endorsed by its largest customer. Wal-Mart, responsible for 15 percent of Rubbermaid's sales, dug in its heels and refused to accept the increased prices. In fact, Wal-Mart, which had already been cherry-picking Rubbermaid's product line, now punished Rubbermaid by reducing its marketing support, slashing SKUs, and moving Rubbermaid products away from high-volume aisle end-cap displays.

In December 1995, Rubbermaid announced that it was abandoning incremental efforts to cope with its slow sales growth and plunging profits and instituted a wholesale rethinking of its strategy. The company discontinued 45 percent of its SKUs (accounting for only 5 percent of sales), reduced its supplier base by 70 percent and cut the color palette to fifty-eight shades. Perhaps the most important change was reflected in the company's revised product vintage sales goal, which now targeted only 10 (not 30) percent of sales to be from products introduced in the past five years.

Though a bit late to the game, Rubbermaid did change its formula, but only after alienating its largest customers and allowing some extremely potent new competitors to attack and erode its franchise from below.

STRATEGIC ASSUMPTIONS BEHIND
INNOVATION MANAGEMENT
BREAKDOWN

Once again, in looking across the many ways in which problems in the innovation management process can eventually produce major revenue stalls, one is struck by the fragility of the chain of activities and how vulnerable the whole process is to management decisions made for perfectly valid corporate goals. In the stalls we examined in this category, decisions that eventually produced breaks in innovation-led revenue ramps were based on a set of weakening (and eventually, failing) assumptions about competitors and customers and these organizations' own capabilities. Four of these dangerous assumption sets are presented below:

Product proliferation. Successful, long-term innovators such as Rubbermaid can find themselves overreaching their core markets' appetites for ever-more iterations and improvements in their core product lines, disqualifying underlying assumptions about limitless market appetite for differentiation and product performance.

Investment requirements. The roster of companies that have temporarily used fluctuations in their R&D investments and innovation funding to produce improvements in their earnings growth ramps is long. Ford, Heinz, Kellogg, Disney, Apple, and others found that their assumption that short-term cuts in innovation investments would not materially affect long-term revenue growth was shaky, at best.

Organizational structure. For the best of reasons, several case study firms had strongly decentralized their R&D and product innovation activities, driven by the assumption that the consistency of returns is best achieved through tighter, direct links to business unit priorities. As 3M can attest, however, overdependence on business-unit controlled innovation can improve the consistency of innovation returns, but at the cost of slowly starving the development of substantial new growth platforms for the firm as a whole.

Siting of disruptive new businesses. The temptation to place new, potential replacement products for existing core products in the same business unit is strong for incumbent firms. The assumption is that self-cannibalization and a smooth transition to the new core product can be best managed by the business unit at risk. As history at Eastman Kodak, IBM, Siemens, and other technology-driven innovators shows, however, existing business units can find a host of principled reasons to slow the growth of the new disruptive product in favor of existing technology.

INNOVATION MANAGEMENT
BREAKDOWN DEFINED

The second largest stall factor identified in our analysis, present in 13 percent of stalls, was Innovation Management Breakdown, chronic problems in managing the internal business processes responsible for renovating existing products and services and creating new ones. We identified six root cause factors that reflect the complexity of the activities contained in this category: Curtailed/Inconsistent R&D Funding; Over-Decentralized R&D; Slow Product Development; Inability to Set New Standard; Conflict with Core Company Technology; and Over-Innovation. The root cause challenges that present most commonly in our experience concern the nature of R&D investment (and therefore its resource allocation and focus between incremental and breakthrough innovation) and the self-cannibalization challenge inherent in the conflict of a new innovation with existing technology and business models.

Self-Test for Executive Leadership

1. Do we budget R&D and other innovation resources at the corporate level in a process that is separate from business unit-level (and therefore largely incremental) innovation funding?
2. Do we maintain adequate visibility into business unit-level funding decisions to monitor the balance between incremental and next-generation investment?
3. Do we allocate some portion of innovation funding to lower-cost versioning of our products and services, as well as enhancements for price premiums?
4. Do our market research and R&D arms maintain strong, real-time coordination of their efforts?
5. Do we expose the executive team regularly and directly to emerging customer and product trends?

Interpreting the Results

The questions above cleave into inquiries concerning level and direction of funding (questions 1–3) and internal coordination (questions 4, 5). Of the funding issues probed, a negative response to question 1 would be the most concerning—our experience suggests that few organizations are able to defend the process they use for determining central innovation funding. Question 4 probes a deceptively difficult challenge; on examination, it is common to discover few formal or informal linkages between R&D and market research. Last, direct experience of customer and product trends is helpful at accelerating senior-level deliberations on pricing, value migration, and innovation.

Chapter 8 Premature
Core Abandonment

The last of the three principal categories of stall factors related to strategy is a category we've labeled Premature Core Abandonment: the failure to exploit fully growth opportunities in the existing core business. Its telltale markers are acquisitions or growth initiatives in areas relatively distant from existing customers, products, and channels, with an accompanying neglect of growth issues in the company's core businesses.

This category of stalls is the third largest in our analysis and has received the most attention in recent business literature. Perhaps as a result, revenue growth stalls attributable to this factor cluster in the years before 1990: we cataloged fewer across the past sixteen years. We are tempted here to credit the management consulting industry generally (and certain business books, specifically!) for having hammered home the lesson of attention to core businesses. Although many strategy consultancies have developed valuable, penetrating perspectives on how to exploit the growth possibilities in the core, Chris Zook of Bain and Company deserves mention for having stayed on this issue with ferocity. Our analyses on rekindling growth in mature businesses suggest that most restarts happen in existing businesses rather than farther afield in new growth platforms.[1]

This is not to say that Fortune 100–sized firms have mastered the art of generating continuous growth in their core businesses. Quite the contrary—the phenomenon of private equity takeovers suggests that public companies suffer from the same problems as ever in extracting growth from perceived mature businesses. Almost without exception, these takeovers are based on fixing growth in the core business, with basic strategy solution sets that public company executive teams are either unable or unwilling to pursue.[2] With their preference for clarity, the capital markets no longer allow the wilder diversification strategies pursued by a relatively large set of major public companies across the 1960s, 1970s, and 1980s.

CONGLOMERATE THEORY—BUT ALSO THE SEARCH FOR "EASY" GROWTH

At first blush, one might be tempted to think that many of these diversification binges—whether they ended badly or just inconsequentially—were driven by classic conglomerate theory and a desire to balance business cycle or profit swings within the portfolio. For a substantial set of stall case studies this was true—to a point. But perhaps just as important, many of these diversification initiatives that ended up causing revenue stalls in core businesses were not only portfolio engineering to smooth performance but also undisciplined hunting trips aimed at finding easier growth businesses than those currently forming the core.

They also present as the adventures of leadership teams of individual companies rather than movements that take place within entire industries (fig. 8.1). As the diversity of companies here demonstrates, this misstep can occur in any industry or geography. As great a growth company as Gillette, for example, began to doubt the value of its flagship shaving business as early as the 1960s. In 1962, incoming chairman Vin Ziegler responded to slowing growth in shaving equipment and new advances by longtime rival Wilkinson Sword by announcing a diversification program the company called "planting seeds for growth." And these seeds were cast pretty widely: the program included acquisitions in more than fifteen businesses, including calculators, watches, potting soil, and leather goods. The consequent battles for corporate control between takeover artists Ron Perelman and Coniston Partners and Gillette's executive team would rage for decades.

Company	Original Positioning	New Businesses	Case Summary
Gillette	Shaving equipment—blades and razors	More than fifteen new businesses including calculators, watches, potting soil, and leather goods	• In the early 1960s, the company faces slow underlying growth in the shaving equipment market and new advances by rival Wilkinson Sword • Incoming chairman Vin Ziegler successfully argues for a massive diversification campaign to "plant seeds for growth"; the revenue goal is reached, but margins—and market capitalization—plummet • Takeover artists Ron Perelman and Coniston Partners fight for control of Gillette in the mid-1980s, citing inattention to core business
BankAmerica	Retail banking	International commercial lending	• In the early to mid-1970s, CEO Tom Clausen directs the company's resources and best talent to international lending; California retail operations fall behind as rivals modernize and upgrade • An early 1980s Boston Consulting Group analysis finds that Clausen should have expanded—not milked—retail operations, the company's most profitable business • One executive notes that for ten years "the bank just drifted"

Fig. 8.1 Representative stalls due to premature core abandonment

Company	Original Positioning	New Businesses	Case Summary
Volvo	Automobiles	Oil exploration, food products, biotech, leisure products	• By the late 1970s, Volvo executives lose faith in the potential of the auto industry to sustain growth, and they set out on a buying spree in a wide-ranging set of businesses • The ensuing shift in resources and attention away from autos is reflected in performance • By the mid-1990s, the new CEO divests all nonauto businesses, noting that "the automotive business demands total attention"

Fig. 8.1 Continued

One has to observe with a retrospective wince the strategic choices made by CEO Tom Clausen at BankAmerica in the mid-1970s when he chose to divert resources and focus away from retail banking expansion (which would soon enter a three-decade hypergrowth run) in favor of transitory growth and profits in the very different business of international lending. Core California retail operations fell behind as the bank's rivals modernized and upgraded. The bank hit its stall point in 1981 and lost ground across the 1980s. It would be twenty years before BankAmerica would regain its stature in U.S. retail banking.

Last, consider the case of Volvo in the late 1970s: assuming that growth rates in the worldwide auto industry were not favorable to the company's growth ambitions, Volvo's executive team used built-up cash reserves to diversify into a weirdly unrelated portfolio of oil exploration, food products, biotech, and leisure industry businesses. This adventure into unrelated acquisition would take more than a decade to unwind, sapping executive focus from the core automotive business all the while.

In our review of company stalls due to Premature Core Abandonment, we identified five root cause manifestations of the problem: Financial Diversification; Misperceived Market Saturation; Misperceived Operational Impediments; International Growth Masks Core Problems; and Earnings Growth over Core Reinvestment.

FINANCIAL DIVERSIFICATION

Across the middle decades of our study period—the 1960s through the 1980s—we identified a number of revenue stalls that had conglomeration-driven neglect of a core business as a central factor. Boeing's recurring problems in balancing its commercial aircraft business with defense contracting were a major contributor to a revenue stall as early as 1957—a pattern destined to be repeated. Goodrich abandoned the tire industry for the presumably faster-growing terrains of aerospace and specialty chemicals, only to be bogged down in unfocused acquisition-led growth. United Technologies found itself distracted by simultaneous strategy problems in all its new growth businesses, creating drift in its core industrial divisions. All these were cases where searches for presumed higher growth actually caused slow-growing core businesses to collapse through management distraction. Conglomeration theory always had its weaknesses from a financial point of view; the more meaningful perspective, as offered by history, may be that it compounded strategy challenges by adding new issues for management teams to deal with without relieving them of the burden of solving too-familiar problems in the core.

One of the most intriguing underlying causes of premature core abandonment is the executive belief that the core business market of the firm has matured and can no longer support the growth rate targets of the organization. The simpler form of this is when the executive team conflates the overall industry growth rate (accompanied by the firm's high market share) with the possible growth rate limit for the firm. So, for example, in its diversification binge in the late 1970s, Volvo management cited the worldwide auto industry's prevailing growth rate of 2 percent annually as justification for shopping around for a more favorable growth environment.

It's a common analytical sin, no doubt repeated in hundreds of conference rooms in the course of strategic planning retreats across the past half century. Of course, a variety of management consultancies and academic inquiries have pointed out the obvious fact that, whatever an industry category's overall growth rate, hidden within it lies a surprising range of individual company growth rates.[3] That said, most of us can at least identify with the "growth rate envy" of executive teams, bored with their familiar problems and peering over the fence at the novel terrain of a higher growth-rate industry category.

MISPERCEIVED MARKET SATURATION

More intriguing, perhaps, than growth rate envy is the straightforward mistake of just getting it wrong analytically. Several of our stall case study histories of premature core abandonment are stories of executive teams, deep in the numbers and the competitive dynamics of their industries, making the call that their industry is saturated and that no new innovations or new market opportunities are likely to unlock new growth. In a surprising number of cases, this kind of strategic judgment was made on the eve of veritable, multidecade growth revolutions in the industries about to be discounted.

Two particularly fascinating cases of this involve stalls at companies in the consumer electronics industry, choosing to turn their attentions away from this core market and toward other, presumably faster-growing opportunities—just as a two-decade hypergrowth run was to launch in their home turf. Philips Electronics, for example, made the unfortunate decision to shift its product line away from consumer products and toward industrial and military products in the mid-1960s. As a business press entry at the time sagely noted, "It's not a case of de-emphasizing a sure thing in favor of products with more prestige or large price tags. Rather, it's a case of recognizing the growth limitations of the consumer market as it looks tomorrow."[4] Led by its shift in R&D and product development efforts, the organization's top-line growth started a two-decade glide pattern downward, ending in a revenue stall in 1978.

Philips was not alone in this judgment of the saturated, moribund future of consumer electronics. No less an insider than Robert Sarnoff, chairman of RCA and son of the legendary General David Sarnoff, who led the company for more than forty years, came to the same belief. A *Fortune* magazine piece in the late 1960s reported Sarnoff's view that "the age of the big breakthroughs in consumer electronics—the age in which [the General] had built RCA—had passed. 'The physicists have discovered about all they are going to for consumer application in the near future,' says James Hillier, himself a renowned physicist who oversees RCA's labs in Princeton, NJ."[5]

One can hardly blame Sarnoff when even the physicists were advocating moving on. And move on, he did. From the mid-1960s on, Sarnoff pursued initiatives in three new, presumably higher-growth directions. Mainframe computers was a first big bet and seemed of a piece with the technology-driven "big bets" that had powered RCA's growth since the 1920s. He also decided that marketing was the future and deployed huge resources against acquisitions of companies in the consumer products sector. Beyond acquisitions, the company redirected internal resources away from consumer electronics research into marketing and brand management projects. Meanwhile, Steve Jobs and Bill Gates were just finishing up high school and about to begin companies and careers that would launch a revolution in both Philips's and RCA's former core markets.

MISPERCEIVED OPERATIONAL IMPEDIMENTS

Just as interesting as getting it wrong on core market growth prospects is the tendency of executive teams simply to give up on apparently intractable problems in their core businesses. Frustrated by years of slow (or no) progress against a persistent problem, the management team decides to end run it by moving on to new, presumably easier, competitive terrain.

Among our stall company cases, the most intriguing case of giving up prematurely on a core business because of operational challenge has to be that of Kmart across the late 1970s and early 1980s. Kmart, of course, was the highly successful challenger to Sears as a general merchandise big box retailer. Kmart emerged in the 1960s to compete directly against Sears, stealing market share relentlessly across the 1970s, and, as we documented in an earlier chapter, forcing Sears into a series of confusing up- and down-market strategy moves.

Kmart, for its part, reached its high point in new store openings in 1976, adding 271 new facilities to its countrywide network. It would prove to be its expansion limit. Across the next decade, Kmart would rein in its expansion plans in its core retailing business, convinced that the U.S. market was already too densely covered. Instead, its chairman, Robert Dewar, created a "special group on strategy" whose purpose was to study new growth avenues and, in the parlance of the time, "far out ideas." He also established a new performance goal for the company of 25 percent of sales from new ventures by 1990.

What's most disturbing about Kmart's activities is not necessarily the temptation of the management team to diversify in search of growth (however misguided this appears in retrospect, given Wal-Mart's concurrent gathering of strength). Rather, it is how the executive team failed to monitor and match operational capabilities in its core business then being pioneered in Bentonville, Arkansas, in distribution and inventory management.

While Wal-Mart was installing its first point-of-service system with a satellite link for automatic reorders in the early 1980s, Kmart was acquiring Furr's

Cafeterias of Texas, Bishop's Buffet chain, and pizza-video parlors as outlets for its retained earnings. Across the remainder of that decade, Wal-Mart continued to invest in its cross-docking distribution system while Kmart pursued a range of disparate businesses, such as Payless Drug Stores, the Sports Authority, and OfficeMax. By the end of the decade, Kmart was at least a decade behind Wal-Mart in its operational capabilities in logistics, handing Wal-Mart a "gimme" advantage of more than 1 percent of sales in inbound logistics costs. As Kmart fell ever further behind, its need for outside-of-the-core growth platforms became a self-fulfilling prophecy.

INTERNATIONAL GROWTH MASKS CORE PROBLEMS

An interesting minority factor within this category of stalls due to premature core abandonment appears at several firms that enjoyed strong—but temporally limited—growth runs in international markets, even as their core businesses in home markets were entering serious trouble. Both Digital Equipment, with its revenue stall in 1989, and Compaq Computer, with its apogee year in 1991, illustrate the phenomenon. Digital, for instance, saw a double-digit domestic sales growth rate fall off a cliff across the late 1980s, even as international sales exploded, eventually accounting for 75 percent of the firm's total sales growth. Management attention naturally migrated to the hot growth opportunity rather than to fixing the competitive issue in the U.S. core domestic market. Likewise with Compaq, whose phenomenal run of overseas sales growth masked a nosedive in core domestic sales. It's hard to argue with management attention to thorough exploitation of international opportunities; at the same time, it's impossible to avoid the lesson here of not letting those opportunities distract from fixes to problems in the core. Wal-Mart, of course, is currently the interesting case to watch closely, as its management team splits its attention between international growth markets and the conundrum of continued domestic growth.

EARNINGS GROWTH OVER CORE REINVESTMENT

Last, we saw in a number of stall cases instances where management teams slowed down core business reinvestment in order to fuel earnings growth rates.

Typically this was done with the intention of buying time from dissident share-holders and unhappy analysts to fix core business problems. Of course, the lags in necessary reinvestment in R&D, capital expenditures, and advertising set up ever-increasing gaps between top- and bottom-line growth rates.

Ford's stall in 1996 was the lagged result of a series of management decisions made across the 1980s, years where Ford's margins were the lowest among the Big Three automakers in the United States. Rebuilding those margins took two forms: first, postponing major design changes to the company's Explorer line of sport-utility vehicles (SUVs) for nearly eleven years; and second, slowing down investments in Chinese production facilities, which management had correctly (and presciently) identified as a key future growth market. The strategy was successful at lowering the company's cost base—cost reductions averaged between 10 percent and 12 percent annually in the early 1990s—but by 1994 the impact of this strategy on franchise value had become clear: by 1994, the company was trading at six times earnings, valuing the entire enterprise at $29 billion, despite having $14 billion in cash.

STRATEGIC ASSUMPTIONS BEHIND
PREMATURE CORE ABANDONMENT

As mentioned earlier, it's highly doubtful any executive team at a Fortune 100–sized organization could be unaware of the danger of prematurely giving up on the core in favor of adventures in unfamiliar, new terrains, given the writing, consulting engagements, and admonitions of capital markets throughout the past decade. That said, as our cases would authenticate, there is something perennially appealing about the dangerous strategic assumptions that drive executive teams to look elsewhere for new growth.

Across the five decades of cases we examined, three dangerous assumption sets reappeared with some consistency.

Industry growth rate as firm growth rate limiter. Few executive teams would state explicitly that their industry's growth rate is a speed limit for their firm's prospects, but it lurks in their collective mind-set as a constant temptation. It's especially powerful as a constraint on executive teams in oligopolistic markets where they already enjoy high market share.

The literature here can be confusing. Many consulting studies have high-lighted the broad variance in individual firm growth rates within industries growing modestly overall. At the same time, powerful arguments have been made that very large firms still able to support high growth rates are located mostly in sectors with similarly high growth rates, such as health care and high technology.

A McKinsey and Company analysis of large, high-growth firms suggests that the odds are strongly against firms seeking to maintain top-line growth rates above the low single digits for a multiyear period if they are not located in a sector that is growing disproportionately faster than the economy as a whole—in their metaphor, sailing with the "tradewinds."[6]

On the other hand, further analysis (and private equity strategy) suggests that higher growth rates can be maintained by focusing in on faster-growing, "granular" subsegments of larger, stodgy markets. Our own strategy work on growth has revealed cases of industry-leading firms (Alcoa, for example) disaggregating their markets and identifying multiple high-growth opportunities to pursue. Alcoa found through its approach to microsegmentation analysis that it had a less than 10 percent market share in more than half the markets it was addressing, leading to significant changes in its marketing and sales strategy and a resumption of higher core market growth.[7]

Operational and business model impediments to reinventing the core. A more modern flavor of premature core abandonment is that of incumbent firms finding that their core businesses now require competencies and even entirely new business models that appear too daunting in terms of stretch to current capabilities. Executive teams thus put on the defensive can become tempted in this circumstance to abandon the core in search of markets where current capabilities can be further exploited.

The likeliest outcome of such searching is, however, disappointment—the realization that current capabilities are far less fungible than the team imagined and that the better course of action would have been to stand and fight in their home markets through substantial business model change, no matter how painful. (Indeed, a beneficial impact of private equity owners is that they move aggressively to change out existing management in favor of new talent with the new competencies required to meet changing core business challenges.) A current exemplar of this "stand and fight" posture is Hewlett-Packard, which has adapted elements of the business models of its longtime rivals (Dell's order execution processes and Apple's priority on design elegance) to drive the unfolding turnaround in the personal computer business. The moral? Change the business model, not the core.

Cash cow reinvestment rate requirements. The final strategic temptation here is to assume that mature businesses have steady—or even declining—reinvestment rate requirements, allowing them to fund new growth opportunities (or pump up earnings ramps) with the harvest of their cash flows. It is intuitively powerful as a theoretical precept for portfolio management.

Unfortunately, the reality, as observed in stall cases across time, is that mature businesses are rarely stable—and seldom capable of being starved of substantial, continuous reinvestment for long. (In this respect, the disinvestment in the core implied by the "cash cow" cell of the growth-share matrix does modern managers no favor.) Mature, profitable businesses have a tendency to attract competition, and the breaks in R&D, capital expenditures, and advertising incurred to harvest cash for use elsewhere have a dangerous history of setting up multiyear revenue growth drop-offs within an alarmingly short time.

PREMATURE CORE ABANDONMENT
DEFINED

The third most common strategy factor leading to multiyear revenue stalls is Premature Core Abandonment—the failure to exploit fully the growth opportunities remaining in the current core business. This factor accounts for 10 percent of all stalls and presents in five variants: Financial Diversification; Misperceived Market Saturation; Misperceived Operational Impediments; International Growth Masks Core Problems; and Earnings Growth over Core Reinvestment. Despite convincing and voluminous academic and consulting evidence, the temptation remains for the executive team almost literally to run from challenges in its core business in favor of other, supposedly easier, opportunities. Decades of experience counsel otherwise: as rewarding as new ventures may, at first blush, appear, there is generally (always?) "more in the core."

Self-Test for Executive Leadership

1. Do we have significant revenue growth, as well as earnings growth, goals for our core businesses?
2. Do we avoid using the term "mature" to describe any of our product lines, business units, or divisions?
3. Is our core business reinvestment rate (R&D + CAPX + advertising divided by revenue) at least equal to historic levels?
4. Do we redefine our core market boundaries outward regularly, such that we position ourselves as having a small share of a large addressable opportunity?

5. Are we actively exploring new business models within our current core businesses?

Interpreting Your Results

A negative response to any of these questions should be taken as cause for concern. Questions 1 and 2 probe management attitudes and expectations for the core business and are of particular significance in identifying areas in the business that are likely to reward renewed scrutiny. Question 4 represents an extremely powerful discipline for ongoing core renewal—redefining addressable markets outward to create "running room" in the business. Readers interested in learning more about redefining core markets or redesign of business models should consult our Web site, www.stallpoints.executiveboard.com.

Chapter 9 Other Strategic Factors

We round out our census of the strategic factors causing growth stalls with a review of the five remaining factors in this, the "trunk" of our root cause tree (see fig. 4.1). Taken together, these factors account for 24 percent of growth stalls—and so are less significant than the three strategic missteps we review in chapters 6, 7, and 8—but they are worthy of analysis nonetheless. The factors we review here run the gamut from the familiar (the failure of an acquisition to bear out its promise) to the terrifying (dependence on a key customer for continued growth) to the surprising (the unexpected long-term consequences of deciding to take a "time-out" from growth).

The five factors are: Failed Acquisition; Key Customer Dependency; Strategic Diffusion/Conglomeration; Adjacency Failures; and Voluntary Growth Slowdown.

FAILED ACQUISITION

The first is a category we've called Failed Acquisition, accounting for 7 percent of stall factors cataloged. At a glance, this seems an intuitively obvious category, given the business press coverage that surrounds failed megamergers such as AOL–Time Warner or the business journal coverage of the persistent difficulties in acquisition integration. But as revealed in our longer time-frame analysis of revenue stalls, single acquisitions and problems with integration rarely produce more than short-term growth hiccups. And when acquisitions do affect the multiyear growth trajectories of large companies, it has far less to do with the operational challenges of integration than it does with what we would call the misconceived economic model underlying a serial pattern of acquisitions.

In many, if not most, of these cases, the usual suspect is generally also the responsible party. A more direct way of expressing this thought is that the "story" behind the combination, as conceived and sold by bankers to one or both of the parties, simply failed to capture the underlying realities of the businesses to which it was being applied. Two classic examples are the stalls of AutoNation and BancOne.

AutoNation's stall in 1999 interrupted a pattern of serial acquisition of auto dealerships captained by Wayne Huizenga, the entrepreneur behind Waste Management and Blockbuster. The roll-up logic that lay behind each of his earlier ventures—becoming the lowest-cost provider of the service through the acquisition of scale—would not transfer to this latest foray. Operating through his controlling interest in Republic Industries, AutoNation acquired 108 dealerships in 1996 alone, with a stock price supported by both sheer acquisition-led growth and a supporting theory of used car superstores. Unfortunately, AutoNation's superstores were beset with high inventory costs and overhead related to value-added services that undercut the supercenters' ability to compete simply and directly with lowest price. Competing dealership and car manufacturer lawsuits also played a role in AutoNation's stall, but the fundamental problem was a flawed cost model for the used car superstores.

BancOne, similarly, was a stock-fueled acquisition roll-up, originally supported by a Wall Street story of cost and revenue synergies. What was distinctive in the BancOne approach to acquisitions was what John McCoy (father and then son) dubbed the "Uncommon Partnership"—the promise to potential acquisitions of continuing local operating autonomy balanced by back-office compliance—centralizing paper and decentralizing people, in the phrase of the time. And the promise was compelling in the heady market of the late 1980s and early 1990s, allowing BancOne to gobble up more than a hundred regional banks. The conventional wisdom on BancOne's stall is that the bank's sally into derivative financing undercut the Street's confidence in McCoy's leadership. More persuasive from some historical distance is that BancOne simply failed to realize cost efficiencies in its acquisitions where other contemporaries, such as Hugh McColl's NationsBank, were clearly succeeding. The underlying economics of these "unconsummated partnerships" simply didn't work.

Certainly there are individual horror stories of a single acquisition poisoning a company's growth future for a significant number of years (think Sealed Air Corporation and its highly unfortunate acquisition of W. R. Grace's packaging business in 1998, just as asbestos litigation was about to create a new legal industry), but the reality is that single acquisitions do not generally create real, historical revenue stalls. Wall Street–enabled "roll-up" theories untethered to reality are more often to blame.

KEY CUSTOMER DEPENDENCY

Slightly less important in the aggregate but intriguing in its implications and remedies is a category of stall factors we've labeled Key Customer Dependency, accounting for 6 percent of stalls. This category of stall factors is highlighted in the historical shift in the balance of power between manufacturers and distribution channels partially created by the rise of Wal-Mart. Without hammering on the obvious, there are any number of major companies whose growth strategies are now, in some sense, hostage to Wal-Mart's fortunes and plans.

The phenomenon of voluntary or involuntary dependence on a single large customer (or very few large customers) is a central issue in large company growth history since 1990. As more companies seek to avoid commoditization through key customer integration, the resilience of strategy to market shocks is reduced proportionately to the reduced diversification of customer revenue streams.

Many readers will think of defense contractors such as Lockheed Martin in the mid-1990s whose growth fate was hugely affected (despite efforts to diversify) by the monopsony buying power of the U.S. government. But the perhaps more troubling (and growing) phenomenon is that illustrated by very large— but still highly dependent—suppliers such as Dana, the truck and auto parts manufacturer, which stalled in 1999.

Across the 1990s, Dana had steadily increased sales in both light truck chassis and heavy truck assemblies. And when the surge in light truck chassis-mounted sports utility vehicles hit in mid-decade, Dana made the "big bet" to ride the SUV wave, supplying chassis for these high-margin vehicles to the U.S.

market through the Big Three. By late decade, light truck-based vehicles were capturing nearly 50 percent of new vehicle sales.

Simultaneously with this market phenomenon, the Big Three were aggressively moving to consolidate their supplier networks, applying accelerating pricing pressure in return for preferential status—and in the process, transferring product development costs and submanufacturing responsibilities to "modular" partners. Dana aggressively pursued the role, acquiring dozens of smaller suppliers and moving aggressively into the design and manufacture of large subassemblies.

When the abrupt downturn in light-truck vehicles commenced at the end of the 1990s, Dana found itself in a position of highly leveraged exposure to the SUV-dominated strategies of its key customers Ford and GM. Its management team had, in the mid-1990s, recognized the importance of at least geographic diversification, with beachheads in Europe, but the requirements of its domestic light- and heavy-truck key accounts absorbed most of senior management's time. When the revenue stall came, it struck violently. In 2000 and 2001 alone, sales declined 6 percent and 17 percent, respectively. Laden with debt from acquisitions taken on to serve its key customers, and with a simultaneous downturn in its heavy truck business, Dana declared bankruptcy in 2006.

Not all key customer integration bets produce eventual bankruptcy, but sacrificing growth strategy flexibility for integration and deep reliance on a very few key accounts should give management pause. As an insurance policy against such abrupt surprises, leaders of businesses that find themselves structurally separated from the ultimate end customer, as was Dana and as are many manufacturing organizations, should redouble market research efforts to gather insight on their "customer's customer." Voice of the Customer and other structured processes that enable upstream players to peer through the periscope to spot and quantify emerging trends in end-use customer preference can provide early warning of changes that would otherwise be opaque.[1]

STRATEGIC DIFFUSION

Historically, and especially through the heyday of conglomeration in the 1970s and 1980s, a somewhat common stall factor was just the opposite—overdiversification, leading to a set of problems we've labeled Strategic Diffusion. Here, management teams suffered from *too many* strategy problems to solve (often, simultaneously), rather than *too few* strategic bets. This category accounted for 6 percent of stall factors cataloged.

Illustrative here is the stall of United Technologies in 1980. UT had its origins in the break-up of the United Aircraft and Transport Company from an antitrust action in 1934. Starting life from that point as the United Aircraft Company, it charted its history until the 1970s as a manufacturer of air transport vehicles and engines. The company became the premier maker of jet engines in the United States on the back of impressive R&D and technical talent.

But faced with the limitations of military contracting, the company chose an outsider for the first time in its history in 1971, Harry Gray of Litton Industries, with a charter to introduce new sources of growth. Gray took on acquisitions rather than operations as his personal mission, with a decided opportunistic rather than strategic logic. As chairman of the company as well, Gray oversaw board approval of proposed acquisitions on relatively thin presentations of evidence, relying on personal credibility with a board dominated by ex–military officers. As with so many stalling companies, UT and its leadership were celebrated right up to the precipice. In 1979, *Business Week* noted that Chairman Gray "has become a role model for other aspiring conglomerate builders, a hero to UT stockholders, a darling to arbitrageurs who have profited handsomely from his acquisitive efforts, and a terror to a raft of vulnerable companies that may very well be subjects of those dossiers that he keeps in his office. He has also transformed an ailing, inbred corporation highly vulnerable to the vagaries of a single market into a vital and diversified growth company."[2]

After engineering a decade of acquisitions of unrelated technology companies, the company's executive team entered the 1980s with ferocious strategy challenges on all fronts. These challenges presented across the portfolio and were distinct to each of the company's (fairly) unrelated divisions:

• Otis Elevator was confronted with new, lower-cost Japanese competition;
• Sikorsky Helicopters was facing renegotiation pressures with the Pentagon;
• The company's Pratt and Whitney unit was in a death match with General Electric, which was winning away major sole-source aircraft engine contracts;
• The Hamilton Standard operating unit itself struggled with overdiversification and overreliance on the U.S. government as its single customer;
• The Mostek semiconductor business faced new low-cost competitors; and
• UT's industrial division was facing a slowdown in the auto industry.

With financial resources focused on acquisitions and servicing existing debt load, UT cut back on R&D across its portfolio, aggravating competitive positions. Perhaps more important, coherent individual company strategies were never formed, as corporate attention was focused on a "conglomerate answer" of even more businesses to counterbalance the puzzling confluence of troubles in its existing portfolio. UT strategy retreats (if indeed operating management had the stomach, or time, to hold them) must have been terrifyingly complex affairs. Across the following decade after the chairman's departure in 1986, the company shed thirty-three thousand employees and multiple businesses as it sought to recover strategic focus.

ADJACENCY FAILURES

Interestingly enough, a small percentage (4 percent) of stalls were identified with what is usually presumed to be a relatively conservative growth strategy: the exploitation of so-called adjacency opportunities. The growth literature of the past decade admonishes companies to exploit those opportunities close to the core business that require relatively small changes to the core business model and to exploit pattern recognition.[3]

Sound advice, on the whole, but we did see a few examples of problems exploiting adjacencies that were large enough and serious enough to perturb growth ramps sufficiently to produce a multiyear stall. The most telling example of this overextension of the formula in our sample was Gillette with its 1996 acquisition of Duracell. For most of its history, since King Gillette invented the disposable razor blade in 1895, Gillette had thrived by acquiring a variety of personal consumer products (Toni Home Permanents, 1948; Paper Mate pens, 1955; Right Guard, Cricket disposable lighters, and Eraser Mate pens, 1960 through the 1970s; Braun, 1979; Oral-B, 1984) and investing R&D resources in them to raise them to premium status in their categories. The model for this formula, of course, was the core razor market, where Gillette lived by its periodic enhancements to build market share and to maintain prices.

Led by CEO Al Zeien, the company in the early 1990s found itself at a size where, in order to maintain double-digit growth rates, it needed a new platform beyond its hygiene and writing products. With the acquisition of Duracell in 1996, Gillette sought to apply its time-tested business model from the shaving business (superior marketing of a technology or engineering advantage that is perceptible to the customer) to small-appliance batteries. It also saw huge potential synergies in distribution between its new battery business and its existing product lines. Across the next five years, Gillette invested in enhanced performance, introducing the Duracell Ultra with a 20% pricing premium and a claimed 50% extension of battery life. But the company found that the formula simply did not apply to this product category, where battery longevity improvements were not valued in accordance with the price premium. A well-timed counteradvertising campaign by a lower-priced, lower-performance Energizer (remember the bunny that keeps going and going?) also diluted Duracell's ability to capitalize on its performance edge. In commenting on the size of the bet that Gillette made with Duracell, then-Gillette president Edward F. DeGraan stated: "We can't have Duracell as an acquisition that doesn't do well, and then we bury it sometime in the future. There isn't a hole big enough for that."[4] Pattern recognition and extension of the business model when targeting adjacencies can give a false sense of security. When the growth bet involved is large enough, it can be a multiyear stall factor.

VOLUNTARY GROWTH SLOWDOWN

Closing out this review, in a very small set (2 percent) of cases we identified a stall factor we've labeled Voluntary Growth Slowdown—the executive team's deliberate decision to take a revenue growth time-out in order to pursue earnings growth improvements, to hit related metrics of EVA (economic value added) or MVA (market value added). This stall factor never appears in isolation; executive teams choosing the growth time-out option are reacting to short-term performance pressures for immediate profitability enhancements.

The riskiest strategy we encountered is the deliberate signal from the executive suite that top-line growth is being set aside for a time. The chief executive at one company that shall remain nameless announced to the Street: "I don't expect sales to grow as rapidly in the 1990s as they did in the 1980s, but our net margin will probably grow faster. We're aiming to get the benefits of this empire that's been put together over time." This statement was uttered in the fourth year of a stall from which the company has yet to recover.

We are struck by how severe and long-lasting the consequences of that honest and well-meaning statement have been. To be fair to our anonymous case example (a leader in its sector), the decision to sequence efficiency and productivity over growth undoubtedly appeared to be the wisest course in the moment. But the lost momentum attendant to "taking your foot off the gas" has caused us to ponder: why it is so hard to turn revenue growth on and off? The historical record suggests undeniably that it is—growth recoveries at stalled companies, if ever successful, are long, painful episodes of cultural and executive team change. The answer lies partly in the obvious distinction between the relative controllability of financial ratios: there are dozens of ethical ways to hit ROIC (return on investment capital) or ROA or margin targets, all of which

draw on experience and skill, but these metrics are ultimately controllable—
they exist within the direct range of management decisions internal to the firm.
Revenue growth, on the other hand, lies in the more mysterious realms of entrepreneurship and innovation. When a firm's executive team and company
culture opt for controllability over growth, the latter skill sets can evaporate
rapidly.

OTHER STRATEGIC FACTORS DEFINED

Five additional strategy stall factors complete the picture of strategy-
based mistakes behind 70 percent of all stalls: Failed Acquisition, typically because of flaws in the underlying economic model; Key Customer
Dependency, particularly when the strategy assumptions of key customers go untested; Strategic Diffusion, stretching an executive team
across too many unrelated strategy challenges; Adjacency Failures, stem-
ming from misapplication of existing, familiar business models; and Voluntary Growth Slowdown, which proves surprisingly difficult to reverse.

Self-Test for Executive Leadership

FAILED ACQUISITION

1. Is our firm's acquisition strategy (if you use this strategy) a "formula"
   (for example, roll-up or tuck-in deals) applied in existing markets, as
   opposed to one of big and/or distant "bets"?
2. Are we "strategy makers" in our relationships with the investment
   banks and other advisers who serve us? (That is, do we approach them
   with the logic behind potential acquisitions?)

KEY CUSTOMER DEPENDENCY

3. Does no single customer account for more than 20 percent of our business?
4. Do we explicitly identify the critical assumptions underlying our key
   customers' growth strategies and monitor them for continued viability?

STRATEGIC DIFFUSION

5. Are we clear (precise, certain) about the value that our corporate center provides to the portfolio of businesses we operate?

6. Are we effective at recruiting, developing, and retaining senior leaders with experience and skill sets suited to the challenges faced by our disparate business units?

ADJACENCY FAILURES

7. Are we able to diagram the logic behind our strategy of adjacent expansion, thereby controlling how much risk we take on in any individual move?
8. When we pursue adjacencies, do we plan adequately for differences in the business model or management capabilities required to win in the new sector?

VOLUNTARY GROWTH SLOWDOWN

9. Do our earnings growth plans require cost-cutting and/or productivity improvements for more than 50 percent of year-on-year growth?
10. Do we segregate ("picket fence") business reinvestment funding to protect it from diversion to short-term earnings management targets?

Interpreting Your Results

The questions in this section go to markers of risk that have led to stalls in a variety of consumer and industrial businesses, so although none is commandingly important, they are all significant. Perhaps obviously, negative responses to both questions in one category highlight an acute concern. Negative responses to questions 1, 3, 6, 8, and 10 are also worthy of examination, since these questions relate directly to the degree of risk inherent in overall strategy and the organization's ability to manage this risk on a continuous basis.

Organization Design Factors

Chapter 10 Talent Bench Shortfall

In our journey across the thicket of root causes of stalls, we move now from the trunk to the thickest branch—from factors related to strategy choice to factors related to Organization Design and to the largest top-line category, Talent Bench Shortfall (see fig. 4.1). Defined as a lack of adequate leaders and staff with the skills and capabilities required for strategy execution, this category accounts for 9 percent of the stall factors we cataloged.

This factor merits careful definition, because to some extent talent shortfalls have become a fact of daily life in many industries and functions. Indeed, shortages of critical high-skill talent are, at this writing, the primary concern of Human Resources departments globally, not just in high-growth markets but in a range of specialty skill categories—and are forecast to get worse.[1] What stops growth dead in its tracks, however, is not merely a shortage of talent—some recruiting failure to reach full staffing levels, for example—but the absence of required skills or competencies in key pockets of the firm and, most visibly, at the executive level. This absence can arise through some shock to the system—a dramatic loss of key talent, for example, that reveals in an instant a degree of crippling dependence—or through the gradual emergence of a need for different-in-kind skills or experience. It is quite common to see companies lagging this shift because of a systemic internal bias in their talent acquisition and development policies and processes. These are the cases we profile in this chapter—and the red flags we set forth for senior management attention.

Talent bench shortfalls of the magnitude we spot in our stall case studies present in four specific root causes: Internal Skill Gap; Narrow Executive Experience Base; Loss of Key Talent; and Key Person Dependence.

INTERNAL SKILL GAP

By far the most prevalent root cause in this category, internal management or talent skill gaps are often self-inflicted wounds, arising as an unintended consequence of too strictly applied promote-from-within policies. Such policies, which are typically adopted most fervently by organizations with strong cultures, can accelerate growth in the early, heady days of an initial run or a formula rollout. But when the external environment presents a novel set of challenges or when competition intensifies, these policies can become an absolute sea anchor to progress.

The 3M company, whose challenges with R&D organization we profiled in chapter 7, suffered from just such a skill gap, which delayed its entry into consumer markets. The firm's lackluster performance in the consumer sector was attributed to its inexperience with the costly launches of mass consumer products (anathema to the "millipede" strategy) as well as to its reluctance to go outside of its ranks to bring in experienced consumer products managers, something 3M had never done. In a 1980 *Fortune* article on the firm's increasingly public challenges with consumer markets, a former 3M executive warned that "a judicious, sparing use of top outside talent would help bring new and fresh ideas forward. Without them 3M is going to have a tough time in consumer products."[2]

What stayed its recruiting hand was the company's long-standing, absolute commitment to a policy of promotion from within. With the exception of managers 3M acquired along with other companies, internal or external observers found it hard to identify midcareer executives brought in from the outside. Talent attraction, development, and retention had always been points of pride for 3M; the firm's now-famous policy of allowing 15 percent of "tinkering" time to its technical staff was but one of the policies contributing to a 97 percent workforce retention rate. The *Fortune* article also notes that policies such as these long made the company impervious to external poaching. One recruiter interviewed for the article lamented, "I've never been successful in getting anyone from 3M."[3]

The interesting question raised by the 3M case, among others in our files, is, when does a towering strength become a weakness? When does a commitment to internal advantage become a liability? After all, as this growth stall was unfolding, two 3M engineers, Art Fry and Spencer Silver, were famously puzzling with potential uses for a glue that "didn't stick very well"—the discovery that launched the Post-It franchise.[4] Could this icon of innovation have maintained its heady rates of top-line growth through greater openness to the external talent markets? What decision rules can guide management here?

Our review of the issue suggests that the bias of promoting from within is almost guaranteed to hinder growth if its implementation requires selecting from a pool of internal candidates that is narrower than that available on the external market. Many firms climbing up the *Fortune* rankings have developed such policies from their earliest days and have maintained them as a driver of culture continuity into midlife. But virtually all continuous growers in the Fortune 100 size range we studied have committed themselves to an open posture toward the external market. Exceptions do exist in the cases of firms that regularly leaven their internal talent ranks through acquisition.

Management teams wishing to perpetuate an internal bias thus must make the investments required to maintain a continuous "mark-to-market" posture, particularly for emerging skill areas that are plentiful in the external market. We review potential investment strategies that we have seen in operation later in this chapter.

NARROW EXPERIENCE BASE

A more acute variant of internal skill gap is the stall factor we've called narrow experience base—excessive homogeneity within the senior executive rank that delays timely response to emerging strategic issues. The most common marker of this narrowness is a tendency to follow a well-worn path internally from a dominant business, market, or function to the executive suite.

We saw this pattern repeatedly in our stall cases—especially in companies with a high degree of market or customer concentration. Boeing's development of commercial market applications was greatly slowed following its 1957 stall owing to the absence of commercial experience, or DNA, in its executive team.

BankAmerica's 1981 stall was prolonged due to what one analyst called a "twisted interpretation" of founder A. P. Giannini's tradition of lifetime employment, adopted during the Depression. Where a comparable major corporate bank might have three or four well-qualified candidates for each senior position, BankAmerica would be lucky to find one. CEO Sam Armacost was unable to effect step-level strategic or organizational changes demanded in the marketplace in large part because of this dearth of top-flight senior talent: "People were not fired, salaries were kept as low as possible. When a fast-rising young executive quit to join another institution at a higher salary, the bank let him go."[5]

Even broad multi-line companies are not immune from this phenomenon of a well-worn path to the executive suite. Proud Hitachi, accounting for 2 percent of Japan's GNP and 6 percent of corporate R&D spending as recently as 1992, has suffered the effects of a growth stall in 1994 that capped decades of sustained growth. The resulting downward slide in earnings has been the most devastating in the company's history since its founding in 1910. Executive management has consistently come up from the energy and industrial side of the company, but the company's growth prospects lie elsewhere. This one-sidedness extends to functional pedigree: none of the firm's top managers has an MBA or other business degree—it is exclusively an engineering culture. As the firm looks toward its centennial in 2010, signs of change may be in the offing. Kazuo Furukawa, named president and chief operating officer in 2006, is the company's first president with no exposure to the company's heavy electrical machinery business, having come up through Hitachi's Information and Telecommunication Systems Group.

LOSS OF KEY TALENT

Although the stall factors we have reviewed so far in this chapter presented with more frequency, instances of loss of key talent are by far the more dramatic. IBM's stumble in 1968 marked the end of 20 percent and up annual growth for the firm. The stall came on the heels of bruising—and unaccustomed—competition from DEC in the emerging minicomputer segment of the market, but one year earlier the firm had also suffered an unprecedented mass exodus of talent. A group of technicians from IBM's San Jose–based storage-products group disgruntled with their compensation resigned en masse to form Information Storage Systems. This "Dirty Dozen," as they came to be known, were followed a year and a half later by a "Gang of 200," lured away by

IBM veteran Alan Shugart to form the core technical team at upstart Memorex. Rubbermaid's stumble in the mid-1990s was followed by the unwanted turnover of fourteen of the firm's sixteen top managers by 1996, including all of the company's international division chiefs, forcing Rubbermaid to abandon its strategy of relying on international sales for top-line growth.

But the story of talent loss that tops all others in our files emerged from the Walt Disney Company—and in particular the sorry state of affairs that greeted Michael Eisner and Frank Wells when they arrived in the mid-1980s to try to restore the magic to Disney.

Reflecting in later years on what he had learned from the turnaround, Eisner held that the center of Disney's finances are its movies, and at the center of its movies are the animated films, and at the center of the animated films is a group of six hundred artists. Eisner pictured those six hundred animators as being a "talent box," and his own view was that he brought almost nothing to bear for those individuals in the box. He couldn't lift a pen, he couldn't suggest a drawing, he couldn't improve the technical product. His task was simply to defend the box: to know every individual therein and to guarantee that they were protected against the corporation—and the world—at large.

Eisner found the box when he joined Disney in 1984—but it took some looking. Specifically, he had to penetrate four levels down into the organization to find it: from the chairman's office, into the filmed entertainment business unit, down into the animated features division, through the production department, and then into lead animation, nestled right next to the production assistants.

Here one would find the box that he spoke of, but it had endured a long, lazy death spiral in the years since control of the company had passed from Walt Disney to Card Walker to Ron Miller, Disney's son-in-law. The last film that Walt Disney himself worked on, *The Jungle Book,* was released in 1967. He died three years later. *The Rescuers* came out in 1977, the last film developed by the original animation team—the so-called Nine Old Men—who drew *Snow White, Pinocchio, Fantasia,* all the classics. Across the 1970s, the animators were put on week-to-week contracts—$600 a week—with the understandable result that features took four to five years to complete, on average.

Then came "Black Monday"—a devastating talent drain—senior animator Don Bluth and sixteen colleagues left to form a rival studio, and total headcount in animation was down to two hundred. By now, the Nine Old Men were well into their seventies and all gone from Disney by 1985—not one lifted a pen to draw *The Black Cauldron,* a strangely un-Disney film of witchcraft and black magic released that year. By Eisner's arrival, the Disney board was rumored to be considering closing the division and purchasing features from the outside.

Utterly unconfused about his own priorities, Eisner and his partner Frank Wells set to work, placing the box under the stewardship of Jeffrey Katzenberg and Peter Schneider, quadrupling the number of animators, investing in computer-based animation technology and commissioning the Robert Stern–designed Feature Animation building to house the function. At the dedication of this soon-to-be landmark, Eisner was quoted as saying, "It all starts here. If it doesn't work here, everything else we do does not matter."[6]

KEY PERSON DEPENDENCE

The last of four root causes in the category of talent bench shortfall, key person dependence, is also the rarest. We've defined this category tightly as "overreliance on the contribution of a single individual (typically a founder) for growth strategies or execution skills." This level of dependence is much more likely in firms well below the size band we examined in our research than in Fortune 100–sized enterprises, and we found ourselves constantly second-guessing our judgments here. We typically ticked this column as a contributory factor and never as the sole factor responsible for a stall.

The classic type of this phenomenon is the passing of a founder, allowing a company to become unmoored from its competencies or driving vision. The decline of animation at Disney in the years following the death of its eponymous founder, discussed above, certainly fits this pattern. Sony's 1994 stall can be attributed to a company suffering in sympathy with its cofounder, Akio Morita, after a stroke on a tennis court a year earlier forced him to retire the chairmanship. Steve Jobs's famous departure from Apple in 1985 preceded that company's stall by three years. (And the renaissance of the firm following his no less famous return after a decade's exile simply underscores Apple's degree of dependence on him.) Though David Sarnoff was not a founder of RCA, his passing in 1970 is generally agreed to mark the end of the golden years of that company.

The remaining cases we flagged were instances of CEOs who, though not wielding the founder's imprint, nonetheless cast such commanding shadows that their passing had an outsized impact on company growth and direction. The easiest of these to spot and flag was the dramatic 1999 stall of Coca-Cola on the death of the irreplaceable Roberto Goizueta two years earlier. The story of the Goizueta years has been much chronicled in the business and popular press, and it is true that any leader coming behind him would have had a tough act to follow: stock price up 3,800 percent across his sixteen-year tenure, creating more wealth for shareholders than any other CEO in history. Even still, the giant has been at sea in the years since his passing, cycling through three CEOs and eking out only low-single-digit revenue growth in the new century.

PREVENTING TALENT BENCH SHORTFALL

In the Corporate Executive Board's membership program for chief human resources officers (CHROs), the myriad challenges of attracting, developing, and retaining scarce high-skill talent are never far from the top of the strategic agenda. This is nowhere more true than at the top of the house, executive succession, for which the CHRO generally maintains personal stewardship. In our research, we identified a simple method for the CHRO to provide an insurance policy on balance in the senior executive rank—what we call "mix management."

Few companies monitor formally the balance in the executive team between company "lifers" and individuals newer to the company who offer novel perspectives and approaches. If anything, large companies have a fairly poor track record at incorporating new voices in senior management. Most studies agree that somewhere from 35 percent to 40 percent of senior hires wash out in the first eighteen months, a statistic that is improving glacially as we learn to innovate new practices in talent management.[7] One executive we interviewed was willing to be unusually candid (if off the record) in describing the situation facing new peers at his company: "We really can't bring people in from the outside, because they are 'rejected' by our culture. They'll come out of meetings where everyone is smiling to their face and agreeing [on a course of action], and as soon as they leave the room the knives come out."[8]

How should human resources accomplish this mix management? What are useful rules of thumb? Analysis from our human resources practice area is beginning to circle in on an answer (fig. 10.1). Although we do not present a comprehensive cross-industry analysis or a commandingly large sample here, the data are intriguing nonetheless—and suggestive of a useful approach. The petroleum company at left sources just 1 percent of its executive rank from the outside and has growth of 3 percent a year. To the right, a computer company has 75 percent of its executives new to the enterprise and a growth rate of 41 percent. Positions at either end of this array are clearly undesirable: the computer

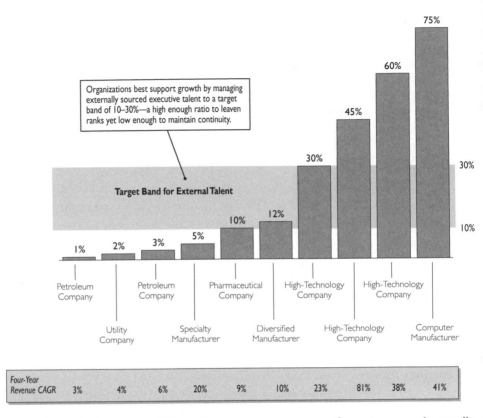

Fig. 10.1 Increasing importance of talent mix management: percentage of executives sourced externally in selected companies

company will have a hard time maintaining any cultural continuity with the demographics shown here. The middle of the band is probably just about right—somewhere between 10 percent and 30 percent of senior management drawn from the outside. This "target band for external talent" is a good metric for the CEO and the board to monitor at the executive committee of the firm and for the human resources organization to monitor for the top 5 percent of the workforce.

You may wish to monitor this metric in your firm, but you'll likely have to calculate it first. In our experience, few companies have included data such as this anywhere on their dashboards.

It might be a point of interest to note that the "diversified manufacturer" in the center of the exhibit—12 percent external talent quotient, 10 percent CAGR (compound annual growth rate)—is General Electric. It's somewhat predictable by now that GE should be in the "sweet spot" on a management metric; what may not be as well known is the strategy that the company adopted to achieve this level of diversity in its most senior ranks.[9]

On becoming CEO in 1981, Jack Welch created the Business Development Program as a management change mechanism within the firm. The program was structured as an autonomous consulting unit reporting to the corporate office and placed under the direction of Gary Reiner, then as now the firm's chief information officer. The intent of the program was to complement the firm's coveted entry-level development programs with an entry portal for top-tier midcareer talent. Candidates were actively sourced from the strategy consulting majors, as well as from a range of investment banks and more specialized professional services firms. Individuals were screened on the basis of analytic horsepower, teamwork, and star quality leadership potential, and successful candidates could then join the internal consulting arm, the Corporate Initiatives Group, or the internal mergers and acquisitions advisory, the Corporate Business Development Group.

Following an eighteen- to-twenty-four-month rotation in these groups, incumbents would be placed in high-profile operations and line positions. One HR manager reported to us: "From the line perspective, we love to see these people. We put them into key jobs, and they hit home runs. . . . Business units get the advantage of the outside perspective along with the certainty that these people are a good internal fit with GE culture."[10]

At our last look into this program, it had been enormously successful at leavening the firm's senior executive band. Approximately 3–5 percent of the top band of the firm had entered through the program, and about 75 percent of the program participants were still with the firm after three years, a very strong performance in what could have been an extended exercise in culture shock.

FAULTY ASSUMPTIONS UNDERLYING
TALENT BENCH SHORTFALL

What unifies the stalls involving talent bench shortfall is a set of assumptions about talent that many executive teams share. They group roughly into three belief systems that are worth the trouble to articulate and use as an internal barometer of any firm's talent management health:

Internal market bias. Most successful, fast-growing firms (or at least those with a recent history of rapid growth) have developed strong, coherent cultures with a predisposition to promote from within for critical positions. Strong company cultures can sometimes repel outsiders who don't enjoy the trust and shared mindset of the executive team. The easiest choice for any firm with strong success in its past is to rely on the known quantity of internal candidates. At best, this can serve as an effective speed limit on growth, if internal talent development isn't operating at peak efficiency. At worst, it hardens into a resistance to the importation of fresh competencies and alternative perspectives on company strategy.

Closure to external perspective in the executive ranks. The perceived need for a "shared perspective" in an organization is strongest in the senior executive ranks. Few organizations find it a comfortable process to mix manage at the most senior level of the firm deliberately for outside perspective. This is probably even more true in periods of duress, when the most natural group instinct is create a singularity of vision and focus on execution rather than a reconsideration of foundational strategy assumptions.

Lack of clarity around critical talent sets. Successful firms have strong formal and informal systems for the development and support of workforce competencies critical to the company's past success and not necessarily to its future needs. Competency models, training programs, and compensation systems all support the skill sets that account for the firm's growth to the present. It is supremely difficult for such organizations, first, to articulate and agree on what future talent sets may be required, and second, to rewire the organization to cultivate and/or recruit and support them.

TALENT BENCH SHORTFALL DEFINED

The most common Organization Design factor driving growth stalls is Talent Bench Shortfall, the lack of adequate leaders and staff with key skill sets to execute the firm's growth strategy, accounting for 9 percent of stalls. It contains four root causes: Internal Skill Gap, particularly of managerial or technical talent; Narrow Experience Base at the executive level; Loss of Key Talent, typically mass defections of scarce skill or core differentiating competence; and Key Person Dependence, either the founder or (more rarely) a visionary leader. Although relatively small in number from the perspective of the overall stall points taxonomy, this category should flash perpetually amber in today's climate of growing talent shortages. Going forward, executive teams at most growth-oriented firms will need to consider the following question areas in setting strategy.

Self-Test for Executive Leadership

1. Are we acting on the need to introduce any new technical or professional discipline into our organization across the coming three years?
2. In recruiting for key positions, are we free to select the best possible candidate, regardless of internal or external sourcing?
3. Do we manage the mix of internal and external perspective in our senior leadership rank to an approximately 30 percent externally sourced talent quotient?
4. Have we identified the internal skill sets (and individuals) that provide our competitive advantage and differentiation in the marketplace?
5. Do we dedicate resources and senior attention to ensuring that these assets (individuals) are internally engaged and safe from external poaching?
6. Do our policies for identifying high-potential employees (HIPOs) select for required future competencies as well as the capabilities required for the current business model?
7. Is our strategic planning closely coordinated with human resources, such that growth plans are explicitly translated into talent acquisition, development, and retention plans?

Interpreting Your Results

The question areas above range from near-in recruitment and sourcing issues to longer-range planning considerations. You should follow a negative response to question 1 with a prod to your recruiting organization—particularly if the discipline you are adding relates to consumer marketing, a fast-moving skill area. Questions 2 and 3 probe openness to the external talent market, and 4 through 6 the amount of focused resource your organization brings to the cultivation of scarce talent. (In this regard, a negative response to question 4 would be particularly concerning.) Question 7 represents a frontier discipline in human resources; readers wishing to examine a model strategic HR plan may consult our Web site, www.stallpoints.executiveboard.com.

Chapter 11 Other Organizational Factors

Beyond talent shortages and mix management problems in the talent ranks of the firm, we cataloged three factors related to organization and human resource policies that figured, collectively, in 8 percent of stall points. While never the primary driver of revenue growth inflections, they typically served as the strong secondary influence that allowed an initial strategy problem—often explicitly recognized by the executive team—to tip over into a multiyear downturn.

The three remaining categories in our stall factor review are: Board Inaction; Organization Design; and Incorrect Performance Metrics.

BOARD INACTION

First among these factors is a phenomenon familiar to modern readers: Board Inaction. At 4 percent of stall factors cataloged, it is one of the more interesting and controversial "major/minor" factors. Our conclusion after reviewing many examples of valiant board action and agency—as well as some notable failures to act—is that, though never the principal cause of a stall, weak boards effectively remove a company's last clear chance to avert a downturn. In fact, we have structured chapter 14 of this book as a direct address to boards and CEOs for precisely this reason: we see in today's current climate unprecedented challenge and opportunity to board engagement with strategy, and we have the utmost admiration for Jay Lorsch and his peers in corporate governance advisory who are exhorting board members to engage constructively and actively with strategy testing and challenge.[1]

Cautionary tales tend to return to the theme of boards that, through their composition or lack of expertise, were not able to exercise this check on headstrong chief executive influence. Commencing in 1940, the Dow board began to be dominated by company insiders to a degree that would not be allowed today. With only two nonemployees on the board, CEO Willard Dow slowed the firm's market and capability expansion and engineered a voluntary growth slowdown in 1956 that exacerbated the company's unfolding stall. Somewhat more recently, Volvo's then-CEO Pehr Gyllenhammer created a hostile environment for dissenters, leading to the resignation of two board members in 1984 and giving management unchecked rein to diversify into unrelated biotechnology, oil, and gas interests. Losing market share in its core auto business, Volvo was reduced to an unsuccessful search for a merger partner by the end of the decade.

By point of contrast, it's interesting to look at the case of Compaq Computer from 1986 through 1993, when the company was headed into—and then pulled out of—a revenue stall. Compaq's executive team, led by one of its founders, Rod Canion, was highly trusted by its largely independent board. Management had earned this trust from the board, since Compaq through the 1980s was highly admired for its ability to counterpunch with its principal rival, IBM, and to establish itself as a legitimate alternative to the much larger incumbent. The Compaq leadership team employed a disciplined management style that avoided the vagaries of decision-making by an iconoclastic, strong-willed entrepreneur-founder. Trouble came to the company from below, in the form of upstart rival Dell. As Dell's new direct sale business model and differentiated marketing message pounded the previously unassailable Compaq, and as the management team avoided and then delayed major changes to its premiumpriced product line and to its increasingly overmatched dealer network, the board intervened firmly and promptly. Led by its chairman (and veteran venture capitalist) Ben Rosen, the board replaced Canion with company officer Eckhard Pfeiffer in 1992 in a move that was shocking for its suddenness. Within nine hours of his appointment, Pfeiffer was taking actions to develop a new, lower-cost product line and a new distribution system to counter Dell. The nose of the plane was pulled up and a revenue stall avoided, even if Compaq continued in a mortal struggle with Dell in the years after. (Rosen continued exercising resolve in his role as chief shareholder advocate, ousting Pfeiffer seven years later, in 1999, after two earnings warnings had shaken the Street's confidence in Pfeiffer's management.)[2]

The activist posture of Compaq's board demonstrates the power of a board, when grounded sufficiently in company strategy, to redirect strategy rapidly and decisively.

ORGANIZATION DESIGN

The second organizational factor we cataloged concerns a set of companies whose stalls derived from deep problems related to Organization Design. Three underlying root causes here: Over-Decentralization, typically manifesting as a commitment to business unit autonomy so absolute as to prevent coordinated capture of growth opportunities; Decision-Making Structure, diffusing owner-ship of growth initiatives in heavily matrixed environments; and No Strategic Planning, which is self-explanatory—but no less surprising for that!

Sometimes these "decentralized to a fault" organization structures are a legacy of history, whereas at others they are a reflection of mere size. The trick for management is to understand how to set the balance between being decen-tralized enough to promote entrepreneurship, ownership, and growth while not creating redundant cost structures and balkanized innovation. Citicorp's travails in the early 1990s are illustrative.

Following the firm's growth stumble as it entered the 1990s, Citicorp man-agement found itself wrestling with a freewheeling culture. With manager compensation tied principally to the performance of the firm's 250 indepen-dent profit centers, it is no surprise that what some characterized as a lawless culture took hold. Most memorable from the era are reports of the terminology that characterized "Citispeak" at the time: "paradising" was the practice of cre-ating one's own back office and computer facilities in pursuit of a larger empire. The Development Division was the ultimate "paradise"—a $100 million R&D enterprise (in a bank!). Most damning was the phrase "the Actuarial Base," long since expunged from the hallways. The term referred to the premise that exec-utives were free to take large risks because the bank was so big and diverse that any problem would be offset by success in another area—sort of the historical equivalent of today's derivatives and securitization-led approach to systemwide credit risk. Reflecting on those days, James Bailey, a Citicorp executive, recalled, "We were like a medieval state. There was the king and his court and they were in charge, right? No. It was the land barons who were in charge. The king and his court might declare this or that, but the land barons went and did their thing."[3]

Another dynamic exasperatingly familiar to many current executive teams is the tangled web of heavily matrixed organizations and the problems this can create in executing quick, crisp decisions on key strategy issues. Philips Electronics stands out in our case files as a firm that got tripped up by a matrix structure that was deeply hardwired into the firm's operating system. Following a growth stall in 1978, management's focus in accelerating growth was to rebalance power between the firm's product divisions and its country management structure, its National Organizations, or "NOs." (This acronym was memorably, if unintentionally, prophetic.)

The NOs were unusually powerful in Philips as a legacy of protectionist measures enacted across Europe during the Great Depression and World War II. The NOs consistently held sway, preventing Philips from achieving scale economies and flexibility in the fast-moving consumer electronics market. As two examples of this power: Philips's television manufacturing was divided among numerous country markets in Europe, with virtually all plants operating below scale, and headquarters unable to convince the NOs of the advantages of pan-European operation. In addition, even though the firm's household appliance business was barely profitable and steadily losing market share, the NOs firmly resisted discussion of central manufacturing. The result was that washing machines and other appliances built in Germany and Italy shared no common parts.[4]

This organizational imbalance was merely an annoyance in the company's heritage businesses of consumer appliances, but the structure effectively blocked the efforts of senior Philips management to recruit new talent and to shift focus to truly global product lines, such as semiconductors.

Many management teams find themselves in some echo of Philips's predicament—structured by product but needing to swing the pendulum over to customers; regionally structured companies trying to move to global product lines or processes. We intend no criticism of Philips in relating this case or their predicament; we are simply impressed by the need to act when structure impedes, rather than impels, strategy.

A final organizational design issue here is the relatively straightforward factor of No Strategic Planning—the absence of any corporate planning function devoted to the portfolio logic or competitive positioning of the firm. The arresting case here is of Ralston Purina in the early 1990s. Across the 1980s, the company had pursued a diversification strategy whose sum was decidedly less than its parts: each acquisition possessed a short-term financial logic, but the resulting portfolio defied categorization—the mix of restaurants, batteries, bakeries, ski resorts, and other unrelated categories thoroughly puzzled external observers.

The constant shifting of the portfolio and the focus on share buybacks for short-term earnings management eventually allowed even the company's iconic businesses in pet food and cereals to drift aimlessly as competitors and markets shifted radically. A company insider at the time confessed that "the main problem we have at Ralston is we have no real strategy." Pressed to explain, William Stiritz, the chairman and CEO, responded to a question about global strategy by stating, "We don't have any global strategy; we don't believe in that stuff. We take it as it comes."[5] And so the company did.

INCORRECT PERFORMANCE METRICS

Completing our journey across the root cause tree is the last of our organizational stall factors: Incorrect Performance Metrics. The two root causes here—Incorrect Competitive Metrics and Inflexible Financial Goals—arise, in large part, for a shared reason: management teams fail to refresh financial and competitive metrics frequently enough to ensure continued relevance and efficacy of the key measures on their dashboards. Our case files are replete with instances of companies that have blinded themselves to an incipient stall through unquestioned reliance on outdated (or simply wrong) performance metrics.

Among our historic stall cases, AMR, the parent company of American Airlines, is an intriguing story of a disciplined, data-driven organization relying on outdated competitive metrics in the face of a decades-long change in the competitive environment. AMR introduced yield management science to the airline industry as early as 1956, with its Magnetronic Reservisor system, to keep track of available seats on flights. Across the 1960s the company partnered with IBM to introduce SABRE, the largest electronic data processing system then in use other than the U.S. government. Beyond its airline business, AMR was a pioneer in the industry in adding aviation and airport service businesses to its portfolio.

As new, lower-cost competitors to the majors appeared in the late 1970s following deregulation, AMR, with its sophisticated data capabilities in yield management, continued to focus on competition with other majors, where such metrics made sense. Missing from the yield management equations, however, were the substantially different cost bases of new, nonunionized competitors with single-model fleets and simplified route structures. CEO Robert Crandall viewed such competition as temporary, niche interlopers, continuing to focus on maximizing revenue per flight with the prevailing cost structures of the major carriers. Three decades of perfecting a yield management tool for competing against competitors with the same cost constraints created the strategic environment that made it difficult to envision a new approach to confronting interlopers.[6]

As for the other manifestation of Incorrect Performance Metrics, the case of Apple Computer is instructive on the strategic limitations that can be imposed by Inflexible Financial Goals. Apple Computer's historical attachment to 50 percent and up profit margins restrained the firm in its early days from product introductions and other investments that might have enabled it to establish at least a double-digit foothold in the personal computer market. Further, following a stall in 1989, and facing higher DRAM costs and spiraling R&D and SG&A expenses, the company attempted to increase margins by raising prices by almost 30 percent, a gambit from which it was forced to retreat three months later. Reflecting on his repeated attempts to refocus the Apple leadership team on market share from gross margin, then-CEO John Sculley lamented, "We took a business that was humming and sent it into a nose dive."[7]

Across all of these organizational factors—Board Inaction, Organization Design, and Incorrect Performance Metrics—we've seen examples of structural issues that, though they do not rise to the level of primary driver of a revenue stall, have been strong supporting causes. Impeded by slow or overly complex designs, unresponsive boards, and misleading metrics, executive teams under the duress of difficult strategy challenges can miss opportunities to redirect the design and dashboards they use to govern the firm.

OTHER ORGANIZATIONAL FACTORS DEFINED

Organizational factors account for a modest 9 percent of our total stall factors, but play a significant supporting role in a number of large company revenue stalls. Root causes include Board Inaction, deriving either from composition or disposition; Organization Design hampering responsiveness to changes in the external environment; and Incorrect Performance Metrics, typically arising from stale metrics or inflexible attachment to an outmoded financial goal.

Self-Test for Executive Leadership

BOARD INACTION

1. Does our board as a whole, or a standing or ad hoc committee, possess adequate industry knowledge or experience to stress-test our strategy assumptions?
2. Does the board use nonfinancial strategic objectives as well as financial outcome measures in determining the CEO's performance plan?

ORGANIZATION DESIGN

3. Does the organization structure we've chosen support us when we need to adapt quickly to an external market or competitive development?
4. Do we have a corporate-level strategy function? Does that function serve as the staging area for development of long-term strategy?

INCORRECT PERFORMANCE METRICS

5. Have we revisited or refreshed our overall company performance metrics in the past two years?
6. Do our financial performance goals help us to capture opportunities to establish a leadership position in important growth markets?

Interpreting Self-Test Results

The six questions above range across broad, politically charged terrain. We discuss the issues raised by questions 1 and 2 on board activities in chapter 13. Negative responses to either suggest the opportunity for a confidential review of the desired role for the board in strategy development and performance evaluation. Question 4 is harder than it looks, thus the two-part question—the focus of the strategy function in many companies is being almost wholly diverted to near-in planning concerns. Questions 5 and 6 probe whether current performance metrics serve the organization well in keeping the focus on growth.

Part III **Avoiding**
(or Recovering from)
Growth Stalls

Chapter 12 Practices for Articulating and Stress-Testing Assumptions

Our analysis to date has taken us deep into the growth experience of a comprehensive set of large firms across the second half of the twentieth century, cataloging the incidence of secular stalls in their growth trajectories and describing the root causes of those stalls—the often-mortal wounds management teams have suffered to their ambitions for the growth of their firms. Our observations have been quantitatively grounded and inductively derived, and our recounting of company experience has, we hope, been respectful of the awesome task of charting a course for—and then leading—multibillion dollar enterprises. (It is tempting to slip into an all-knowing posture when holding a rearview mirror up to experience, and we are conscious that this perspective provides an unfair advantage to the analyst.)

In this third and final part of the book, we change gears significantly, lifting up to the question that lies behind all of this collective experience—what is *really* going on here? What is the ultimate lesson that readers should take away from these findings, and what are the actions that executive leaders should take?

We believe that a powerful observation can be distilled from all of this experience. Behind all the stall points, behind the thicket of root causes, behind the case studies of stall experience, we see one root cause: a lack of effective action on the part of management to close the gap between company strategy and the external environment. This can manifest itself as a lack of self-awareness that the gap exists (or is widening) and as a challenge of prioritization—of all of the problems we face, which is the most important to address?

The lack of self-awareness is particularly vexing because it is so insidious. In chapter 4, we introduced the role and importance of strategic assumptions in grounding strategy. *Stated in the extreme, we have gleaned from our analysis of executive experience with stalls that the assumptions the team has believed the longest or believes the most deeply to be true are the likeliest to be the team's undoing, because these beliefs are so obvious and accepted that it is no longer politic to debate them.*

Given this, we devote this third and final part of our study to a set of process suggestions that leading companies have pioneered to articulate, stress-test, and monitor the assumptions that underpin their strategies. Our hope is that readers will find one or more of the practices we profile here exportable to their own settings—consistent with their industry environments and corporate cultures—and implementable at low upfront cost into operating cadence and calendar.

FROM OBSERVED REALITY TO BELIEF SYSTEM

The very fact that the growth strategies that propelled our case study companies to world-class status were founded on sets of assumptions attests to the fact that they are not necessarily "bad" rigidities and unfounded, blind beliefs. In fact, as pointed out by Peter M. Senge and Daniel H. Kim, they make possible efficient decision-making under conditions of high ambiguity (fig. 12.1).[1] Assumptions begin as direct observation about the world in the formative years of young company history, become incorporated into business planning, are then relied on as operational guidance, and finally pass into unspoken, strategic orthodoxy.

As the continuing success of the company validates strategic assumptions, they cascade into a growing structure of foundational and then supporting assumptions about the competitive environment, forming an ever-more complete worldview for the organization and the senior executive team. A good example here is the world of discount airline competition for U.S. domestic passenger flights (fig. 12.2).

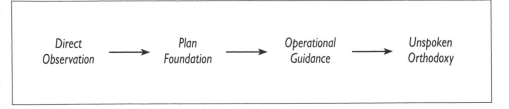

Fig. 12.1 Life cycle of a strategic assumption

Major assumptions—the bets early entrants made to join the competitive fray—concern the power of the strategy to alter customer behavior and thus market share; the cost benefits of equipment standardization; the niche entry opportunity offered by point-to-point itineraries; and the perceived customer benefits of self-service ticketing. These major assumptions decompose into a larger set of foundational assumptions about customer and competitor behavior and business economics. These foundational assumptions are observable, factual phenomena on which strategy decisions can be based—demonstrated customer preference to trade off service levels for low price, say, or the turnaround time advantages of short-hop route networks. And these foundational assumptions give birth, in turn, to supporting sets of subsidiary assumptions that aid efficient operational-level decision-making down through the organization.

THE CHALLENGE OF MAKING STRATEGIC ASSUMPTIONS EXPLICIT

Despite the importance of understanding and monitoring the link between strategic assumptions and the evolving external context, executive teams rarely take the time or care to articulate explicitly the assumptions on which strategy is based. It is even rarer that management will have defined precise metrics around these assumptions that allow them to be tested against external reality. And from a strategy validity point of view, assumptions are rarely triaged or prioritized to identify those few foundational assumptions that are critical to the continuing health of the organization's strategic direction.

The ability to articulate assumptions precisely and to test them continuously is foundational to what Stanford professor Robert Burgelman and former Intel

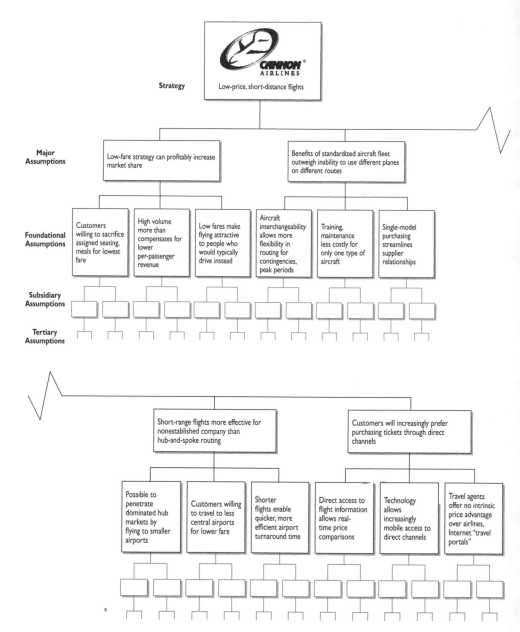

Strategy — Low-price, short-distance flights

Major Assumptions
- Low-fare strategy can profitably increase market share
- Benefits of standardized aircraft fleet outweigh inability to use different planes on different routes

Foundational Assumptions
- Customers willing to sacrifice assigned seating, meals for lowest fare
- High volume more than compensates for lower per-passenger revenue
- Low fares make flying attractive to people who would typically drive instead
- Aircraft interchangeability allows more flexibility in routing for contingencies, peak periods
- Training, maintenance less costly for only one type of aircraft
- Single-model purchasing streamlines supplier relationships

Subsidiary Assumptions

Tertiary Assumptions

- Short-range flights more effective for nonestablished company than hub-and-spoke routing
- Customers will increasingly prefer purchasing tickets through direct channels

- Possible to penetrate dominated hub markets by flying to smaller airports
- Customers willing to travel to less central airports for lower fare
- Shorter flights enable quicker, more efficient airport turnaround time
- Direct access to flight information allows real-time price comparisons
- Technology allows increasingly mobile access to direct channels
- Travel agents offer no intrinsic price advantage over airlines, Internet "travel portals"

Fig. 12.2 Strategy rests on an array of assumptions: structure of strategic assumptions for hypothetical competitor in U.S. discount airline segment

CEO Andy Grove have called strategic recognition, "the capacity on the part of top and senior management to see the strategic implications of new internal and/or external developments for the company's future, usually *after* they have already been initiated but *before* there is general agreement about their implications."[2] This is a leadership competency that was in perilously short supply when they brought the term into the active debate in 1996. Now a decade on, we would argue that the problem is a decade worse.

Our membership of heads of corporate strategy has identified the articulation and monitoring of strategic assumptions as among the weakest areas of current performance in large corporations and as one of the greatest opportunities for impact.[3] In an annual survey, we ask strategists to report how well they believe their organizations are performing against twenty core strategy and planning objectives and how important they believe each area is to overall outcomes. By comparing responses to each area, we can size the gap between performance and importance to help members set their priorities for the coming year.

The two halves of the assumptions challenge (articulation and monitoring), taken together, are the number-one area of performance opportunity as perceived by our members, outstripping even such important focus areas as "embedding strategic thinking in line management" or "understanding customer needs." This is an area of active and urgent experimentation and focus.

In this and the next chapter, we document practices for addressing this challenge that leading organizations have pioneered and that they have allowed us to document for potential emulation by their peers. We turn first to the challenges of articulating and then stress-testing the assumptions underlying strategy.

PRACTICES FOR ARTICULATING
STRATEGIC ASSUMPTIONS

This section profiles two practices that we have documented for articulating strategic assumptions—forcing the senior executive team to make explicit and unambiguous the foundational assumptions behind current firm strategy and to sort critical from noncritical assumptions to allow focus for further inquiry. This work can—and will—feel somewhat remedial when first undertaken but is essential to bring into the open the unstated, infrequently tested beliefs that underpin the senior executive team's worldview. The goal is typically achieved most effectively by including a significant set of company managers in the exer-

Practice in Brief: Core Belief Identification Squad

A cross-sectional employee working group goes on an internal "hunting expedition" to identify the firm's most deeply held assumptions about the company and the industries in which it participates. The process is highly effective at assembling a catalog of accepted wisdom in a compressed time frame.

Mechanics

- Under the guidance of a sponsor from senior management, company staff assemble a working group of 12 to 25 employees. The group should span geographies, operating units, and functions and should be biased toward younger, newer employees less likely to be invested in current firm orthodoxies.
- Across a relatively compressed time period (days or weeks, not months), the members of the team conduct internal research against a narrow list of questions (see illustration, opposite) that probe first principles of company strategy and industry success drivers.
- Individual research is punctuated by meetings of the entire working group to review findings and to identify areas of agreement—and disagreement—within the various management levels of the firm.
- Overall findings of the effort can be used in (at least) two ways: (1) "Edges" of internal convention about the business can be explored to identify franchise-expanding opportunities; and (2) Areas of unanimous agreement among senior management can be assembled into a unitary list for periodic review.

Assessment

- This practice is remarkably effective, in part because the effort to articulate key assumptions is so seldom undertaken. Good questions yield good answers.
- It also represents a healthy compromise between traditional, black box strategy processes and all-inclusive "jams" or other company-wide processes. Striking the right balance in democratization of inputs to the process is a worthy goal.
- Pacing is key: this practice can be very low-cost and very compressed in cycle time, if the correct group of participants is chartered.

Fig. 12.3 Diverse perspectives facilitate the hunt for corporate orthodoxies

Representative Question Areas for Focus in "Core Belief" Identification

Identifying Internal Orthodoxies

1. **What conventions do we hold about...**
   - What industry we are in?
   - Who our competitors are?
   - Who our customers are?
   - What our customers want?
   - What we are good at?
   - How we make money?
   - How we grow the business?
   - How we organize?
   - What values and behaviors we promote?

2. **What 10 things would you never hear these groups say about our business?**
   - Top management
   - Customers
   - Competitors
   - Shareholders

Identifying Industry Orthodoxies

1. **What things are commonly considered "critical success factors" in this industry?**

2. **What do industry leaders believe about...**
   - Who the customer is?
   - How to reach them?
   - The basis for differentiation?
   - Where to take profits?
   - How vertically integrated to be?

3. **Who has succeeded by breaking the established "rules" of the industry?**
   - What conventions did they overturn?

4. **What major innovations of the past 10 years has our company missed?**
   - Who saw them? How did they see the opportunities that we missed?

BALANCING FOCUS AND INCLUSION IN STRATEGY REVIEW

"We used this technique to kick off an inquiry into long-term pathways to growth for our company. It was very helpful in stretching our thinking and challenging our conventions by drawing on the expertise and perspective of a larger cross-section of the organization than we typically involve in strategy review processes."

Vice President
Fortune 100 Consumer
Products Company

cise rather than creating a "star chamber" or having one executive document his or her views. An unintended payoff reported by early practitioners is that the process can be highly motivating to participants, because the outcome is a meaningful level of consensus in the organization around the issues critical to company success.

Core Belief Identification Squad

One innovative approach in use is a practice we've dubbed the core belief identification squad (fig. 12.3). The process is simple to execute and involves commissioning a diverse, cross-sectional working group within the firm to go on an internal "hunting expedition" to identify the firm's most deeply held assumptions about itself and the industries in which it operates. For setting a baseline, the activity is incredibly useful at identifying areas of universal agreement (which, as we note above, are no less important—or suspect—than areas where consensus does not exist), as well as tapping minority views that can leaven strategic deliberations at the senior executive table.

Across a compressed time period, members of the team conduct internal research using a common set of questions; interviewees range across management levels in the business units and in major functional areas of the firm. The process is designed to be conducted quickly—days or weeks, not months— and team members meet periodically across the process to compare notes and to document findings.

Early practitioners report that two aspects of the process are particularly important to get right. Identification of the correct participants is a critical ingredient of success (see fig. 12.3). Although the correct number of participants can range widely depending on organization size, the need for diversity and intellectual independence in the participant set is of universal importance. The best-functioning squads represent a cross-section of the firm but are biased toward younger, newer employees less likely to be invested in current orthodoxies.

As important as the quality of participants is the quality of the questions they are armed with. The art in constructing questions is to arm individuals to raise the thorniest, most entrenched beliefs by ranging across a series of fact-based queries ("What industry are we in?" "Who are our customers?") to more provocative issues of judgment and speculation ("What ten things would you never hear customers say about our business?" "Who has succeeded by breaking the established 'rules' of the industry? What conventions did they overturn?"). The short list of questions in fig. 12.3 probes both internal and industry orthodoxies.[4]

One leading consumer products organization reported that it used this practice to kick off an inquiry into long-term growth pathways for the firm and found it helpful to challenge conventions that had taken hold across the years. We like this practice because it seems to arrive at right answers on two issues that we often see firms struggle with: first, striking the right balance between traditional, closed-door strategy discussions and all-company "jams," which tend to lose credibility and edge in direct proportion with the number of participants involved; and second, constructing a mix of questions that raises both the areas of universal agreement and those that are currently in play.

Pre-Mortem Strategic Analysis

A second practice for articulating key strategic assumptions that leading executives have found both useful and (dare we say it?) fun is pre-mortem strategic analysis (fig. 12.4). The practice charges teams of senior managers with developing competing visions of the future success—and failure—of the company, as they would be reported in a business periodical five years hence. Collation of the issues underlying the respective takes on the company's future enables the working teams to identify the considerations common to both scenarios—and therefore the issues critical to company success going forward.[5]

Most instances of this practice that we have reviewed have taken place across multiple days in an off-site setting for management. The practice has three principal steps. In the first, which can take a half-day or more to complete, teams outline and then write the articles documenting company success and failure. (A best practice here is to have each team member in the working group compose his or her version, and then the team's final product is created using the best elements of individual stories.) We have seen real creativity at this stage in the process; for example, one organization had teams create collages illustrating the major elements of their success and failure scenarios.

After individual visions are complete, team members are shuffled to create new working groups containing a blend of members from the success and failure teams. These groups then deconstruct the articles to identify the "big bets" that went right (or wrong) in each. Last, the entire group assembles and collates individual lists to identify the issues that are common to both scenarios: success and failure. These issues, logically, represent the set of capabilities, uncertainties, and objectives that must be most closely managed.

Practice in Brief: Pre-Mortem Strategic Analysis

Senior managers work in teams to document and then analyze competing visions of the future success—and failure—of their company's strategy. In addition to being kind, the practice immediately enables the team to identify the crucial issues for executive focus and resourcing.

Mechanics

- Senior management sets aside a 1- to 2-day time slot for the top tier of leaders to engage in the exercise. Most companies scale the exercise to include the top 30 to 50 leaders in the firm.
- The group is divided into multiple teams, which are given one of two assignments: "Write the newspaper or business periodical article dated 5 years from now that celebrates our great success" or "Write the newspaper or business periodical article dated 5 years from now that chronicles our abject failure." Distribute the resulting articles to all participants.
- Create new teams that blend members from the respective assignments. Charge them with analyzing the success and failure projections to identify the issues that were material to each. What were the issues we got right that drove our success, and what were the issues we got wrong that caused our failure?
- Collate these lists to identify the items appearing on both the success and failure ledgers. These are the crucial issues on which to focus management attention and resource investment.

Assessment

- Pre-Mortem Analysis is a highly effective way to enfranchise a large portion of the senior rank of the firm in surfacing the key success factors underpinning company strategy. It's a nice balance of creativity and practicality.
- The exercise is, however, time-consuming. Creation of the articles alone typically takes at least a half-day or more, and the entire exercise can easily extend across two days of work.
- An experienced external facilitator is enormously helpful at making the process enjoyable and at navigating the sensitivities that the process can raise. (We would be pleased to share a list of consultancies and solo practitioners we have identified that specialize in facilitating this type of exercise.)

Fig. 12.4 Pre-mortem analysis uses alternative visions of future success to isolate crux issues

Overview of Pre-Mortem Strategic Analysis Process

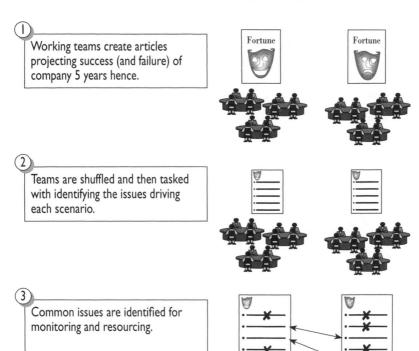

① Working teams create articles projecting success (and failure) of company 5 years hence.

② Teams are shuffled and then tasked with identifying the issues driving each scenario.

③ Common issues are identified for monitoring and resourcing.

--- ADOPTING THE POSTURE OF THE "INVOLVED OUTSIDER" ---

"Our management has been around for such a long time, they know one another so well, they know the business so well. Turning them into consultants was a creative way to use their talent and knowledge and allow them to be more critical of the company's strategy, though in a constructive way. The 'consulting hat' created a third-party feel that was very important."

Vice President,
Planning & Analysis
Fortune 750 Food Company

As we indicate above, one reason that this practice has proven so popular with executive teams is that it *is* fun; writing the articles is a memorable, tangible accomplishment that allows group members to showcase their various skills. In addition, the consequences of the strategy assumptions are made vivid in the articles themselves, lending weight to the activity. It is also extremely selective—a short list of critical issues will surface when teams collate the positive and negative takes on the future. One executive noted that the process allowed his management team to step away from its insider status and to adopt a critical, objective posture toward the company's prospects.[6]

EXPOSING STRATEGIC ASSUMPTIONS
TO INTERNAL AND EXTERNAL SCRUTINY

Perhaps an even thornier problem than surfacing key strategic assumptions for successful firms with highly aligned executive teams is exposing those assumptions to constructive challenge. In the world of corporate practice, there is a long and somewhat shaky history of attempts to invite challenge to prevailing orthodoxy. Practices to raise alternative views of strategy down deep in the ranks typically mutate into exercises to release steam or to communicate existing strategic orthodoxy more profoundly through the organization.[7]

As for external perspectives on management's strategy orthodoxies, the challenge mechanisms most in use currently are proxy battles and private equity offers, hardly evolutionary approaches to changing management's strategic assumption sets.

Even more perversely, suppliers and venture partners—potentially useful interrogators for executive teams' worldviews—are more often absorbed in successfully integrating with their big bet customers or coventurers, rather than questioning the validity of their strategies. In fact, for many companies in the business-to-business sector, operational-level integration planning with their partners has replaced a good deal of their traditional strategic planning activities (a root cause we have flagged as "customer strategy dependence," which could well be in the ascendant as a stall factor for the future).

What's needed are credible, timely challenge mechanisms that can shake management awake when a cherished assumption is under threat. In a *Harvard Business Review* interview, Jeff Bezos, CEO of Amazon, captured the nature of this challenge perfectly: "A lot of our strategy comes from having very deep points of view. . . . Of course there could also come a day when one of those things turns out to be wrong. So it's important to have some kind of mechanism to figure out if you're wrong about a deeply held precept."[8]

Despite these difficulties, we have identified a set of practices for submitting key strategy assumptions to constructive testing by internal and external audiences. We present one targeted to each constituency, below.

Shadow Cabinet

Perhaps the most novel idea we have profiled for challenging strategy assumptions through the introduction of new internal voices to the strategic debate is the Shadow Cabinet (fig. 12.5). We have seen this mechanism implemented in a variety of corporate settings, and we've documented its use for reasons as diverse as strategy challenge, leadership development, and corporate "workout."

The Shadow Cabinet is a standing group of high-potential employees who participate in meetings of the firm's executive committee on a rotating basis as invited attendees. Participants are typically in midcareer and are often in line for promotion to a director level within the firm. Meetings of the group are sequenced to occur in cadence with meetings of the firm's senior executive team, typically on the day before. The agenda of the cabinet meetings matches, as much as is possible, that of the executive committee for the following day, with presenters delivering dry runs of their material to the group (a good rehearsal opportunity!) and then providing whatever follow-on is needed to support the group's deliberations and decision-making. A standard element in most firms is for a subset of the cabinet to attend the next day's executive meeting and to share their discussions and judgments with the full executive committee.

The benefits of this practice are manifold. Because the senior rank of the firm is most captive to the assumptions underlying current strategy—they carry pride of authorship, they are often farthest from the day-to-day of markets and customers, the information they receive is filtered—the perspectives of a creditable, informed constituency such as the Shadow Cabinet offers is incredibly valuable. The executive who originally presented this idea to us reported that the chairman and CEO of her firm regarded the Shadow Cabinet as "extremely good business."

More perhaps than any other practice we have ever profiled, executives have an immediate, visceral response to this idea. Most executives to whom we've presented this respond that it would never work in their organization: "The executive agenda is too confidential," "Our executive team is too impatient," or, candidly, "It looks like too much work." We completely agree that this practice falls into the "not for everyone" category, and in fact we have visited board-

A standing group of high-potential employees who participate in meetings of the firm's senior executive committee on a rotating basis as invited attendees. The practice provides two-way value, exposing the senior team to novel perspectives and accelerating the development of the junior participants.

Mechanics

- Human resources department identifies a set of 6 to 10 high-potential employees who show exceptional promise in the areas of strategy formulation or execution for participation in this 1- to 2-year experience.
- Across that time period, these individuals are convened regularly (8 to 10 times per year) in meetings timed to coincide with the cadence of the senior executive committee.
- Each meeting cycle typically consists of two half-days: on the first, the Shadow Cabinet convenes as a mock executive committee, considering all the issues slated for the upcoming executive committee meeting and previewing the presentations being prepared for those sessions.
- On the second half-day, a subset of the cabinet attends the executive committee meeting, sharing the cabinet's deliberations and decisions from the day before.

Assessment

- The Shadow Cabinet is a powerful practice for senior executives to be exposed to the views of knowledgeable insiders who are much closer to markets and customers and who are less invested in current orthodoxy.
- A real, if ancillary, benefit of the practice is that it is a powerful accelerant to the development of junior participants, giving them a perspective that they would otherwise not experience until much later in their careers.
- Not for Everyone: The practice is dependent both on demonstrated executive commitment to support the "speaking of truth to power," and on candor in allowing the Shadow Cabinet to participate in virtually all discussions.

Fig. 12.5 Shadow cabinet brings fresh perspective to executive strategy discussions

Overview of Shadow Cabinet Process

1 Prior to regularly scheduled strategy committee, Shadow Cabinet members receive agenda (nearly) identical to that of real executive committee.

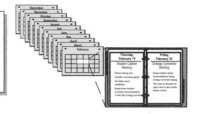

2 Shadow Cabinet conducts mock strategy session, formulates list of recommendations to real executive committee.

Shadow Cabinet

3 Rotating subgroup of cabinet members attends executive committee meeting to present recommendations, participate in session, and report outcomes.

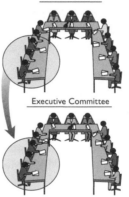

Executive Committee

"EXTREMELY GOOD BUSINESS"

"[The Shadow Cabinet] is extremely good business. It creates a win-win for the company and the employee. For the employee, it provides a chance to see outside his or her particular area of expertise and to understand how the entire company works. For the company, it helps strategy development by drawing young, fresh talent from different layers of the company and bringing those different perspectives to the table."

Vice President
Fortune 250 Manufacturer

┌─ PRACTICE IN BRIEF: VENTURE CAPITALIST STRATEGY REVIEW ─┐

Management invites a qualified venture capitalist to attend
strategy review presentations and to probe investment proposals
for potential weaknesses. The practice provides a useful challenge
in the moment as well as an education in the immediacy and
practicality of considerations that "owners" apply to potential
expenditures of "their" money.

Mechanics

- Executive management selects a venture capital adviser from a list of VC
  firms/partners qualified to offer an informed opinion on company strategy
  (criteria include industry experience, track record in investments in industry,
  and quality of screening methodologies)
- Under a nondisclosure agreement, VC advisers are invited to attend
  strategy and/or investment review sessions and to lead off questioning
  of business unit managers.
- Challenges posed to management by VC interlocutors are then
  incorporated into final strategy summaries and investment proposals.
- VC questions should be cataloged and assembled into a structured
  challenge approach that can live on after the session. The goal can
  be articulated as "learning enough about their method that we can apply
  it without them."

Assessment

- Early adopters of this practice report that the questions and approaches
  that VCs bring add a new flavor of urgency and immediacy to (formerly)
  routine deliberations.
- Given the current activist posture of private equity firms, the practice
  provides a timely opportunity to understand the perspective of this sector
  in considering potential large corporate investments.
- Many management teams can tap current friendly "feeder" relations
  between VCs and R&D or Corporate Development to identify potential
  partner candidates. (But get them to sign the NDAs!)

Fig. 12.6 VCs bring "voice of the owner" into strategy reviews

rooms where speaking candidly about shortcomings of firm strategy had all the
markers of a serious career-limiting move. Organizations in which this is
true—where the required candor does not exist to support this openness with
the next generation—should absolutely pass on this idea. Not only will it not
achieve the desired effect, but it will surely cause more harm than good to the
morale of staff involved in the initiative.

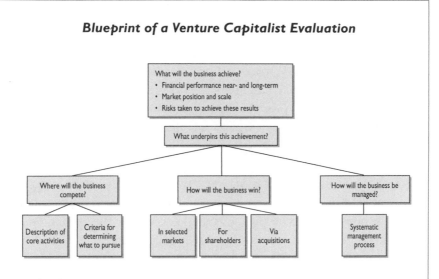

Blueprint of a Venture Capitalist Evaluation

What will the business achieve?
• Financial performance near- and long-term
• Market position and scale
• Risks taken to achieve these results

What underpins this achievement?

Where will the business compete?

How will the business win?

How will the business be managed?

Description of core activities

Criteria for determining what to pursue

In selected markets

For shareholders

Via acquisitions

Systematic management process

─────── A FINE-MESH SCREEN ───────

"The great thing about venture capitalists is that they recognize that only one of ten ideas will eventually survive, and they're trained to identify those that won't. . . . Presenting the proposals to venture capitalists forces us to answer very penetrating questions regarding every aspect of our proposals."

Director, Corporate Strategy
Fortune 250 Electronics
Manufacturer

Venture Capitalist Strategy Review

A companion practice for bringing external perspective into the challenge of strategy assumptions is the Venture Capitalist Strategy Review (fig. 12.6). In this process, management invites a qualified venture capitalist to sit in on the panel that conducts business unit strategy and investment reviews, asking the venture capitalist to bring external market perspective to the conversation and to probe investment proposals for potential weaknesses. The practice provides benefit for business unit managers not only from the substance of the challenges introduced into the dialogue but also from the practical, payback-focused lens that the venture capitalist brings to capital expenditure requests.

The difficult trick to pull off in implementing this practice, obviously, is to identify an external party who is knowledgeable enough to bring value to the conversation but "safe" enough to allow into the room (In the current climate, representatives from the private equity community might sail past the first requirement and fail the second miserably!) The organization that brought this idea to our attention had identified a venture capitalist with whom it was currently coventuring and so had begun to build operating trust. (In fact, unlike corporate investors, venture capitalists are so accustomed to serving on the boards of portfolio companies that the request to participate in a similar capacity with a corporate partner is typically a relatively easy stretch.)

The learning for the corporate partner, in contrast, is often nothing short of eye-opening. The external perspective brought by the venture capitalist partner provides in-the-moment stress testing of assumptions about markets, customers, and competitors and brings an urgency and immediacy to corporate processes that can often feel routine. In considering funding proposals, the venture capitalist brings a fundamentally different lens to the deliberation than does a corporate manager. For a venture capitalist, every funding decision is an option, as opposed to a blanket approval, and his or her natural tendency is to stage-gate funding requests so that additional funding is released only as meaningful milestones are achieved. Freedom to operate for a quarter—not a year—is the norm, conditional on progress against a specific agenda for the management team to work against.

Perhaps the best aspect of this practice is that there is such well-established method to the venture capitalist approach that someone serving as scribe to the early sessions, recording all the questions and strategies the venture capitalist uses to gather information, can essentially capture the essentials of the approach for later reuse (see fig. 12.6). The sessions that have been reported to us have had an impact that lived on well after the venture capitalist had left the room.

All of these practices for articulating and stress-testing the assumptions underlying strategy require effort, and some carry risk (real or perceived) that disqualify them from universal applicability, but they all bring the assumptions behind company strategy into the open. In the next chapter we describe the complement to this activity—monitoring assumptions across time to separate "signal from noise" in the external environment.

Chapter 13 Practices for Mapping the Future: The Role of Signposts and Tripwires

The activity of articulating and testing core assumptions will not provide ongoing guidance unless management teams master the complementary activity of monitoring those assumptions on an ongoing basis. Simply stating assumptions will only draw up sides at the executive level—do you believe the assumption or not? What's needed to bring assumptions into the active debate are objective facts from outside the organization that can support data-based discussion and resolution.

ORGANIZATIONAL STRUCTURE DIFFICULTIES

Obviously, Fortune 100–sized firms have elaborate, sophisticated functions for tracking significant external developments. But disconcertingly, the organizational distance between these sensing functions (market research, competitive intelligence, sales force call reporting, and so on) and the senior executive team seems to be increasing all the time. As ongoing observers of strategy practice, it is always surprising to us to bear witness to the organizational disconnect between the immediate intelligence-gathering organs of companies and the participants in strategy-forming activities. Often this is simply because the freshest and least varnished intelligence is gathered only for highly tactical use within the sales organization of the firm.

Complicating the "distance from reality" problem is the ongoing trend of decentralization of market research to individual business units in a quest to make it more immediately responsive to internal client needs. Representative here is the experience of a major credit card firm with a highly decentralized market research function, driven by a client service mandate. Across a multi-year period, the director of market research saw a drift apart in two key metrics: "project satisfaction" and "overall satisfaction" with the function. Project satisfaction climbed consistently across time, as market research pursued and executed against ever more precise project inquiries ("What is the relation between statement fold variance and customer satisfaction?"). Overall satisfaction dropped off steadily as the enterprise impact and visibility of market research activities dissipated. The obvious lesson is that internal client satisfaction is not necessarily the best guide for setting agendas for these critical sensing capabilities of the firm.

"RATE OF CHANGE" DIFFICULTIES

The second level of difficulty in stress-testing key strategic assumptions stems from the increasingly choppy rate of change in competitive environments. Understandably, executive teams assume somewhat predictable trajectories to changes in customer behavior, competitor capabilities, and market development, and this expectation sets the cadence for the accustomed pattern of annual or biannual environmental reviews that kick off the strategy-making process at most large firms. And yet in each of these areas discontinuous change is rapidly becoming the norm: technological development cycles are becoming terrifically foreshortened; customer behavior patterns are increasingly characterized by the sharp departures of "tipping points"; surprise entrants are bringing disruptive new business models to upset the competitive balance in many established industries. Yet despite our recognition of these developments, the pattern of strategy review "every three years, whether we need it or not" lives on.

Or, of course, there is its somewhat popular counterpart, the strategy-on-demand approach of addressing issues as they appear and become critical. Variations on quick reaction strategy formulation have proliferated in the past few years.[1] They seek to replace pro forma, scheduled strategy activities with a needs-based approach of mobilizing resources and senior management attention for intensive activities around market developments as they occur. Although these approaches are laudable in their attempts to implement strategy in real time, they can carry the danger of focusing too heavily on immediate market events in a reactive stance rather than alerting the executive team to critical phenomena that might signal incipient cracks in their strategic assumptions.

FACT-BASED METRICS AND EXECUTIVE
TEAM OWNERSHIP

Despite this general swinging back and forth between stately, periodic (and sometimes pro forma) strategy reviews and unscheduled, reactive "crash" strategy development, some institutions have moved to establish processes for a more consistent approach to monitoring key assumptions behind their strategic positions. They combine the continuity and consistency of traditional periodic strategy reviews with the real-time sensing and reaction of strategy-on-demand approaches. Two critical components distinguish them.

First, they establish fact-based metric systems for moving the monitoring of key assumptions out of the realm of argument and differing perspectives and into the realm of measurable, objective change. The best approaches establish *signposts* for individual assumptions—measurable phenomena that validate or invalidate key beliefs shared by the executive team and that support current strategic direction (fig. 13.1).

In our example of *signposts* for a retail bank's deposit-gathering strategy, the bank's *strategy* of branch-driven deposit-gathering depends on *assumptions* about its customers' definition of convenience, which drives channel usage patterns, and their comfort with Internet banking. So, the strategy rests on the assumption that high-balance customers define convenience as "proximity to a bank branch," which suits their preference for face-to-face transactions, particularly given their low comfort level with Web-based transactions. These assumption sets can be decomposed into *signposts* relating to customer behavior and market demographics: balance levels of customers with different transaction patterns, the rate of personal computer penetration and broadband connectivity, increasing levels of comfort with commercial transactions. These signposts can ultimately be monitored through *tripwires* set to alert bank man-

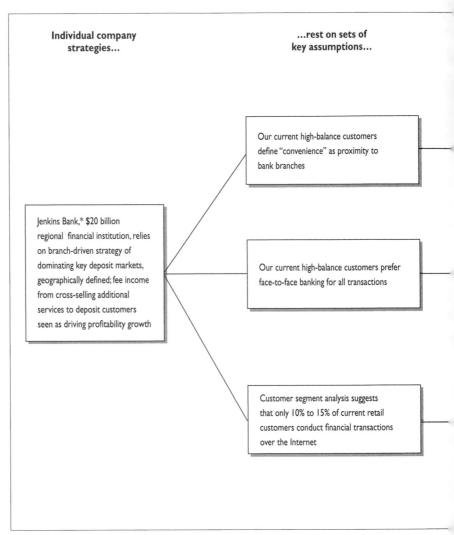

Individual company strategies...

...rest on sets of key assumptions...

Jenkins Bank,* $20 billion regional financial institution, relies on branch-driven strategy of dominating key deposit markets, geographically defined; fee income from cross-selling additional services to deposit customers seen as driving profitability growth

Our current high-balance customers define "convenience" as proximity to bank branches

Our current high-balance customers prefer face-to-face banking for all transactions

Customer segment analysis suggests that only 10% to 15% of current retail customers conduct financial transactions over the Internet

Fig. 13.1 Signposts and tripwires: metrics to gauge "approach speed" of the future

agement to a meaningful change in customer behavior: Have our high-balance customers begun to conduct two transactions per week or more over the phone? Have monthly branch visits in this segment declined by more than 2 percent per quarter? Has broadband penetration exceeded 60 percent in our target segment households?

These signposts and tripwires are finite in number and decompose naturally from the overall strategy and its major assumptions. In total, these systems of *signposts* and *tripwires* take executive conversations around critical strategy be-

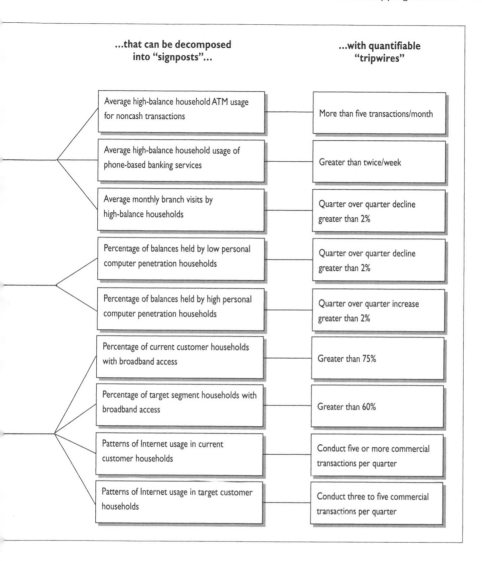

...that can be decomposed into "signposts"...	...with quantifiable "tripwires"
Average high-balance household ATM usage for noncash transactions	More than five transactions/month
Average high-balance household usage of phone-based banking services	Greater than twice/week
Average monthly branch visits by high-balance households	Quarter over quarter decline greater than 2%
Percentage of balances held by low personal computer penetration households	Quarter over quarter decline greater than 2%
Percentage of balances held by high personal computer penetration households	Quarter over quarter increase greater than 2%
Percentage of current customer households with broadband access	Greater than 75%
Percentage of target segment households with broadband access	Greater than 60%
Patterns of Internet usage in current customer households	Conduct five or more commercial transactions per quarter
Patterns of Internet usage in target customer households	Conduct three to five commercial transactions per quarter

liefs out of the realm of subjective or anecdotal argument and bring it into the realm of tracked, objective facts.

The second critical component of the following practices is that they eliminate the distance between the sensing mechanisms of the firm (market research, sales force reports, service center data) and the senior executive team by assigning individual ownership of key strategy assumptions and their monitoring. Better practices here thus force the members of the executive team to have top of mind the continuing, objective validity of critical components of their worldview. Taken together, fact-based metrics and executive monitors of strategy assumptions can at least allow for the hope of evolutionary strategy shift to changing conditions rather than the delayed—then sudden—breakdowns of strategy validity responsible for the multiyear revenue stalls we have documented.

Annual Key Bets Contract

A direct way of forcing senior executives to engage with critical assumptions is to turn the assumptions into annual "key bets" for individual executive ownership and monitoring (fig. 13.2). The critical uncertainties behind a business unit's strategy are illuminated through the strategy function's interaction with a network of internal managers and external objective experts and are then translated into "bets" the organization has placed on developments within each of them. After the senior executive team signs off on the list, finance staff are assigned to monitor each one, with a full review of developments across all uncertainties at year's end.

The first, critical task of this practice is to assemble a network of objective experts who can identify the critical uncertainties in customer behavior, technology trajectories, and competitor strategy that could affect the business unit's strategy in the coming year. The burden is then on the strategist to narrow these factors to a finite list of ten to twelve uncertainties for monitoring. These are then translated into measurable "bets" that the business is placing and that can be evaluated factually each year.

Practitioners report three key elements for ensuring that the activity stays focused and relevant in real time. First, the "bets" to be monitored should be divided into Tier One concerns (immediate and critical to strategy within the year) and Tier Two issues (critical to longer-term, multiyear strategy). Second, having the strategist review the bets on a six-month "pull-up" basis ensures both that fast-changing issues don't wait for an annual address and that obsolete issues are retired. Third, it's important to carry over "bets" on uncertainties that remain critical to longer-term strategy from one year to the next rather than losing focus if meaningful changes are absent within the annual time frame.

At one large natural resources firm where this practice has been in place for several years, the chief strategist reports that the process has been successful in forcing attention on about half the critical market and environmental factors that have ultimately affected strategy success in the same period. The company has moved to increase significantly the number of monitored "bets" in the future.

Competitive Disruption Modeling

The traditional planning methodology of scenario planning has been rightly criticized for being too ponderous, too expansive in its focus, and too concerned with a few large, external threats that have reasonably low probabilities of occurring (all legacy traits from its origins in national security planning). One leading organization has streamlined and focused the process on the more strategically relevant terrain of potentially "disruptive" actions of existing and new competitors in their businesses (fig. 13.3). A finite set of game-changing scenarios driven by competitor moves is generated by the strategy function, and business unit teams then evaluate the adequacy of current strategic initiatives to respond to new competitive realities. Metrics of the "rate of approach" for scenarios are then prepared for use in briefing the executive committee of the firm.

By articulating a small but realistic number of scenarios within a medium-term time frame, the organization focuses on those moves by competitors that are likely to be both most disruptive and most probable. In considering potential countermoves, business unit teams construct realistic views of shifts among suppliers, existing competitors, and customer segments. Strategy initiatives in place can then be evaluated with "robustness" scores—and, potentially, resources shifted to counter the most likely disruptions.

At the organization engaged in this process, the "war-gaming" it has produced has led the company to take concrete initiatives ranging from targeted acquisitions and partnerships to a nicely anticipated crash cost-cutting program in a particularly "disrupted" period. Although the language of "disruptive innovation" typically refers to technology-enabled cost-based competition, the practice is equally useful in industries where new entrants are crossing blurry industry boundaries.

Web-Enabled Signposting

Another organization has moved aggressively to incorporate the entire organization in monitoring critical factors that could influence the validity of company strategy. We've named it Web-Enabled Signposting because of its use of the firm's intranet to serve as a catchment for intelligence on a select set of issues from across the company (fig. 13.4). The practice both broadens tremendously the listening posts for information on key issues and democratizes judgments about the rate of change occurring in them.

At the technology company where we first encountered the practice, the planning department extracts from business unit strategy a set of key assump-

┌─── PRACTICE IN BRIEF: ANNUAL KEY BETS CONTRACT ───┐

A structured process for surfacing and monitoring the small
number of measurable bets that are implicit in business unit
or corporate strategic plans. Relatively high year one setup
costs are offset by much lower ongoing operating and refresh
requirements.

Mechanics

- The corporation's senior strategist or planner drives this activity, timed to coincide with the annual strategy review process. The process begins with the selection of a diverse set of objective experts to serve as an interview network. The best candidates are highly specialized subject matter experts (scientists, economists, consultants) as well as senior operating managers.

- Strategist and team conduct one-on-one and group interviews across this network to gather perspectives on key uncertainties facing the company's business units in the major industry areas in which it participates.

- With the findings from these interviews as backdrop, senior management of each business unit develops a list of 10-15 measurable key bets that they are placing against the uncertainties. These lists are then collated and approved at the senior executive level.

- Finance staff at the corporate and business unit levels then track (measure) these bets across the year to spot material adverse developments, with a full review conducted with each business unit at the end of the year.

Assessment

- This process of requiring business managers to be explicit about the bets implied by their strategies is incredibly useful at surfacing the small set of key assumptions for ongoing monitoring.

- The practice is also very scalable and can be accomplished by a solo practitioner in a small or focused company or can be coordinated globally for large, complex multibusiness enterprises.

- The principal liability of the practice is the setup cost attendant to year one startup—ongoing monitoring and subsequent annual reviews will be greatly eased by the internal strategy education and assumption surfacing involved in the first year of operation.

Fig. 13.2 Annual "contract" acts as forcing function to articulate key uncertainties

Overview of Annual Key Bets Process

Component #1: Network of Experts

Strategist establishes standing network of internal, external industry experts; highly diverse group represents different types of marketplace uncertainty

Component #2: Annual Interviews

Strategist interviews network of experts and elicits input to develop an understanding of key uncertainties facing company

Component #3: Key Bets Contract

Negotiations between business managers and senior executives organized to convert strategist's findings into list of 10–15 measurable key bets each business will place against uncertainties

Component #4: Ongoing Monitoring System

Key bets tracked (measured) across year by corporate staff and analysts within each business; at year-end business strategy reviews, all bets are reexamined

---

A POSTURE OF HUMBLE WATCHFULNESS

"Suppose we fast-forward ten years and take a look at the things that have really shaken and moved this company around. I would expect we'd get at least 50% of them. There are always going to be things we can't anticipate or afford to spend a lot of time on . . . so we're going to be a little humble about this. A lot of the things that [have caused company downturns] could easily have been identified with a scheme like this. They were not bolts from the blue that came out of nowhere."

Vice President, Strategic Planning
Fortune 500 Natural Resources Company

┌─ Practice in Brief: Competitive Disruption Modeling ─┐

A structured approach to identify vulnerable strategic assumptions
through the creation of concrete, role-based scenarios that define
plausible industry disruptions for preemptive treatment. The
approach is highly practical and actionable, enabling immediate
and ongoing monitoring of readiness.

└──┘

Mechanics

- The strategy team generates four near-term scenarios (3 to 5 years out),
  each assuming that a different industry participant (suppliers, competitors,
  disruptive entrants, and buyers) drives a "game-changing" disruption in the
  current competitive balance.
- The team then articulates the implications of each scenario, focusing on
  potential strategy and positioning shifts among current participants.
- These scenarios are then used to test the adequacy of the firm's current
  portfolio of strategic initiatives using a Robustness Scorecard (see
  illustration, opposite). Results are used to redirect resource allocation
  and overall composition.
- Scenarios are then continually monitored for rate of approach, with periodic
  updates to the firm's executive committee.

Assessment

- Competitive disruption modeling is distinctive from traditional scenario
  planning processes in the "groundedness" of the scenarios, as well as in the
  immediacy of their focus.
- These qualities enable the scenarios to be translated into ongoing
  operations and strategy reviews, as well as into ongoing "signposting"
  activities.
- Although this practice could be undertaken as the focus of a consulting
  intervention, the broadest benefit arises from ongoing monitoring and
  testing of scenario emergence.

Fig. 13.3 Competitive disruption modeling—scenario planning gets real

Illustration of Strategic Initiative Robustness Scorecard

Initiative	Portal Power	Solidarity	Newcomers	Global Cocooning	Total
Strengthen Lead in Core Business					
Strategic Cost Management	5	4	2	5	16
One-to-One Marketing	2	1	2	3	8
Virtually There	4	2	4	1	13
Pursue Adjacent Opportunities					
Financial Settlement					7
CRM					15
Content Leadership					19
Manage Industry Turbulence					
Agency Yield Management					9
Dynamic Travel Packaging					11
Total	29	23	14	34	

Executive committee assesses robustness of initiative portfolio for three "horizons" of strategy under all four scenarios.

Scoring Key

5	Very Promising
4	Suitable
3	Neutral
2	Vulnerable
1	Too Risky

"A FRAMEWORK TO THINK ABOUT THE WORLD"

"We have found using the set of scenarios and tracking tools effective in trying to manage the chaotic environment that's happening around us. A lot of our customers and business partners come to us for our vision and for clarity about what's happening, and I have to say that in large part due to our driving these scenarios we have a framework to think about the world... and what we need to do to increase shareholder value."

Director of Strategic Planning
Fortune 750 Services Company

Practice in Brief: Web-Enabled Signposting

An intranet-based system for tracking measurable external events that validate or invalidate assumptions underlying firm strategies or scenarios. The practice is relatively inexpensive to implement and is particularly useful for organizations in fast-moving or cyclical sectors.

Mechanics

- The planning team decomposes company and business unit strategies into key assumptions and signposts—measurable phenomena or events that validate or invalidate key strategy assumptions. Signposts can be based on current strategies or can be early warning indicators from scenarios that the firm is monitoring.
- These signposts are then entered into an intranet portal offering role-based access to business unit, functional, and executive leaders responsible for strategy development or execution.
- The site owner refreshes the site on an ongoing basis, appending links to internal and external sources of data related to the signposts and noting significant changes in signposts or assumptions.
- Periodic reviews ("traffic light" monitoring reports, signpost redefinition) help to ensure that significant developments are noted and acted upon.

Assessment

- This practice is very effective for animating the strategy conversation in the firm; for a relatively small investment, management can increase key staff awareness of the critical underpinnings to strategy and, effectively, deputize the broader team in ongoing monitoring of assumptions.
- The investment is particularly advisable for organizations with a decentralized approach to strategy, where executives responsible for monitoring and responding to changes in the business environment are dispersed throughout the organization.
- Organizations that have found it difficult to make scenario planning "real" will likely find that signposting on the Web helps overcome the perceived low value of such exercises.

Fig. 13.4 Engaging the organization in monitoring change

Rendition of a Signposting Web Page

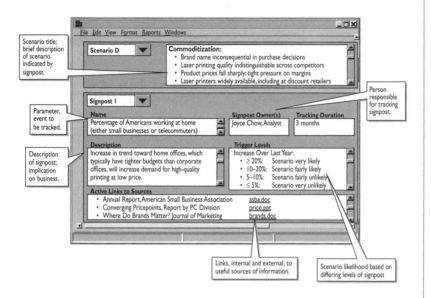

Scenario title; brief description of scenario indicated by signpost.

Parameter, event to be tracked.

Description of signpost; implication on business.

Person responsible for tracking signpost.

Links, internal and external, to useful sources of information.

Scenario likelihood based on differing levels of signpost

STRATEGY AS A CONTINUOUS PROCESS

"People think that once they have a strategy in place they can ride on it. They neglect all the hard work of developing scenarios, setting up signposts and triggers, tracking the triggers, and finally taking action on them. There is no sense creating scenarios if you ultimately do not track the triggers and act on them."

Strategic Change Consultant
Fortune 50 Electronics Company

tions that can be turned into observable phenomena for monitoring. These factors are then posted on the firm's intranet portal as "signpost" sites for individual issues. (A mock-up of a signposting Web page is included in the practice description on the public Web site for this book, www.stallpoints.executive board.com.) Assigned owners then allow access and contribution to these signposts and ensure that they are regularly refreshed and linked to new internal and external sources of information. Signpost owners are also responsible for the preparation of periodic "traffic light" reports to alert business owners to significant developments or changes.

The practice is particularly effective for organizations with multiple, outward-facing functions likely to be early observers of meaningful changes in strategy assumptions but organizationally (and psychically) far from the strategy process. At the technology company where we observed it, it was also driving the strategy conversation considerably deeper and broader across the firm.

We reported in a prior chapter the intense level of concern that the strategy profession brings to the work we have documented here. What drives this community is the conviction that there is some way, short of stalling, to alter foundational beliefs (the strategic assumptions of the senior executive team), some structured approach to altering the mental models controlling corporate ambition in a systematic, incremental fashion. We thank the strategists whose innovations we have documented in this part of our study and hope that our readers will find in this abbreviated toolbox of practices some useful models for emulation.

Chapter 14 Locating Stewardship for Growth Strategy

The activities we advocate in this book compete for space on an already overcrowded executive agenda. What gives force to our advocacy is the wildly positive payback from effort invested to avoid a growth stall: stalls bring down even the most admired companies; they exact a sizable financial and human toll; and their impact can be permanent. Once a stall sets in, the odds against recovery rise dramatically with the passage of time.

Compounding this urgency, all signs point to increased stall risk in coming years. Particularly concerning in the current environment is the shrinking half-life of established business models. As these continue to shorten, the premium on spotting change early enough to react in time will rise exponentially. The practices we profile in chapters 12 and 13 create that early warning capability: signposts and tripwires to signal emerging discontinuities; the removal of hierarchy and boundaries that inhibit strategic recognition. Structured conversations enabled by these practices arm the executive team to test the continuing accuracy of its worldview and to flag, early, those few critical assumptions that could trigger a stall if not corrected.

FINE ACTIVITIES—WHO SHOULD OWN THEM?

Given the shared, tight conceits of the senior team and the weaker credibility of junior staff, who in the organization can take on the sensitive task of stress-testing company strategy? In our view, the ideal owner of this mandate is a robust corporate strategy function. The strategy planning functional model, with responsibility for strategy development, corporate visioning, strategic planning, and internal consulting, has the requisite charter and perspective to perform this work admirably. In light of the mission drift we have documented in many strategy organizations across the past several years, leadership teams will want to make sure that their group has both the clarity and the resources to lead this effort.

To be as effective as possible, strategy functions will need two additional forms of support from the executive teams they serve. First is a concerted effort to build assumptions monitoring and testing into the overall operating cadence and calendar of the organization. Second, we see a real opportunity for the chief executive to involve the board of directors in this work. Although this cuts against emerging patterns in board oversight and focus across the past several years, we believe that board members should view such strategy challenge as a critical form of risk management rather than as meddling in management's proper terrain.

Although it is tempting to prescribe an exact allocation of roles and responsibilities across all of these constituencies, we recognize that the decision of where to locate stewardship for growth strategy is very much organization- and culture-dependent. To help individual executive teams make the correct decisions for their organizations, we describe in this chapter a foundational diagnostic exercise we have created that we believe is a relevant starting point for all organizations concerned about stall risk. We then discuss the opportunities that the executive team and the board of directors have to embed the process of assumptions monitoring and testing into the workflow of the enterprise.

A STARTING EXERCISE: "RED FLAG" WARNINGS
OF AN IMPENDING STALL

How should executive teams first engage with the task of diagnosing their vulnerability to a growth stall? Although the practices of chapters 12 and 13 are relatively modest in their requirements of senior executive time, they certainly require robust "hearts and minds" support if they are to serve their desired purpose. And we recognize that many organizations may neither have the resources nor be ready for this level of commitment. Thus, a first-order task for the senior team can be that of a general checkup of the revenue growth health of the organization.

In appendix 5, we provide just such a checkup, a self-test consisting of fifty "red flag" indicators, spread across seven functional areas of the firm, that can be used as a diagnostic to indicate the need for more extensive examination. We compiled the set of red flags by working back from the stall case studies to ask, "What clues could the leaders of stalling companies have spotted in their markets, their competitors' behavior, and in their own internal practices that might have alerted them earlier to an impending stall?" These flags are a mix of empirical metrics, available from most management information systems, and subjective judgment questions to be posed to the relevant functional experts in the firm. The process is useful as an early warning indicator of incipient stalls as well as a marker of increasing internal dissonance around key strategic assumptions held by the senior team. (Interested readers might wish to take this self-test using the confidential survey tool that we have placed on the Web site for this book, www.stallpoints.executiveboard.com.)

For metrics from finance, for instance, the general goal is to sense the organization's comfort with the relation between revenue growth arising from organic sources and that coming from acquisitions, as well as the relation between relative revenue and income growth rates. Questions on strategy seek to understand the level and focus of resources dedicated to strategy formulation, as well as the currency of market and competitor definitions.

The red flags in marketing and marketing research are meant to probe how fully and frequently customer segmentation schemes are validated and how each segment values the product and service attributes on which strategies are based. From the sales force itself, indicators are meant to sense both potentially dangerous, untracked shifts in core market size and behavior and business model shifts of potentially disruptive competitors. The metrics for human resources are designed to reveal emerging mismatches between the competencies critical to prevailing strategy and those emerging in importance for the future, as well as to gauge the mix management of internally and externally sourced talent in the senior executive team.

For R&D/innovation management, the questions are meant to probe the validity of the organization's reliance on iterative innovation to maintain pricing premiums, as well as the balance between incremental and new platform investments. And last, metrics related to the board are designed to test directors' engagement with the risks embedded in the firm's *strategy.*

Again, the goal is to use the red flags exercise as a starting point for the more intensive, ongoing activities of assumptions articulation and monitoring. Organizations can apply these questions at the individual business unit level or to the enterprise as a whole, as instinct and facts require.

EMBEDDING IN THE WORKFLOW OF THE FIRM

The work of guarding against growth stalls must go beyond a one-off diagnostic activity such as the self-test described above to a continuous conversation in the upper echelons of the firm. The goal here is not to make assumption monitoring and testing showcase elements of the occasional management offsite but rather to embed these activities into the core operating processes and cadence of the enterprise. This requires charging line managers at all levels of the firm with leadership in that conversation.

As we noted in the introduction, the ability and discipline to question current strategy do not come naturally to executive teams and line managers. In part, this reflects an atrophy of strategy skill in the executive suite. Harvard Business School professor Clayton Christensen has observed that management teams become deeply competent with activities that recur frequently, such as preparing annual operating plans and delivering on those plans, but are less competent at the occasional—and often outsourced—tasks of strategy development.[1] Also responsible here is the nature of the mandate of an executive team, which is charged with developing a vision and then working back from that desired state to chart the operational steps to its achievement. Few formal opportunities to question the continuing relevance of that vision and plan arise in the packed agenda of a busy executive team.

That said, executive teams have clear opportunities to embed strategy challenge into the workflow of the firm, incorporating the responsibility into job descriptions at all levels. Although different organizations will face different opportunities, we see three that we suspect are nearly universal in their applicability.

1. *Building real strategy challenge into operating plan review.* Perhaps the clearest signal that executive management can send about the importance of senior line engagement is to focus attention on strategy challenge during annual operating plan reviews. This is deceptively difficult to do well. Even though almost all plan templates currently have a section entitled "Assumptions and Risks,"

veterans of the process of presenting such plans know that these events suffer in several regards. First, the information presented tends to be limited to "safe," noncontroversial data, such as macroeconomic and other planning assumptions. Second, even when risks are presented, they tend to be superficial and "manageable," such as internal execution risks, rather than more fundamental customer or competitor concerns. And, since this issue is typically placed last in most templates, and therefore in most presentations, this portion of the review is typically given short shrift.

Executive teams can provide real encouragement to operating unit managers to think through and present the major risks to their plans systematically and honestly. An abbreviated version of the Red Flags diagnostic presented above would serve as a useful starting point for spotting the major external and internal uncertainties. Further, reorganizing plan review to give priority to the risk analysis conversation would help to spread the message that the executive team is serious about the activity. One strategy head we spoke with even suggested that the executive team organize a competition among business units, with such awards as "most thorough review of strategy assumptions," "most plan assumptions questioned," "hardest issues addressed," and the like.

2. *Elevating assumption review to the executive calendar.* An alternative to dialing up the strategy challenge conversation in annual operating plan reviews is to make assumption review and challenge a distinct event on the executive calendar. In the same way that many senior teams go offsite for an annual talent review or budget review, the senior team could set up a periodic assumptions review, perhaps using our Red Flags diagnostic as a catalyst and guide.

There are several advantages to this approach, not least among them the creation of a "safe space" for frank executive exchanges. By making this a dedicated and stand-alone activity, limiting conversation to the senior team, rules and norms can be established that will tend to encourage candor in the search for right answers. In addition, making it an annual process can serve as a great forcing function for assigning rotating owners for key assumptions, leading to the creation of an institutional memory around key assumptions and preventing ossification of views by function.

3. *Focusing management development program participants on strategy challenge.* Most organizations have an ideal resource for "skip-level" strategy challenge in the form of the participants in their management development programs. These individuals are well placed for the activity because they have deep investment in the future success of the enterprise yet are not themselves authors of the current strategy and can thus approach it objectively. They are also valu-

able enough to the enterprise that their criticisms and concerns can typically secure and hold a senior executive's attention and respect.

An additional benefit in involving these individuals in strategy challenge is that executive teams can avoid the common temptation merely to stamp out the next generation of leadership in its own image. Rising executives in the current dynamic environment are likely to face careers involving much more frequent revision to strategies and business models; executive teams thus send a powerful signal when they invite introspection and challenge from the ranks of their current high-potential staff.

The practices we present in chapter 12 for articulating and stress-testing strategic assumptions would serve as strong models for management development programs to emulate. In particular, the "Core Belief Identification Squad" and "Pre-Mortem Analysis" practices would lend themselves well to such adaptation. The "Shadow Cabinet" practice profiled in that chapter explicitly targets the rising stars of the next generation and is therefore also worthy of consideration.

A RETURN TO CLARITY
FOR THE STRATEGY FUNCTION

We began this chapter by observing that the strategy function is the natural home to organize the activities involved in strategy challenge. As acute observers of corporate strategy have noted, the strategic planning process itself does not necessarily create strategy; this sometimes seems to be done mysteriously, incrementally, and informally by the CEO and a small set of close advisers. Rather, what the strategic planning process *does* produce is, in the words of one close observer, *prepared minds.*[2] We strongly agree with this sentiment and, in fact, would argue that this is the key responsibility of corporate strategists in large firms. Putting issues on and taking issues off the executive agenda is a central task of the corporate strategist; clearly, strategic assumptions monitoring has its natural home here. Whatever other responsibilities the strategy function assumes, guarding against growth stalls should be at the core of its agenda.

THE CHALLENGES OF CAREER TENURE
AND RESOURCING

A few practical difficulties, however, need to be faced—we have noted several in our tracking of the particulars of strategy departments across the past

decade.[3] The first is the increasingly short tenure of the seniormost strategy officer of the firm. Across ten years of interactions with a membership of strategists
from several hundred companies—most global in reach—we have observed a
slow decline in the population of professional strategists in service and a corre-
sponding rise in rotational executives in these positions. This is confirmed by
our regular survey results, showing that currently 48 percent of head strategists
at our surveyed organizations have been in chair for less than two years, with an
average tenure (dragged up by a few long-term solons) of 2.9 years.

This marks a slow decline in tenure that we've tracked for a decade, and it
obviously reflects a secular trend toward strategy as a development opportunity
for senior managers. From the perspective of monitoring strategic assumptions, however, this decline becomes troubling when combined with data on
how frequently major corporate strategy reviews are conducted, which at most
large firms is approximately every five years. Clearly, at most of these companies, it is a rare accident if the head of strategy has been through more than one
major strategy review process.

The second challenge is posed by the ongoing, gradual devolution in large
firms of much strategy activity out to the business units themselves. Our tracking of housing trends in key strategy activities suggests a steady shift in the majority of organizations away from the corporate center and out to the business
units. For all the right reasons of proximity to markets and ownership of initiatives, this makes great sense. At the same time, it increases the shift in the center of gravity of already scarce strategy resources toward client service business
unit work, from the less urgent activities related to long-term strategy. (Our research also indicates that typical staffing for a corporate strategy function at a
$20 billion organization is just over four people. It's hard to wave the banner for
more corporate overhead, but this doesn't seem terribly plush!)

The shift of strategic planning activities away from a steady, predictable
tread of annual reviews and twice-a-decade retreats to a more ad hoc, on-de-
mand schedule poses a third challenge. On the positive side, this allows for
quick mobilization of resources and executive team attention to emerging market realities. We've seen powerful practices here and are great admirers of the
approach at its best.[4] At the same time, at firms without a strong central strategy function to serve as a counterweight, the temptation of reduce costs (both
direct costs and the opportunity cost of executive time) can prove irresistible,
causing organizations to shrivel further already skeleton crews in corporate
strategy, often in favor of the variable-cost alternative of consulting engagements.

Taking all these trends together, it is uncomfortably clear that the easy prescription of putting the strategy function in charge of monitoring early warning flags for future revenue growth problems and for surfacing and monitoring key strategy assumptions of the firm is a necessary, but not sufficient, safeguard. As we have scanned the corporation for natural sponsors and allies in this effort, our attention has been drawn to the chairman and chief executive officer—perennially strong advocates—and beyond, to a new, potentially even stronger sponsor: the board of directors itself.

THE BOARD'S ROLE IN STRATEGIC RISK MANAGEMENT

Since the passage of the Sarbanes-Oxley Act of 2002, conversations about board activities have developed a distinct strain of, in the sentiment and words of McKinsey and Company, "time to move on." Generally, governance advisers have adopted the argument that public company boards need to broaden their role from that of check on executive power (and auditor of last resort on compliance issues) to a deeper engagement with the firm's strategic issues.[5] Some of this is driven by the disarray seen within the boards at several prominent public companies (Disney and Hewlett-Packard, most obviously) over essentially strategic issues. When boards develop schisms over the strategic direction of their organizations, all specific duties of the board's subcommittees become individual, small battlegrounds.

At a more universal level, the desire for public company boards to engage more deeply with strategy is driven by envy of the alignment and purity of purpose of private equity-controlled organizations. Many observers have noted the competitive advantage given to an organization where directors are not indirect fiduciary responsibility players but rather are direct participants in strategy formulation with substantial ownership stakes.

The policy and management recommendations for remedy here have gone in the direction of returning to the CEO some significant power in picking and choosing members of the nominating subcommittee of the board, in order to create a board with deeper, more cohesive strategy experience. McKinsey and Company has noted in its survey work on board activities that, under current circumstances, fewer than a third of senior executives now feel that their board members deeply understand their company's strategy. Driven by a host of outside pressures (outside-inside balance, diversity, audit experience), boards have become "blandly populated with less capable people."[6]

This perspective is persuasive, even if the recommendation to allow CEOs to pack their boards doesn't sound believable from a public policy perspective. Our view is that boards can have a deep engagement with public company strategy without originating it. Their deepest responsibility is to ensure that the company actually *has* a thorough, coherent, and well-conceived strategy. The board's next most obvious responsibility is to ensure that performance management measures and compensation systems for the seniormost executives of the company are aligned with the execution of strategy rather than with short-term financial measures.

But potentially the deepest level of board engagement with strategy lies in the terrain to which we have devoted the last third of this book: the systematic, ongoing stress-testing of the foundational strategy assumptions of the senior executive team. Although strategy staffs can construct red flag metrics and implement best practice for raising and articulating these specific foundational blocks of strategy, they need an ally to backstop them in ensuring that this thinking is hardwired into the decision-making of the firm. If boards at public companies are inescapably about risk management as their first, greatest responsibility, then the risks involved in the growth stalls that are the subject of this book should surely rise to the top of that agenda.

Chapter 15 Postscript:

If You're in Freefall

The run of *Stall Points* has treated revenue stalls as strategic situations that are, in most cases, within the range of management control. Our contention is that executive teams, armed with the knowledge of what repeated patterns of failure have been across time, and with practices for surfacing and stress-testing the assumptions that underlie them, can reduce the likelihood—or at least the intensity and duration—of these major turning points in growth performance. With discipline and continuity of focus, strategies can be evolved and growth runs extended.

But what about firms that already find themselves well and truly in the stall, revenue growth flat-lining and the executive team tentative—or even frozen—at the strategic controls? Well-trained air pilots faced with in-flight stall situations instinctively engage in a four-step process for recovery of control and forward progress: first, they re-orient the plane, pulling the nose down to regain control; second, they add incremental power to increase lift; third, they readjust all trim controls for level flight; and fourth, they replot course.

The terrestrial equivalent for a stalling firm follows roughly the same contours. Firms successfully recovering from serious growth stalls first readdress and reorient the original core business. They then add growth power through the exploitation of incremental adjacencies. If required, they substantially alter the "trim" of the core business model. And finally, they reset their growth course toward opportunities still related to the core.

To assist executive teams that find themselves currently grappling with a stall, we describe in this postscript the results of analysis we have done on the strategies of a set of companies that have been able to restart and sustain growth following a stall.[1] Our intention here is not to delve deeply into their specific strategies or stories but rather to study the group's experience for patterns that might guide management teams seeking to set priorities in a confusing time.

The exhibit that organizes this chapter plots the "location" of strategies underlying the restarts of forty-two large companies since the early 1980s (fig. 15.1). Each dot on this chart represents the growth strategy initiative of one of these restart companies. We plot each initiative on two dimensions: we display distance from the original core business model on the Y-axis and distance from the original industry on the X-axis. So, in other words, in the quest to restart, what degree of change was required to the core business model, and how far afield was the company required to look for new markets to exploit?

A squint at the exhibit, with its density of dots in the bottom left quadrant, makes the point visually: advantaged strategies for restarting growth typically lie close to home. Significantly more than half (59 percent) were located in the company's original core business, addressing essentially the same customer base and same customer need. We've labeled this lower left quadrant "core value maximization." Another 19 percent fell in the lower right quadrant labeled "adjacency extension"—lengthening the core business growth run with obvious, close-in opportunities. The upper left quadrant labeled "core transformation" accounted for 6 percent of restarts, including two powerful restarts that involved major changes to the business model, while still addressing the same core customer base and customer need. And finally, within the quadrant labeled "new business creation," 16 percent of restarts involved the leverage of existing assets to exploit opportunities outside of, but still related to, the core. Significantly, no restarts involved opportunities unrelated to the company's existing core business.

Based on an examination of individual company restarts located in each of these quadrants, we offer five foundational recommendations for executive teams seeking to recover top-line growth momentum.

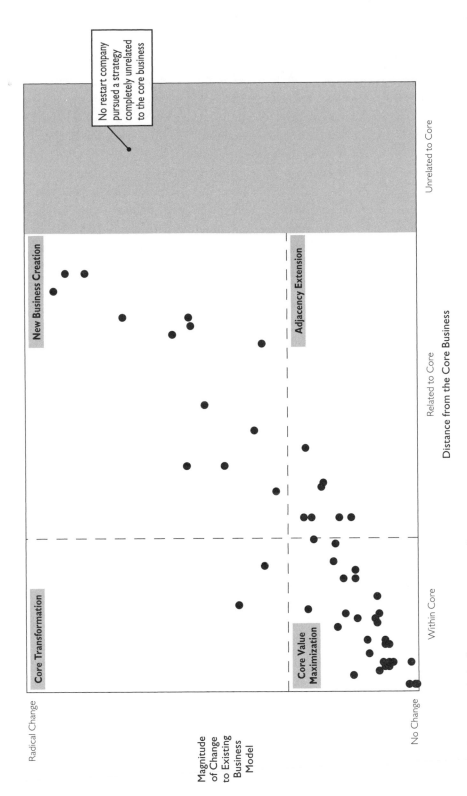

Fig. 15.1 Location analysis of restart company strategies

CORE VALUE MAXIMIZATION

The first stop for any restart strategy has to be the original core business. The re-vitalization of "the core" has been generally recognized and intensively worked over by management literature for the past decade. Yet the urge to look else-where for new growth platforms when the core has underperformed for multi-ple years is almost irresistible for frustrated executive teams.

Recommendation 1. Build consensus about the sources of weakness in your core business strategy between the top executive team and "skip-level" management. Just as the aircraft pilot must assess the stall situation crisply and correctly before taking corrective action, so too must executive teams diagnose precisely the flaws in the current strategy. The goal here is to expose the blind spots the se-nior executive team may have to weakened strategic assumptions and under-serving business processes that were once sources of strength—and now shield at least the senior executive team from new realities.

Because the senior team is often too invested in the current strategy to eval-uate it dispassionately, we strongly recommend that stalling firms begin their situation analysis by collecting and examining the perceptions of the high-po-tential emerging leadership rank in the organization. These individuals operate closer to customer, market, and competitive realities than does the senior team, and they are likely to have formed a coherent, if sometimes dissonant, view of the strategic situation. An ideal first exercise here would be to have this group and the executive team take the Red Flags diagnostic exercise presented in ap-pendix 5 and then to compare differences in perspective between the two groups.

Recommendation 2. Confront the operational and/or business model challenges in your core business that you previously have avoided. It's striking how many of the major stall factors we identified as "strategic" had stubborn, persistent "op-erational" challenges behind them. Premium positions are adhered to because cost structures require them. Innovation returns go into multiyear declines be-cause R&D and market research simply can't coordinate their activities. Core businesses decline because technology or manufacturing reinvestment require-ments are avoided. Outdated business processes, aging business models, and uncompetitive cost structures are the breeding ground of bad strategy.

The activities of new private owners of formerly public firms are instructive here. They hew closely to direct engagement with operational-level challenges in the core. Fix legacy costs that were allowed to creep. Reinvest in required technology and/or manufacturing capabilities. Reduce or eliminate cost struc-tures that do not leverage revenue growth. Rarely do new private owners buy legacy businesses to introduce adventures in new strategy. Most often, they return with bulldog intensity to the original core business and its perennial challenges.

Michael Hammer has argued persuasively that aggressive, targeted investments in core business operations can be a growth strategy itself, if the capability being addressed differentiates the firm significantly from its competitors on a dimension that is important to customers. Such "operational innovation," as he labels it, is less often copied by close competitors with essentially the same strategy than one would assume. Operational innovations have "legs" in his view that actually favor first movers than fast followers.[2] Any reader familiar with Wal-Mart's accelerating advantages over Kmart across the 1980s and 1990s should be nodding strongly in assent. Our view is that aggressive attention to core operational characteristics is a strong preventative to "bad" strategy created by running away from shortfalls in core business processes.

Hammer offers several prescriptions to management teams boxed in by a rigid understanding of the limits in their core operations. In particular, he encourages teams to identify what he calls the "constraining assumption"—the operational constraint within the core business model that more than any other prevents differentiated performance. This constraint then becomes the target of the team's operational innovation efforts.

ADJACENCY EXTENSIONS

After exploiting the potential remaining in the core business, the next most advantaged focus area for companies seeking to extend their growth runs—or to restart growth in a moribund core—is the pursuit of opportunities close to the original business. Such "adjacencies" are often described as manageable step-outs from the core business along a single dimension: offering your current products to a new customer segment, modifying your products or services for your current customers, and so on. Yet even apparently closely related opportunities can hold hidden challenges. Chris Zook of Bain and Company has estimated that only 20 to 25 percent of adjacency plays actually create meaningful new growth.[3] Our own research substantiates this and, beyond the obvious problem of incumbent firms having exploited the easy adjacencies, points to the hidden operational challenges in addressing even apparently "close" adjacent opportunities.

Recommendation 3. For even the closest of adjacency extensions, conduct a careful "gap analysis" to identify required changes to the core business model. Opportunities within the same industry can prove frustratingly difficult when they require significant changes to elements of the core business model such as marketing, distribution, or servicing. A salient example here is the challenge that Brazilian jet manufacturer Embraer faced in moving from its core business of regional jet manufacturing and sales into the private executive jet market across the past four years. The change seemed to require only moderate modifications to aircraft design, especially to interior furnishings and fuel systems. But as Embraer management plotted the firm's entry strategy, it found numerous "gaps" in its current business model that would make pursuit of the seemingly close adjacency extremely challenging. Target markets were much larger, with prospecting much less certain. Product design and manufacturing would involve a whole new set of unpredictable cost factors. Sales would be single, rather than fleet-sized. And finally, servicing would require partnership with new, widely distributed third parties.

Embraer management decomposed these challenges to their current business model into a discrete set of gaps, and the company engaged in the creation of solution paths for each missing or incomplete element (fig. 15.2). Figure 15.2 summarizes Embraer's charter to its strategy function for addressing predicted and discovered gaps in company capabilities as they moved (quite successfully) into the executive jet market.

First, Embraer charged its strategy team with building out its understanding of the new business model requirements, starting with obvious competitors but also moving out to "cognate" markets serving executives, such as luxury cars and boats. This extended business model analysis was done to ensure that, not only would the firm not miss obvious required changes, but it might even discover competitive advantages to apply in its new adjacency.

Second, strategy was asked to go beyond the obvious work of modeling financial pro formas to creating predictive analyses of how competitor countermoves might affect its assumptions about the adjacency's performance. It was also asked to investigate direct and opportunity costs that would be sustained to the current business model, as it made modifications for the adjacency. At the execution level, strategy also was charged with looking forward several time frames to model decisions that would need to be made about the service network and product line extensions, as the business grew.

Beyond these more predictable gaps in their knowledge base, Embraer management discovered new challenges for the leadership team to address as the initiative progressed to execution. The structure and timing of the market—so closely linked to the ebb and flow of corporate profits and executive compensation—required more marketing budget flexibility than had been budgeted.

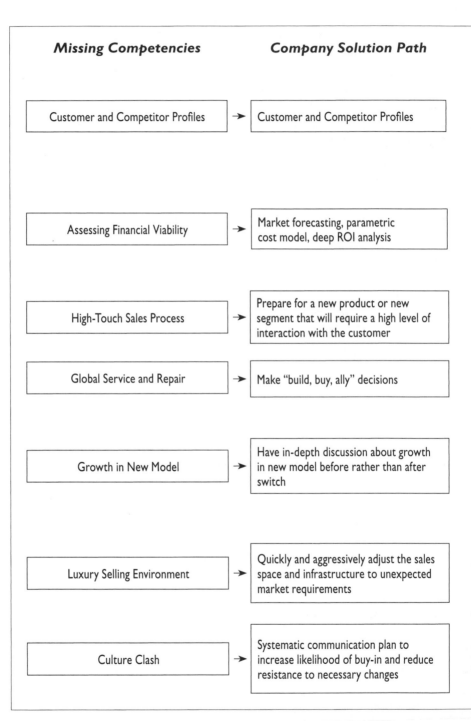

Missing Competencies

- Customer and Competitor Profiles
- Assessing Financial Viability
- High-Touch Sales Process
- Global Service and Repair
- Growth in New Model
- Luxury Selling Environment
- Culture Clash

Company Solution Path

- Customer and Competitor Profiles
- Market forecasting, parametric cost model, deep ROI analysis
- Prepare for a new product or new segment that will require a high level of interaction with the customer
- Make "build, buy, ally" decisions
- Have in-depth discussion about growth in new model before rather than after switch
- Quickly and aggressively adjust the sales space and infrastructure to unexpected market requirements
- Systematic communication plan to increase likelihood of buy-in and reduce resistance to necessary changes

Fig. 15.2 Filling in the gaps at Embraer: modifying the business model for adjacent expansion

The Strategy Role

- ✔ Consult or hire outsiders with expertise in new business model
- ✔ Ensure that research is not limited by assumptions from core business model
- ✔ Ensure that research is broad-based
- ✔ Conduct parallel analysis of cognate markets: luxury cars, luxury boats, etc.

- ✔ Bottom-up and top-down modeling
- ✔ Project costs from "ripple effect" of business model change
- ✔ Project market and competitor reaction
- ✔ Perform reality check: business plan scenarios may be too optimistic

---

- ✔ Include possible higher per unit sales costs in business case

---

- ✔ Consider allying to learn about the business and costs rather than building or buying

---

- ✔ Test cost assumptions for future new product development
- ✔ Test if new market segments fit under the new model
- ✔ Cross-check the new product with the company's portfolio: check and push for synergies and sharing opportunities

---

- ✔ Benchmark competitors and conduct market research to identify skill or infrastructure gaps and include those in financial models
- ✔ Include significant "post-launch costs" in business case to avoid conflict over budget for necessary changes

---

- ✔ Bring in outside experts to explain and advocate changes that the market requires but that go against company culture

Further, in a corporate culture used to rigorous cost controls even in sales, the introduction of a luxury sales model facility for executive jets needed organizational change management planning to ease and explain the cultural exception.

Embraer's adjacent expansion has captured attention in the industry; the trade journal *Flight International* noted that "corporate aviation has been the most significant new market for Embraer in recent years."[4] The salient restart discipline illustrated by the Embraer experience is as follows: before venturing into what appear to be even the closest of adjacency extensions, break down the business model requirements of the new opportunity and dispassionately compare them to current capabilities. In point of fact, adjacencies should be prioritized by the degree of change required to the core business model rather than by degree of industry relatedness.

CORE TRANSFORMATION

With increasing frequency, the restart challenge facing executive teams comes down to transforming a business model in the existing core. In particular, a product-centric firm can find itself trapped by its own product innovation process, assuming that its existing approach to design, prototyping, sourcing, manufacturing, and distributing represent its only options. Higher-yielding, alternative go-to-market models can be locked out early on.

Recommendation 4. Examine opportunity for new business models early in the new product development process. For many product-centric firms, the smoothest, most efficient approach to business model innovation can be to integrate business model design into the product development process. An effective practice we saw in our research is that of a large industrial materials company that was attempting to capture shifting profit pools in the businesses it was serving. The organization had experimented with retail sales, shared product development with partners, and service add-ons, but the technology development decisions of its material sciences R&D shop often eliminated options for richer margins before they could be developed or scaled up.

The company redesigned its materials innovation process in a way to force the consideration of new business models very early on in the technology development cycle (fig. 15.3). Essentially, business model options are now developed on a parallel track with product development, ensuring that the technology requirements of the new material do not shut out promising, higher-margin ways of bringing the product to market.

The company has now adopted a new seven-step innovation process. When

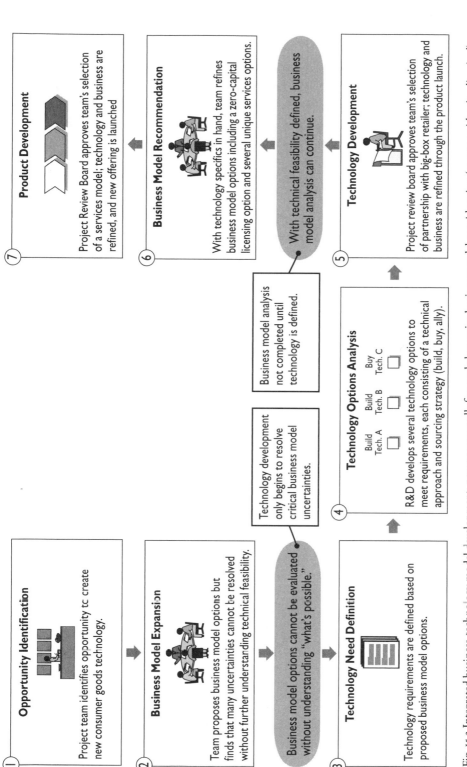

Opportunity Identification ①

Project team identifies opportunity to create new consumer goods technology.

Business Model Expansion ②

Team proposes business model options but finds that many uncertainties cannot be resolved without further understanding technical feasibility.

Business model options cannot be evaluated without understanding "what's possible."

Technology development only begins to resolve critical business model uncertainties.

Technology Need Definition ③

Technology requirements are defined based on proposed business model options.

Technology Options Analysis ④

Build Tech. A   Build Tech. B   Buy Tech. C

R&D develops several technology options to meet requirements, each consisting of a technical approach and sourcing strategy (build, buy, ally).

Business model analysis not completed until technology is defined.

With technical feasibility defined, business model analysis can continue.

Product Development ⑦

Project Review Board approves team's selection of a services model; technology and business are refined, and new offering is launched

Business Model Recommendation ⑥

With technology specifics in hand, team refines business model options including a zero-capital licensing option and several unique services options.

Technology Development ⑤

Project review board approves team's selection of partnership with big-box retailer; technology and business are refined through the product launch.

Fig. 15.3 Integrated business-technology model development: new process pulls forward alternative business model consideration (company identity disguised)

the material sciences lab proposes new product line possibilities, a project team is created to develop a matching set of potential business models with different revenue structures, target markets, and potential partners. The early consideration of alternative business models forces the project team to consider options for business partners, value chain position, and revenue source alternatives before the firm locks in the relevant technology development challenges.

Now armed with a set of business model possibilities, the technical team can work out technology versions and cost/production alternatives for each. Armed with these technical pro formas, the project team can further build out the cases for business model alternatives and whittle down the possibilities to a few best candidates. Last, a project review board can make the final "best case" choice and empower both the material sciences lab and the full project team to proceed apace.

As an important aside, project teams are supported by a corporate-level set of "coaches" with skill sets in business model alternatives. These coaching positions are reserved for high-potential managers considered to be on the fast track to business unit general manager posts, further embedding alternative business model literacy at a high level across the organization.

NEW BUSINESS CREATION

Finally, most large companies will face the challenge of restart initiatives located in the quadrant we've labeled "new business creation"—growth bets that require both changes to the existing business model and the pursuit of opportunities beyond the existing core business. Operating in these high-risk conditions, successful restart strategies in this space were based on proprietary insights into potential customer needs and deep capabilities developed across time in the original core business.

Recommendation 5. Exploit "privileged insight" into customers in building new growth platforms. Other observers have highlighted the important role that fallow assets in the core business (brand, business processes, manufacturing capabilities, and so on) can play in serving as the building blocks for businesses outside the current core. Chris Zook of Bain and Company has rigorously examined this opportunity. [5] Here we observe that fallow assets are most powerful as the basis of new, sustainable growth platforms when they combine "privileged insight" on customers with a strong, differentiated organizational competency. When both are present, the organization has an advantaged competitive basis for winning in the new arena.

A good example of the power of this combination of assets is provided by Manpower Inc. across the past decade. Manpower's core business of providing temporary clerical and light-industrial staffing grew steadily across the 1990s as many companies moved to more flexible staffing structures. In the course of growing this core business, Manpower created strong capabilities in recruiting, skills assessment, employee selection, training, and payroll processes, as well as an in-depth understanding of what best practice is in each. It also developed, through its work with a wide range of clients (both geographically and industrially), deep and proprietary insights into projected staffing needs, skill gaps, and emerging corporate activities.

As growth leveled off in its core temporary staffing business late in the decade, Manpower combined its accumulated expertise in human resources activities with its insight into proprietary customer needs to launch its Empower HR consultancy in 2000, made up of five geographically distributed entities worldwide. In addition, Manpower used its "early warning" insights from customers to acquire Jefferson Wells, an auditing service company. This acquisition, completed in 2001, timed perfectly the coming wave of demand triggered by the Sarbanes-Oxley act in the United States. Both new businesses took Manpower out of its traditional core, but both played to the combination of proprietary insight into customer activities and existing core capabilities. As Annalisa Gigante, Manpower's director of global strategy and business development, commented, "With the Empower Group, we extended our HR services portfolio from staffing to HR consulting, allowing us to respond to customer requests for a broader range of value-added workforce solutions."[6] Even as the firm surpassed the $19 billion mark in late 2007, it continued to maintain a strong double-digit revenue growth rate.

THE NEED FOR SPEED IN RECOVERING FROM STALLS

We are well aware that the five recommendations presented above are but the barest brush with a topic that deserves its own book-length treatment, but we offer this framework in the hope that management teams facing a difficult growth stall will find guidance in the strategies followed by exemplary peers. To management teams in this situation, we encourage immediate, diligent attention to the restart challenge; as peer experience amply demonstrates, restarting growth *is* possible, but it doesn't get any easier with the passage of time.

Appendix 1: Companies in the Sample

Company	Stall History
ABB Ltd	Stalled 2000
Abbott Laboratories	Continuous grower
ABN AMRO Holdings NV	Continuous grower
Adecco SA	Stalled 2000, recovered 2001
Aegon NV	Continuous grower
Aerojet General Corp.	Stalled 1962
Aetna Inc.	Stalled 1985
Agway Inc.	Stalled 1984
Akzo Nobel NV	Stalled 1989
Albertson's Inc.	Stalled 1979, recovered 1980; stalled 1999
Alcan Inc.	Stalled 1956, recovered 1958; stalled 1974, recovered 1994
Alcoa Inc.	Stalled 1955, recovered 1985
Allegheny Technologies Inc.	Stalled 1968, recovered 1999
Allied Stores	Stalled 1968
Allis-Chalmers Energy Inc.	Stalled 1955, recovered 1993
Altria Group Inc.	Stalled 1994
Amax Inc.	Stalled 1955, recovered 1969; stalled 1979, recovered 1985

Amerada Hess Corp.	Stalled 1974, recovered 1993
American Airlines Inc.	Stalled 1992
American Cyanamid Co.	Stalled 1980
American Electric Power	Stalled 1981, recovered 1990; stalled 2001
American Express Co.	Stalled 1988
American Financial Corp.	Stalled 1989
American General Corp.	Stalled 1984, recovered 1988
American International Group	Continuous grower
American Motors Corp.	Stalled 1962, recovered 1968; stalled 1979
American Standard Companies Inc.	Stalled 1956, recovered 1958; stalled 1973, recovered 1993
American Stores Co.	Stalled 1985
AmerisourceBergen Corp.	Continuous grower
Ameritech Corp.	Continuous grower
AMF Inc.	Stalled 1957, recovered 1958; stalled 1979
Amoco Corp.	Stalled 1981
AMR Corp.	Stalled 1968, recovered 1975; stalled 1993
Amstar Corp.	Stalled 1981
Anaconda Co.	Stalled 1969
Anderson Clayton and Co.	Stalled 1957
Anheuser-Busch Companies Inc.	Stalled 1986
Apple Computer Inc.	Stalled 1988, recovered 1997
Aquila Inc.	Stalled 2001
Archer-Daniels-Midland Co.	Stalled 1975, recovered 1976
Armco Inc.	Stalled 1959, recovered 1964; stalled 1981
ASARCO Inc.	Stalled 1974, recovered 1985
Ashland Inc.	Stalled 1955, recovered 1956; stalled 1975
Associated Dry Goods Corp.	Stalled 1967, recovered 1977
AstraZeneca PLC	Stalled 1999, recovered 2000
AT&T Corp.	Stalled 1979
AT&T Inc.	Stalled 2000
Atlantic Richfield Co.	Stalled 1981
Australia and New Zealand Banking Group Ltd	Continuous grower
AutoNation Inc.	Stalled 1999
Avatex Corp.	Stalled 1979
Avco Corp.	Stalled 1968, recovered 1972; stalled 1981
Aventis SA	Stalled 1991, recovered 1997
AXA	Stalled 2000
Banco Bilbao Vizcaya	Continuous grower
Banco Central Hispano	Stalled 1992
Banco Santander SA	Stalled 2000
Bank of America Corp.	Continuous grower

Bank of New York Co. Inc.	Stalled 1989
Bank One Corp.	Stalled 1998
Bank Tokyo–Mitsubishi	Stalled 1992
BankAmerica Corp. (Pre-1998)	Stalled 1981, recovered 1988
BankBoston Corp.	Stalled 1981, recovered 1983
Bankers Trust Corp.	Stalled 1974, recovered 1976
Barclays PLC	Stalled 1990, recovered 1996
Baxter International Inc.	Stalled 1986
Bayer AG	Stalled 1998
BCE Inc.	Stalled 1989
Beatrice Companies Inc.	Stalled 1984
Bell Canada	Stalled 1988, recovered 1994
BellSouth Corp.	Stalled 2000
BellSouth Telecommunications	Stalled 1980, recovered 1984; stalled 1994
Bendix Corp.	Stalled 1955, recovered 1958; stalled 1974
Bergen Brunswig Corp	Stalled 1969, recovered 1972
Berkshire Hathaway	Continuous grower
Best Buy Co. Inc.	Continuous grower
Best Foods	Stalled 1974
Bethlehem Steel Corp.	Stalled 1957
BG Group PLC	Stalled 1991, recovered 1998
BHP Billiton Ltd	Stalled 1990, recovered 1997
Bicoastal Corp.	Stalled 1968
Boeing Co.	Stalled 1957, recovered 1960; stalled 1986, recovered 1987; stalled 1998
Borden Chemical Inc.	Stalled 1974
BorgWarner Inc.	Continuous grower
BP PLC	Stalled 1979, recovered 1990
Bristol-Myers Squibb Co.	Stalled 1968, recovered 1979; stalled 1998
British Airways PLC	Stalled 1996
British American Tobacco Ltd	Stalled 1979, recovered 1994; stalled 2000
Broadway Stores Inc.	Stalled 1986
BT Group PLC	Stalled 1989
Burlington Industries Inc.	Stalled 1968
Burns International Services Corp.	Stalled 1955
C&S/Sovran Corp.	Continuous grower
Cable and Wireless PLC	Stalled 1999
Cadbury Schweppes PLC	Stalled 1990, recovered 1997
Campbell Soup Co.	Stalled 1990
Canadian Pacific Railway Ltd	Stalled 1981, recovered 2001
Canon Inc.	Stalled 1991

Capital Cities/ABC Inc.	Stalled 1986
Cardinal Health Inc.	Continuous grower
Caremark Rx Inc.	Continuous grower
Carnation Co.	Stalled 1974
Caterpillar Inc.	Stalled 1975, recovered 1985
CBS Corp.	Stalled 2001
CBC Inc.	Stalled 1978
Centerpoint Energy Inc.	Stalled 1984, recovered 1988; stalled 2001
Ceridian Corp.	Stalled 1982
Champion International Corp.	Stalled 1973
Chevron Corp.	Stalled 1980, recovered 1991
China Mobile Hong Kong	Continuous grower
Chiquita Brands International Inc.	Stalled 1975, recovered 2000
Chrysler Corp.	Stalled 1955, recovered 1958; stalled 1972, recovered 1979
Chubb Corp.	Stalled 1988, recovered 1994
Cigna Corp.	Stalled 1985
Cisco Systems Inc.	Stalled 2000
Citicorp	Stalled 1981, recovered 1994
Cities Service Co.	Stalled 1981
Citigroup Global Markets Holdings	Stalled 1982, recovered 1996
Citigroup Inc.	Stalled 1998, recovered 1999
City Investing Co.	Stalled 1972, recovered 1975
CAN Financial Corp.	Stalled 1995
Coca-Cola Co.	Stalled 1966, recovered 1967; stalled 1978, recovered 1987; stalled 1997
Coca-Cola Enterprises Inc.	Stalled 2001
Coles Myer Ltd	Continuous grower
Colgate-Palmolive Co.	Stalled 1978
Collins and Aikman Corp.	Continuous grower
Columbia Energy Group	Stalled 1960, recovered 1968; stalled 1982
Comcast Corp.	Continuous grower
Commonwealth Edison Co.	Stalled 1983
Compaq Computer Corp.	Continuous grower
Conagra Foods Inc.	Stalled 1989
ConocoPhillips	Stalled 1955, recovered 1964; stalled 1981, recovered 1992
Consolidated Edison Inc.	Stalled 1981
Continental Bank Corp.	Stalled 1981
Continental Corp.	Stalled 1986
Continental Group	Stalled 1956
Cooper Industries Ltd	Stalled 1981, recovered 1982
Corus Group PLC	Continuous grower
Costco Wholesale Corp.	Continuous grower

Countrywide Financial Corp.	Continuous grower
Courtaulds PLC	Stalled 1974
Covanta Energy Corp.	Stalled 1961, recovered 1962; stalled 1976, recovered 1986; stalled 1996
Crane Co.	Stalled 1956, recovered 1960; stalled 1974
Creole Petroleum Corp.	Continuous grower
Crown Zellerbach	Stalled 1955
CSZ Corp.	Stalled 1980
Curtiss-Wright Corp.	Stalled 1955, recovered 1992
CVS Corp.	Stalled 1986, recovered 1989
Daiei Inc.	Stalled 1994
DaimlerChrysler AG	Stalled 1998
Dana Corp.	Stalled 1979, recovered 1988; stalled 1999
Deere and Co.	Stalled 1978, recovered 1985; stalled 1997, recovered 1999
Delhaize America Inc.	Stalled 1992
Dell Inc.	Continuous grower
Delta Air Lines Inc.	Stalled 1973, recovered 1975; stalled 1993
Deutsche Bank AG	Continuous grower
Deutsche Telekom AG	Continuous grower
Diageo PLC	Stalled 2000
Digital Equipment	Stalled 1989
Disney (Walt) Co.	Stalled 1972, recovered 1974; stalled 1997
Dow Chemical	Stalled 1981, recovered 1995
Dresser Industries Inc.	Stalled 1956, recovered 1958; stalled 1981, recovered 1987
DuPont (E. I.) de Nemours and Co.	Stalled 1983
Duke Energy Corp.	Stalled 1982, recovered 1987; stalled 2001
Dunlop Holdings PLC	Stalled 1979
Dynegy Inc.	Stalled 2001
E.ON AG	Continuous grower
Eastern Air Lines	Stalled 1985
Eastman Kodak Co.	Stalled 1973
Eaton Corp.	Stalled 1972, recovered 1987
Edison International	Stalled 1980
El Paso CGP Co.	Stalled 1977, recovered 1991; stalled 1996
El Paso Corp.	Stalled 1981, recovered 1987; stalled 2001
Electrolux AB	Stalled 1989
Electronic Data Systems Corp.	Stalled 1994
Emerson Electric Co.	Stalled 1981
Endesa SA	Continuous grower
Eni SpA	Continuous grower
Enron Corp.	Stalled 1985, recovered 1987
EnviroSource Inc.	Stalled 1974, recovered 1982; stalled 1994

Ericsson (L. M.)	Stalled 1974, recovered 1977; stalled 2000
Exxon Mobil Corp..	Stalled 1956, recovered 1964; stalled 1980, recovered 1993
Fannie Mae	Stalled 1979, recovered 1986; stalled 2000
Farmland Industries Inc.	Stalled 1979, recovered 1985; stalled 1996
Federal Home Loan Mortgage Corp.	Stalled 2001
Federated Department Stores	Stalled 1980, recovered 1988; stalled 2000, recovered 2001
FedEx Corp.	Continuous grower
Fiat SpA	Stalled 1990
Firestone Tire and Rubber Co.	Stalled 1955
First Chicago Corp.	Stalled 1974
First Interstate Bancorp	Stalled 1981
First National Stores Inc.	Stalled 1962
Flagstar Corp.	Stalled 1974
FleetBoston Financial Corp.	Stalled 1974, recovered 1975; stalled 1995, recovered 1996
Fleming Companies Inc.	Stalled 1989
Florida Power and Light Co.	Stalled 1981, recovered 1999
Fluor Corp.	Stalled 1955, recovered 1956; stalled 1982, recovered 1986; stalled 1997, recovered 2001
FMC Corp.	Stalled 1967
Foot Locker Inc.	Stalled 1973
Ford Motor Co.	Stalled 1972, recovered 1982; stalled 1996
Ford Motor Co. of Canada Ltd.	Stalled 1972
Ford Motor Credit Co.	Stalled 2001
Fort James Corp.	Stalled 1986
Fortune Brands Inc.	Stalled 1975, recovered 2001
FPL Group Inc.	Stalled 1981, recovered 1996
France Telecom	Continuous grower
Fuji Photo Film	Stalled 1987, recovered 1992
Fujitsu Limited	Stalled 1999
Galen Health Care Inc.	Stalled 1986
Gamble-Skogmo	Stalled 1972
GenCorp Inc.	Stalled 1962
General Dynamics Corp.	Stalled 1961, recovered 1972; stalled 1985, recovered 1992
General Electric Capital Corp.	Stalled 2000
General Electric Co.	Stalled 1974, recovered 1985; stalled 2000
General Foods Corp.	Stalled 1981
General Mills Inc.	Stalled 1975, recovered 1994
General Motors Corp.	Stalled 1955, recovered 1958; stalled 1971
Genesco Inc.	Stalled 1971, recovered 1994
Georgia-Pacific Corp.	Stalled 1972

Getty Oil Co.	Stalled 1966, recovered 1969
Gillette Co.	Stalled 1955, recovered 1957; stalled 1974, recovered 1983; stalled 1996
GlaxoSmithKline PLC	Stalled 1973, recovered 1977
Goodrich Corp.	Stalled 1979, recovered 1989; stalled 1999
Goodyear Tire and Rubber Co.	Stalled 1955, recovered 1961; stalled 1973
Grace (W. R.) and Co.	Stalled 1973, recovered 1998
Grand Met PLC	Stalled 1991
Grant (W. T.) Co.	Stalled 1969
Great Atlantic & Pacific Tea Co.	Stalled 1961
Great Western Financial	Stalled 1986
Grumman Corp.	Stalled 1968
GTE Corp.	Stalled 1966
Gulf Canada Corp.	Stalled 1981
Gulf Corp.	Stalled 1957, recovered 1963; stalled 1974
Halliburton Co.	Stalled 1978, recovered 1988; stalled 1998, recovered 2000
Hanson PLC	Stalled 1995, recovered 1998
Hartford Financial Services	Continuous grower
HCA Inc.	Stalled 1995
Heinz (H. J.) Co.	Stalled 1974
Hewlett-Packard Co.	Continuous grower
Hitachi Ltd	Stalled 1994
Home Depot Inc.	Continuous grower
Honeywell Inc.	Stalled 1970
Honeywell International Inc.	Stalled 1983, recovered 1996
Hormel Foods Corp.	Stalled 1974
Host Marriott Corp.	Stalled 1985, recovered 1994
HSBC Finance Corp.	Stalled 1969, recovered 1971; stalled 1981, recovered 1988
Hydro Quebec	Stalled 1988
IBP Inc.	Stalled 1979
Ikon Offiice Solutions	Stalled 1974, recovered 1975; stalled 1995
Imperial Chemical Industries PLC	Stalled 1974
Imperial Group PLC	Stalled 1980
Imperial Oil Ltd	Stalled 1956, recovered 1963; stalled 1976, recovered 1994
INA Corp.	Stalled 1976
Inco Ltd	Stalled 1955, recovered 1958; stalled 1974, recovered 1997
ING Groep NV	Stalled 2001
Ingram Micro Inc.	Stalled 2000
Intel Corp.	Stalled 1996
International Business Machines Corp.	Stalled 1968, recovered 1974; stalled 1984
International Paper Co.	Stalled 1956, recovered 1982; stalled 1995

Ito Yokado Co. Ltd	Stalled 1994
ITT Industries Inc.	Stalled 1976, recovered 2001
IU International Corp.	Stalled 1974
Japan Airlines Corp.	Stalled 1994
Jewel Companies Inc.	Stalled 1969
Johnson and Johnson	Stalled 1979, recovered 1984
Johnson Controls Inc.	Stalled 1966, recovered 1968
JPMorgan Chase and Co.	Stalled 1980, recovered 1983
Kaisertech Ltd	Stalled 1955, recovered 1956; stalled 1980
Kellogg Co.	Stalled 1975, recovered 1982; stalled 1992
Kennecott Corp.	Stalled 1974, recovered 1975
Kerr-McGee Corp.	Stalled 1981, recovered 1995
Kimberly-Clark Corp.	Stalled 1961, recovered 1985; stalled 1995
Kirin Brewery Ltd	Stalled 1995
Komatsu Ltd	Stalled 1994, recovered 2000
Koninklijke Ahold NV	Stalled 2001
Koninklijke Philips Electronics NV	Stalled 1978
Korea Electric Power Co.	Continuous grower
Kraft General Foods	Continuous grower
Kroger Co.	Stalled 1985, recovered 1989; stalled 2000
Kubota Corp.	Stalled 1977, recovered 1981; stalled 1994
Lehman Brothers Holdings Inc.	Continuous grower
Levi Strauss and Co.	Stalled 1977, recovered 1984; stalled 1996
Lilly (Eli) and Co.	Stalled 1974, recovered 1987
Limited Brands Inc.	Stalled 1991
Lincoln National Corp.	Stalled 1987
Litton Industries Inc.	Stalled 1966, recovered 1994
Lockheed Martin Corp.	Stalled 1959, recovered 1976; stalled 1996, recovered 2001
Loews Corp.	Stalled 1975, recovered 1978; stalled 1995
Lowe's Companies Inc.	Continuous grower
LTV Corp.	Stalled 1968
LTV Steel Co. Inc.	Stalled 1957, recovered 1971; stalled 1981
Lucent Technologies Inc.	Stalled 2000
Lucky Stores Inc.	Stalled 1976
Lykes Corp.	Stalled 1968
Lyondell Chemical Co.	Continuous grower
Macy (R. H.) and Co.	Stalled 1989
Manufacturers Hanover Corp.	Stalled 1981
Marathon Oil Corp.	Stalled 1981, recovered 1990
Marriott International Inc.	Stalled 1997
Martin Marietta Corp.	Stalled 1962, recovered 1975
Matsushita Electric	Stalled 1992

Maxus Energy Corp.	Stalled 1955, recovered 1957; stalled 1983
May Department Stores Co.	Stalled 1986
McCrory Parent Corp.	Stalled 1969
McDermott International Inc.	Stalled 1978, recovered 1999
McDonald's Corp.	Continuous grower
McDonnell Douglas Corp.	Stalled 1967, recovered 1975; stalled 1991
MCI Communications	Continuous grower
MCI Inc.	Stalled 1998
McKesson Corp.	Stalled 1966, recovered 1982
Medco Health Solutions Inc.	Stalled 2001
Merck and Co.	Stalled 1974, recovered 1978; stalled 2001
Merrill Lynch and Co. Inc.	Stalled 2000, recovered 2001
Merritt Chapman and Scott Corp.	Stalled 1955
Microsoft Corp.	Continuous grower
Millea Holdings Inc.	Continuous grower
Mitsui and Co. Ltd	Stalled 1994
Mobil Corp.	Stalled 1956, recovered 1961; stalled 1980
Moneygram International Inc.	Stalled 1973
Montedison SpA	Stalled 1990
Morgan (J. P.) and Co.	Stalled 1982, recovered 1986
Morgan Stanley	Continuous grower
Motorola Inc.	Stalled 1966, recovered 1970; stalled 1995
Nabisco Brands Inc.	Continuous grower
Nabisco Group Holdings Corp.	Stalled 1988
Nabisco Inc.	Stalled 1975
National Australia Bank	Stalled 1992, recovered 1993
National Tea Co.	Stalled 1969
National Westminster Bank	Stalled 1990
Navistar International Corp.	Stalled 1979
NCR Corp.	Stalled 1973
NEC Corp.	Stalled 1994
Nestle SA	Stalled 1987, recovered 2001
News Corp.	Stalled 1991, recovered 1993
Nippon Telegraph and Telephone	Stalled 1994
Nissan Motor Co. Ltd	Stalled 1994, recovered 2000
NL Industries Inc.	Stalled 1956
Nokia Corp.	Continuous grower
Norfolk Southern Corp.	Stalled 1968, recovered 1972; stalled 1988, recovered 1997
Norsk Hydro ASA	Stalled 1990, recovered 1992
Nortel Networks Corp.	Stalled 2000
North American Philips Corp.	Stalled 1977

Northrop Grumman Corp.	Stalled 1955, recovered 1960; stalled 1970, recovered 1972; stalled 1985, recovered 1991
Northwest Airlines Corp.	Stalled 1968, recovered 1970; stalled 1988
NYNEX Corp.	Stalled 1989
Occidental Petroleum Corp.	Stalled 1974, recovered 1978
OfficeMax Inc.	Stalled 1969, recovered 1994; stalled 2000
Olin Corp.	Stalled 1966, recovered 1998
Owens-Illinois Inc.	Stalled 1977
Pacific Bell	Stalled 1960
Pan Am Corp.	Stalled 1968, recovered 1970; stalled 1980
Paramount Communications Inc.	Stalled 1968, recovered 1985
Penney (J. C.) Co.	Stalled 1973
PepsiAmericas Inc.	Stalled 1980, recovered 1997
PepsiCo Inc.	Stalled 1995, recovered 2000
Pfizer Inc.	Stalled 1966, recovered 1969; stalled 2001
PE&E Corp.	Stalled 1960, recovered 1967; stalled 1985, recovered 1988; stalled 2000
Pharmacia Corp.	Stalled 1962, recovered 1997
Phelps Dodge Corp.	Stalled 1956, recovered 1959; stalled 1973, recovered 1982; stalled 1995, recovered 1996
Pillsbury Co.	Stalled 1979, recovered 1981
Plains All American Pipeline L.P.	Continuous grower
POSCO	Continuous grower
PPG Industries Inc.	Stalled 1955
Price Co.	Continuous grower
Primerica Corp.	Stalled 1980
Procter and Gamble Co.	Stalled 1992, recovered 2000
Public Service Enterprises Group Inc.	Stalled 1980, recovered 1998
Publix Super Markets Inc.	Continuous grower
Pullman Inc.	Stalled 1957, recovered 1964
Quaker Oats Co.	Stalled 1989
Qwest Communications International Inc.	Stalled 2001
Ralston Purina Co.	Stalled 1974
Raytheon Co.	Stalled 1960, recovered 1962; stalled 1981, recovered 1988; stalled 1998
RCA Corp.	Stalled 1955, recovered 1956; stalled 1967
Repsol YPF SA	Continuous grower
Republic Steel Corp.	Stalled 1956
Revlon Group Inc.	Stalled 1958, recovered 1980
Rexam PLC	Stalled 1957, recovered 1962; stalled 1974, recovered 1984

Reynolds Metals Co.	Stalled 1955, recovered 1960; stalled 1974
Rio Tinto Ltd	Continuous grower
Roche Holdings Ltd	Stalled 1998
Rockwell Automation	Stalled 1957, recovered 1958; stalled 1988
Royal Dutch Petroleum	Stalled 1957, recovered 1963; stalled 1980, recovered 1994
Royal Dutch Shell PLC	Continuous grower
Ryder System Inc.	Stalled 1956, recovered 1961; stalled 1987
Ryerson Inc.	Stalled 1974, recovered 1998
Safeway Inc.	Stalled 1955, recovered 1964; stalled 1978, recovered 1991; stalled 2001
Santa Fe Pacific Corp.	Stalled 1985
Sanyo Electric Co. Ltd	Stalled 1994
Sara Lee Corp.	Stalled 1969, recovered 1975; stalled 1997
Schlumberger Ltd	Stalled 1980, recovered 1987
Scott Paper Co.	Stalled 1955, recovered 1957; stalled 1989
Seagram Co. Ltd	Stalled 1975, recovered 1980
Sealed Air Corp.	Stalled 2000
Sears Holdings Corp.	Stalled 1976
Sears Roebuck and Co.	Stalled 1969, recovered 1979; stalled 1989
Security Pacific Corp.	Stalled 1981
Sempra Energy	Stalled 1962, recovered 1969; stalled 1985, recovered 1993
7-Eleven Inc.	Stalled 1985, recovered 1995
Shell Oil Co.	Stalled 1981
Shell Transport and Trading Company	Stalled 1979, recovered 1994
Siemens AG	Continuous grower
Signal Companies	Stalled 1967, recovered 1971
SmithKline Beckman Corp.	Stalled 1963, recovered 1968; stalled 1982, recovered 1983
SmithKline Beecham PLC	Stalled 1991
Sony Corp.	Stalled 1994
South Central Bell Telephone	Stalled 1982
Southern California Edison	Stalled 1980
Southern California Gas Co.	Stalled 1982
Southern Co.	Stalled 1984
Southwestern Bell Telephone	Stalled 1982
Spartan Industries Inc.	Stalled 1965
Spelling Entertainment Group Inc.	Stalled 1979, recovered 1991
Sperry Corp.	Stalled 1959
Sprint Nextel Corp.	Stalled 1974, recovered 1975; stalled 1993, recovered 1995
St. Paul Travelers Companies Inc.	Continuous grower
St. Regis Corp.	Stalled 1960
Standard Oil Co.	Stalled 1981

Stevens (J. P.) and Co.	Stalled 1965
Stone Container Corp.	Stalled 1990
Stop and Shop Companies	Stalled 1966
Sunoco Inc.	Stalled 1982, recovered 1993
Supervalu Inc.	Stalled 1994, recovered 1996
Svenska Cellulosa AB	Stalled 1990, recovered 1992
Swiss Reinsurance Co.	Continuous grower
SYSCO Corp.	Continuous grower
Target Corp.	Continuous grower
Tech Data Corp.	Stalled 2000
Telefonica SA	Continuous grower
Telefonos de Mexico SA	Stalled 1999
Tenneco Corp.	Stalled 1981
Tenneco Inc.	Stalled 1981
Tennessee Gas Pipeline Co.	Stalled 1986
Tennessee Valley Authority	Stalled 1982
Texaco Canada Inc.	Stalled 1983
Texaco Inc.	Stalled 1981
Texas Eastern Corp.	Stalled 1984
Texas Eastern Transmission	Stalled 1982
Texas Instruments Inc.	Stalled 1966, recovered 1967; stalled 1981, recovered 1985; stalled 1995, recovered 2001
Textron Inc.	Stalled 1968, recovered 1982; stalled 1994
Thales	Stalled 1990
Thomson Corp.	Stalled 1997
3M Co.	Stalled 1973
Tidewater Inc.	Stalled 1980, recovered 1985; stalled 1997, recovered 1999
Time Warner Inc. (AOL Time Warner)	Stalled 2001
Time Warner Inc. (Pre-AOL merger)]	Stalled 1965, recovered 1969
TJX Companies Inc.	Stalled 1967, recovered 1975; stalled 1987, recovered 1988
Tosco Corp.	Stalled 1976, recovered 1984
Toshiba Corp.	Stalled 1994
Total SA	Stalled 2000, recovered 2001
Toyota Motor Corp.	Stalled 1987, recovered 1997
Toys "R" Us Inc.	Stalled 1992
Transamerica Corp.	Stalled 1967
Transco Energy Co.	Stalled 1982
Travelers Corp.	Stalled 1987
TRW Inc.	Stalled 1968, recovered 1989
TXU Corp.	Stalled 1956, recovered 1957; stalled 1984, recovered 1988; stalled 2001
TXU Gas Co.	Stalled 1983, recovered 1990

TXU US Holdings Co.	Continuous grower
Tyco International Ltd	Stalled 2001
Tyson Foods Inc.	Stalled 1990, recovered 1991
U.S. Air Inc.	Stalled 1990
U.S. Bancorp	Stalled 1972, recovered 1975; stalled 1986, recovered 1987; stalled 2001
U.S. Industries	Stalled 1973
U.S. Trust Corp.	Stalled 1964, recovered 1965; stalled 1981, recovered 1994
U.S. West Communications Inc.	Stalled 1961, recovered 1967; stalled 1979, recovered 1980
UAL Corp.	Stalled 1969
Unicom Corp.	Stalled 1983
Unilever NV	Stalled 1956, recovered 1964; stalled 1974, recovered 1983; stalled 1995
Unilever PLC	Stalled 1974
Union Carbide Corp.	Stalled 1981
Union Pacific Corp.	Stalled 1983
Uniroyal Inc.	Stalled 1973
Unisys Corp.	Stalled 1956, recovered 1958; stalled 1974, recovered 1976; stalled 1987
United Airlines Inc.	Stalled 1993
United Energy Resources	Stalled 1981
United Parcel Service Inc.	Stalled 1992, recovered 1997
United States Steel Corp.	Stalled 1957, recovered 1994
United Technologies Corp.	Stalled 1957, recovered 1960; stalled 1981, recovered 1999
UnitedHealth Group Inc.	Continuous grower
Unocal Corp.	Stalled 1974
USF&G Corp.	Stalled 1988
Valero Energy Corp.	Stalled 1984, recovered 1986
Varity Corp.	Stalled 1955, recovered 1956; stalled 1975
Verizon Communications Inc.	Stalled 2001
Vodafone Group PLC	Continuous grower
Volvo AB	Stalled 1995, recovered 1999
Wachovia Corp.	Continuous grower
Walgreen Co.	Stalled 1968, recovered 1977
Wal-Mart Stores	Continuous grower
Warner Communications Inc.	Stalled 1974, recovered 1975
Warner-Lambert Co.	Stalled 1974, recovered 1987
Washington Mutual Inc.	Stalled 2001
Wellpoint Health Networks Inc.	Continuous grower
Wells Fargo and Co.	Stalled 1981, recovered 1985
Westpac Banking Corp.	Continuous grower
Wetterau Inc.	Stalled 1986

Weyerhaeuser Co.	Stalled 1957, recovered 1958; stalled 1973, recovered 1994
Whirlpool Corp.	Stalled 1972, recovered 1980; stalled 1992, recovered 1997
Williams Companies Inc. S	talled 1974, recovered 1975; stalled 2001
Winn-Dixie Stores Inc.	Stalled 1957, recovered 1964; stalled 1978
Wyeth	Stalled 1974, recovered 1985; stalled 1995
Xerox Corp.	Stalled 1972

Appendix 2: A Note
on Methodology

Because this research sought to understand longer-term, secular growth rate shifts in individual company revenue growth performance, as opposed to shorter-term performance volatility caused by economic cycles or operational missteps, we assembled a set of companies for which we could compile multiple decades' worth of data. We began with a set of all companies that had ever appeared in the Fortune 100 since that list's inception in 1955. Early versions of that list excluded services firms and large companies headquartered outside the United States, so we added to our data set any firm that had revenues large enough to have been included within the Fortune 100—or more specifically, firms with annual revenues greater than or equal to those of the 100th largest firm on *Fortune*'s list. Regardless of current parentage or disposition (acquisition, merger, bankruptcy), companies stand as historical entities in Compustat's, and thus in our, data set.

We worked with Standard and Poor's Compustat data group to get the "as reported" financial performance numbers for all publicly traded U.S. companies who met the revenue size threshold of a Fortune 100 firm—whether *Fortune* included them on their list or not. We collected all available revenue, margin, and market value data on those firms from 1950 to 2006, even if such firms were only "Fortune 100 eligible" for part of that period. Additionally, by including foreign companies for which Compustat had data because those companies trade American Depository Receipts (ADRs), we expanded our set internationally. In total, we examined the growth histories of 503 firms, of which 82 percent were headquartered in the United States and 18 percent were headquartered outside the United States.

DEFLATED TO REFLECT REAL PERFORMANCE

We used the implicit price deflator from the U.S. Bureau of Economic Analysis to inflation-adjust all data to constant 2006 dollars. For any comparative market value analysis, we additionally deflated market value performance by that of the S&P 500 Index to remove the temporal effects of major bubbles or downturns the better to see the impact of a stall.

DETERMINING "STALLS"—INFLECTION POINTS
IN LONG-TERM PERFORMANCE

As explained in chapter 2, we developed a methodology for identifying stall points—those moments when firms encounter a significant downward, enduring inflection in revenue growth—and applied this analysis to the population of Fortune 100–sized firms across the past fifty years.

We determined stall points by comparing the ten-year growth rate before and after each year of the company's history. The point where the most significant difference—or delta—existed between the growth rates of those ten-year blocks is the stall point. For a company to qualify as "stalling," pre-stall growth must have been at least 2 percent in real dollars for the ten prior years; the delta, or difference, in pre- and post-stall growth rates must have been at least 4 percent; and the post-stall growth rate must have fallen below 6 percent, again in real dollars.

This methodology permitted us to screen out bad quarters and bad years and focused our attention on those discontinuous moments where growth gives way to prolonged stagnation or decline and on the critical managerial activities in place during the years immediately before and after a stall. Similarly, we were able to screen out the effects of even sizable one-time events, such as acquisitions or divestitures, using this methodology, because no single transaction unduly influenced a company's revenue growth trajectory.

ADJUSTING FOR RECENCY

For each year which data was available, we calculated the ten-year forward and ten-year backward compound annual growth rate (CAGR) for the deflated revenues of each firm. As we got closer to the edges of the available data for a company, we would adjust the ten-year period to a five-year period for the CAGR calculations. If a company had data from 1950 to 2006, for the 1957 data, we calculated a seven-year backward CAGR and a ten-year forward CAGR, but in 1999, we calculated a ten-year backward CAGR and seven-year forward CAGR. This means that no stall can be calculated earlier than 1955 or after 2001.

We are pleased to discuss any aspect of our methodology or findings with analysts who wish to learn more or to replicate our approach. We maintain an updated list of Frequently Asked Questions on our Web site, www.stallpoints.executiveboard.com.

Appendix 3: Case Study Companies for Stall Factor Taxonomy

Business Market	Stall Period	
	Before 1990	After 1990
Asset-Intensive	3M	Borden
	BFGoodrich	Dana Corp
	Boeing	Lockheed Martin
	Caterpillar	
	Daimler-Benz	
	DuPont	
	Fluor	
	GE	
	ITT	
	Tenneco	
	Toyota	
	United Technologies	
Business-Service	Unisys	Supervalu
Consumer-Focused	Coca-Cola	Altria (Philip Morris)
	ConAgra	AMR
	Disney	AutoNation

Business Market	Stall Period	
	Before 1990	After 1990
	Eastman Kodak	Campbell Soup
	GTE	Coca-Cola
	Sears Holdings (Sears/Kmart)	Gillette
		Heinz
		Kellogg
		Kimberly-Clark
		Levi Strauss
		Matsushita
		Procter and Gamble
		Ralston Purina
		Sony
		Toys "R" Us
Financial Services	Citibank	Bank One
	American Express	
	BankAmerica	
Tech-Intensive	Apple	Hitachi
	DEC	Motorola
	IBM	NEC
	Philips	Toshiba
	RCA	
	Xerox	

Appendix 4: Stall Factor
Definitions

Regulatory Actions
Government intervention aimed at reducing or controlling market power of individual firms, limiting freedom of action for revenue growth

Antitrust
Regulatory activity that constrains competitive tactics firms can apply

Government Subsidized Overcapacity
Government funding that stimulates overproduction, driving prices down

Economic Downturn
Severe national or sectoral slowdown in real growth rates, affecting (virtually) all participants in an industry or a geographic market

National Labor Market Inflexibility
Labor regulations restrict employers' freedom to adjust size or activities of workforce in response to market conditions; particularly relevant in European and Japanese labor markets, as well as in highly unionized industries

Geopolitical Context
Exogenous geopolitical events—such as outbreak of war, entry of state-sponsored competitor, impact of pricing cartel, and "acts of God"—that curtail company revenue growth and/or threaten continuing operations

Premium Position Captivity
Failure or inability to shift tactics in response to advent of low-cost competitor or changing customer preferences

Disruptive Competitor Price/Value
Competitor's market entry significantly displaces the existing market leader's proposition on price/value

Overestimation of Brand Protection
False security derived from perception of power of brand image to retain a loyal customer base

Gross Margin Captivity
Self-restriction of top-line growth opportunities to those that shore up or enhance current gross margins

Innovation Captivity
Serial repetition of innovation cycles to maintain pricing premium

Missed Strategic Inflection in Demand
Failure to recognize and respond appropriately to material changes in the value proposition preferences of customers

Innovation Management Breakdown
Failure to achieve desired or required returns on investments in new products and services

Curtailed/Inconsistent R&D Funding
Deliberate decision to reduce R&D funding from project-sustaining levels to fund non-growth initiatives or to engineer overall earnings performance

Over-Decentralized R&D
Allocation of R&D decision-making within business silos restricts pursuit of cross-unit "white space" opportunities

Slow Product Development
New product development cycle time is fundamentally uncompetitive with leading market practices

Inability to Set New Standard
Company lacks market influence necessary to establish a technology standard for which it possesses innovative offerings

Conflict with Core Company Technology
Company resistant to support emerging technologies due to core business cannibalization threat or incompatibility with existing technology investments

Overinnovation
Incorrect perception of market appetite for a new product innovation and the competitive differentiation opportunity it could profitably provide

Premature Core Abandonment
Failure to maximize the existing and potential growth opportunities in existing core franchise (products/customers/channels)

Financial Diversification
Company shifts investment away from core in order to diversify financial structure away from dominant industry

Misperceived Market Saturation
Diversification based on inaccurate internal assessment of saturation of core market(s); underlying error generally revealed by strong subsequent sales gains by new or existing competitor

Misperceived Operational Impediments
Management assessment that some insurmountable operational impediment in core business requires diversification; impediment later overcome by more committed or creative competitor

International Growth Masks Core Problems
High international growth rates lead managers to postpone attention to domestic market challenges, which ultimately serve as drag on growth to entire firm

Cost-Cutting Disruption to Core Business
Focus on spending reductions diverts management attention from core growth initiatives

Failed Acquisition
Revenue growth rates materially slow after acquisition(s)

Misconceived Economics
Company overestimates the financial contributions of the acquisition target or its own capacity to combine business models

Unsustainable Financial Acquisition Model
Scale or frequency of acquisitions prove larger than company can manage

Unrealized Synergies
Company is unable to realize the top-line growth premium expected from combined organization

Key Customer Dependency
Failure to diversify revenue stream beyond the strategies of a few key customers or loss of market power to distribution channel partners

Distribution Channel Shift
Company misses the rise in importance of alternative distribution channels offering greater perceived value to current customer base

Customer Strategy Dependence
Limits of revenue growth determined by success of a particular strategy bet made by one or more dominant customers

Monopsony Buyer
Revenue is contingent on one customer, such as a government

Strategic Diffusion/Conglomeration
Overabundance of strategic initiatives undertaken by management team, resulting in dilution of efforts and results

Adjacency Failures
Attempt to expand revenue base through entering adjacent markets fails to meet intended growth goals

Overextension of the Formula
Unable to reap rewards in adjacent markets from existing competitive advantages or operational failure to support competition at larger scale

Unable to Manage New Model
Inability to adjust business model to new exigencies of adjacent markets

Incorrect New Business Siting/ Stewardship
New product or business launch hampered or delayed through incubation within more mature business unit whose principal product(s) it is intended to cannibalize

Voluntary Growth Slowdown
Deliberate decision on part of executive management team to slow top-line growth; generally arises following period of intensive acquisition activity

ORGANIZATIONAL FACTORS (CONTROLLABLE)

Talent Bench Shortfall
Lack of adequate leaders and staff with the skills and capabilities required to execute strategy successfully

Internal Skill Gap
Insufficient competencies across the ranks of general management or technical talent critical to a particular growth strategy; generally an unintended consequence of strict promote-from-within policies

Narrow Experience Base
Excessive homogeneity within the executive team—expertise from one dominant business, market, or function—delays timely response to emerging strategic issues

Loss of Key Talent
Mass retirement or defection of critical management or technical talent directly required for successful strategy execution

Key Person Dependence
Over-reliance on contributions of single individual (typically a founder) for growth strategies or execution skills

Board Inaction
Board of directors fails to exercise mandate to redirect or replace chief executive when clear signs of flawed growth strategies are present or at early evidence of misconduct

Organization Design
Structural design of organization hampers competitiveness by slowing response times or limiting range of strategic considerations

Over-Decentralization
Excessive focus on business unit autonomy prevents company from seizing opportunities that would require coordinated effort across business units

Decision-Making Structure
Business unit governance structure diffuses responsibility for and ownership of growth initiatives; characteristic of some heavily matrixed environments

No Strategic Planning
Absence of any formal, corporate-level planning function

Incorrect Performance Metrics
Company focuses on incorrect financial outcomes and/or competitive indicators to support growth plans

Incorrect Competitive Metrics
Company monitors wrong indicators on internal "dashboard," masking market share losses or other markers of deteriorating revenue growth

Inflexible Financial Goals
Adherence to outmoded or unrealistic metrics "engineers" growth stall—present in cases where overly aggressive goals drive staff defections and in instances where overly modest goals produce inadequate results

Appendix 5: "Red Flag" Warnings of an Impending Stall: A Self-Test for Management

After months of quantitative research and examination of individual company stall point histories, we found ourselves returning to the question, "What could they (company senior management) have foreseen in their markets, their competitors' behavior, in their own organizational practices that might have alerted them earlier to an impending stall?" The following fifty possible "red flags," rendered as a self-test, represent our attempt to compile the early warning signs and questions that management teams should guard against. The list is neither exhaustive nor universally relevant, though the issues it raises are worthy of management examination and discussion.

We suggest that each member of the team take this test privately, registering individual degree of concern for each of the issues raised here, and then collate those responses with those of other senior peers. Three patterns are interesting to spot and discuss: areas where all team members share substantial concern; areas where team members are unanimously unconcerned (check for groupthink!); and areas where individual team members have begun to become uneasy.

Following the self-test is an abbreviated facilitator's guide, which describes the intent behind each functional area covered in the instrument. In the Web site associated with this book (www.stallpoints.executiveboard.com), we have created a downloadable form, as well as benchmarking and discussion management tools to guide executive team deliberations.

We would be pleased to answer any questions readers might have. Simply contact the Corporate Executive Board through the Web site or call us directly.

STALL POINT "RED FLAGS" SELF-TEST

	No Concern	Moderate Concern	Substantial Concern
Finance and General Management			
1. Our earnings growth rate has outstripped our revenue growth rate for five or more years.	_____	_____	_____
2. Cost-cutting and/or productivity improvements account for more than 50 percent of our year-on-year earnings growth.	_____	_____	_____
3. More than 50 percent of our revenues derive from "formula roll-out" businesses that are five years old or more.	_____	_____	_____
4. [*If publicly held*] Our firm's PEG rate (price/earnings to growth) is 1.0 or under.	_____	_____	_____
5. Our core business reinvestment rate (R&D + CAPX + advertising divided by revenue) falls below its historic range.	_____	_____	_____
6. We rely on acquisitions to meet current-year revenue growth targets.	_____	_____	_____
7. Our dividend payout ratio exceeds 30 percent.	_____	_____	_____
8. Our revenue projections for our three- to five-year planning horizon do not explicitly link back to our one- to three-year operational plan.	_____	_____	_____
Strategy and Business Planning			
9. We have no formal corporate-level strategic planning function.	_____	_____	_____
10. Our strategic planning function's budget and staff are in multiyear decline.	_____	_____	_____
11. Time and resources meant to be allocated to long-term strategy and top-line growth drivers are routinely diverted to annual planning and near-term earnings concerns.	_____	_____	_____
12. Our core assumptions and beliefs about the marketplace and about the capabilities that are critical to support our strategy are not codified or otherwise written down.	_____	_____	_____

	No Concern	Moderate Concern	Substantial Concern
13. Major issues relating to our strategy are "off the table" for consideration; executives have intimated that dissent is unacceptable.	_____	_____	_____
14. We haven't revisited our core market definition (and, therefore, our list of relevant competitors and calculation of our market share) in several years.	_____	_____	_____
15. We have not revisited or refreshed our overall company performance metrics in the past two to four years.	_____	_____	_____
16. We describe our core market as "mature"—a source of earnings or cash flow; growth comes elsewhere.	_____	_____	_____
17. We are not actively exploring new business models within our existing core businesses.	_____	_____	_____
18. Our organizational structure hinders us when we need to adapt quickly to an external market or competitive development.	_____	_____	_____

Marketing and Market Research

	No Concern	Moderate Concern	Substantial Concern
19. We test only infrequently for shifts in key customer groups' valuation of product or service attributes.	_____	_____	_____
20. Key customers are increasingly unwilling to pay a premium for brand reputation or superior performance.	_____	_____	_____
21. Our executives lack effective (immersive, experiential, or otherwise visceral) mechanisms to directly engage with emerging customer and product trends.	_____	_____	_____
22. We do not formally track the trajectory of emerging technologies with the potential to disrupt our core businesses.	_____	_____	_____
23. We do not track customer perceptions of the quality differential between our offerings and those of low-end and emerging competitors.	_____	_____	_____

	No Concern	Moderate Concern	Substantial Concern
24. New entrants with new business models or disruptive technologies are garnering an accelerating share of the total market value of all companies in our sector.	_____	_____	_____
25. Market research and R&D do not have close, regular coordination of their activities and agendas.	_____	_____	_____
26. We are less effective than our competitors at translating customer insights into new product and service categories.	_____	_____	_____

Innovation and R&D

27. We've recently cut our R&D budget well below its historical range and below that of competitors.	_____	_____	_____
28. We lack adequate visibility into the business unit–level R&D bets being made across the company.	_____	_____	_____
29. R&D spending is so decentralized that we struggle to direct sufficient resources to significant opportunities for differentiation and growth.	_____	_____	_____
30. We view many market opportunities as "subscale": our R&D shop and innovation processes are geared for larger, more complex customer problems and opportunities.	_____	_____	_____
31. We are terminating too many product or service initiatives because their "time to material impact" is too long.	_____	_____	_____
32. Too many of our new product or service introductions fail to achieve expected returns, due to volume and/ or pricing shortfalls.	_____	_____	_____
33. We have not been able to synchronize our internal innovation cycle with the requirements of the external marketplace.	_____	_____	_____

Sales and Sales Force Management

34. More than 70 percent of our sales are dependent on a single, dominant distribution channel.	_____	_____	_____

	No Concern	Moderate Concern	Substantial Concern
35. More than 25 percent of the sales growth in our industry over the past years is through a product/service category or distribution channel we do not currently utilize.	_____	_____	_____
36. We are largely unable to self-cannibalize existing revenue streams in favor of new products and services.	_____	_____	_____
37. Our new product and/or service sales are slowed by housing them within existing business units.	_____	_____	_____

Human Resources and Talent Management

38. We have a stated or unstated bias to promote from within that disadvantages highly qualified external candidates.	_____	_____	_____
39. Our formal HR systems (e.g., job descriptions, competency models, and promotion criteria) lag our emerging strategic and operational requirements.	_____	_____	_____
40. In identifying our high-potential employees (HIPOs), we overweight current business model competencies and underweight required future competencies.	_____	_____	_____
41. Employee engagement scores (or other proxy for employee commitment) for our most critical talent groups are low and/or declining.	_____	_____	_____
42. Our future success is highly dependent on the continued productivity and contribution of a core group of specialized, hard-to-replace employees.	_____	_____	_____
43. More than 60 percent of our senior leaders have twenty or more years' tenure with the company.	_____	_____	_____
44. Our leadership team has been stable for many years; all but a few members of the group have worked together now for years—if not decades.	_____	_____	_____

	No Concern	Moderate Concern	Substantial Concern
45. We are not effective at recruiting/on-boarding/retaining senior hires with new skill sets and profiles.	_____	_____	_____
46. Our CEO has such force of presence and influence that his or her views on strategy tend to discourage discussion and debate.	_____	_____	_____

Board of Directors and Governance

	No Concern	Moderate Concern	Substantial Concern
47. Our board does not include strategy challenge and assumption-testing in the list of risks it manages.	_____	_____	_____
48. Our board considers only financial objectives, and not attainment of strategy goals, in performance management and incentive schemes for senior management.	_____	_____	_____
49. Our board lacks sufficient market knowledge and diversity of experience to challenge our strategy.	_____	_____	_____
50. We do not actively identify and manage gaps between our stakeholders' expectations and their current perceptions of our operations, policies, products and markets.	_____	_____	_____

"RED FLAGS" SELF-TEST FACILITATOR NOTES

Finance and General Management (Questions 1 to 8)

Although aggregate financial measures are retrospective indicators of performance and therefore not the best measures of the strategic health of the business, this first group of red flags is valuable for spotting general weakening of the economic foundations of the company's growth model.

Questions 1 and 2 are not indicators of a growth problem per se (margin enhancement is a good thing!) but highlight that a reliance on earnings growth, and in particular earnings growth fueled by cost cutting, can indicate that top-line strategies are either lacking or absent.

Question 3 attempts to place the firm in the life cycle of a typical growth run; dependence on a formula run beyond its early stages can be a signal of looming trouble.

Question 4, for public companies only, probes the external market's confidence in the firm's growth strategy through the PEG ratio. More precise guidance could be obtained by comparing individual firm PEG ratios to industry peers.

Question 5: When a company's financial commitment to foundational growth drivers is curtailed, this generally takes the form of long-term growth being sacrificed for short-term profit. The argument here is not that you can or should try to spend your way out of a stall (studies show no relation between R&D spending levels and growth) but that ratcheting back on growth investments should always be cause for concern.

Last, if this scaling back of activity is a trigger for anxiety, the scaling *up* of activity flagged in question 6 should provoke outright distress. With disturbing regularity, companies approaching a stall will attempt to use the event of an acquisition—or a series of acquisitions—to buy time (and, presumably, assets and capabilities) to solve problems that are cropping up in the core business.

Strategy and Business Planning (Questions 9 to 18)

A primary role of the strategy function, and the process it typically administers, is to translate long-term strategy into a concrete plan of action. In parallel to this planning focus, the strategy group's role is to challenge and stretch thinking to assist management in questioning the beliefs and assumptions supporting strategy. Questions in this section probe the resourcing and positioning of the function, as well as the state of the strategy dialogue in the organization.

Questions 9, 10, and 11 audit the time and accountable resources devoted to strategy activities. The absence of a strategy group should not automatically cause alarm, just as the presence of such a function should not wholly reassure. The much more important test is whether someone—a "strategist" or other capable function—is prompting executives regularly to check their own collective thinking against emerging market realities.

Questions 12 and 13 probe whether the core beliefs beneath strategy are formally articulated and, if so, whether an honest challenge to their continued viability is permissible. (Reservations in "speaking truth to power" are more common than you might think in large corporate cultures.)

The remaining questions are designed to push teams to revisit core assumptions, each focused more sharply on a single aspect of the business system: what business we are in (question 14); our definition of winning (question 15); and our perspective on the sources of growth, business model, and organizational structure needed to succeed (questions 16, 17, and 18).

Marketing and Market Research (Questions 19 to 26)

We have concluded from our review of stall case histories that the market research and competitive intelligence functions rarely provide the early warning capability that they could or, arguably, should. Too much effort and resource tends to be expended on tracking customer satisfaction and market share movements and not nearly enough on shifts in customers' preferences and competitors' capabilities. Questions in this section probe the targeting and performance of these functions, as well as their integration with other key functions in the firm.

Questions 19 and 20 focus on customer sensing around trade-offs: do we really understand what product attributes or features customers are willing to pay a premium for or how they'd trade off one set of benefits (for example, convenience, reliability) for another (for example, lower price)?

Question 21 tests whether organizations are able to communicate emerging insights to executives directly and powerfully enough to overcome deeply rooted beliefs and instincts.

The complement to robust customer sensing is strong competitor tracking, especially of competitors with "disruptive" business models or technologies and with low-end value offerings. Multiple dimensions of competitive intelligence are beneficial here, including growth trajectories (question 22), brand and quality differentials (question 23), and share of market value growth (question 24).

Finally, in questions 25 and 26, we probe for the tightness of linkage between the market research and R&D functions, a joint in the large corporation that typically works surprisingly poorly.

Innovation and R&D (Questions 27 to 33)

Repeated, reliable success in innovation requires coordination across a complex, time-lagged set of processes, and the innovation-related stalls in our study were driven by a multitude of specific failures within and across every aspect of these processes. As such, the diagnostic questions here address every component of the innovation process, from the basics of R&D funding to the biases that influence how those dollars are deployed.

Questions 27 to 29 probe overall funding levels and their allocation across the organization. Cutting back on R&D (question 27) is of greatest concern to firms where R&D remains critical to strategy (in a rapidly maturing market with fewer opportunities for new products, scaling down the R&D investment could well be the right move). Pushing R&D deeper into the organization to improve business relevance and short-term impact can decrease transparency into R&D bets (question 28) and the ability to redirect resources to the most important future sources of growth (question 29).

Questions 30 and 31 focus on the ability to explore and exploit emerging opportunities characterized by uncertain visibility into their ultimate size or impact. Is there a systematic preference for chasing the (ever more complex) needs of current customer groups over the less certain returns from emerging customer segments (question 30)? Moreover, are we "patient" enough in our management of emerging innovations, waiting to apply rigorous financial metrics until opportunities have developed to a point where they can be evaluated correctly (question 31)?

Finally, questions 32 and 33 probe the problem of "getting paid" for innovation. Most industries experience a predictable pattern where returns to innovation decline as more and more core needs of customers are met. Companies stall in such situations when they fail to shift their innovation model to reflect this market reality, or when they fail to find enough new market opportunities. This problem initially presents as an "innovation" problem, but over time is recognized as a strategy shortcoming.

Sales and Sales Force Management (Questions 34 to 37)

The sales function bears the enormous responsibility of managing the firm's go-to-market strategy, including which products, channels, and customers receive the most attention. Because decisions about the product/channel/customer mix are so significant to an organization's strategy, sales is a part of the organization with perspective and influence on a multitude of potential stall factors.

Questions 34 and 35 probe for degree of dependence on a particular customer segment or distribution channel. High dependence often results in decision-making or resource allocation that cuts off the ability to move into new or emerging channels.

Questions 36 and 37 are meant to raise a similar bias in current product offerings, in which new product or business offerings are ignored or delayed due to fear of self-cannibalization.

Human Resources and Talent Management (Questions 38 to 46)

The role of human resources in preventing stall points is multifaceted. Critical functions include ensuring that organizational skills and capabilities support shifts in strategy, that critical technical and managerial talent is engaged and retained, and that the next generation is positioned to assume positions of leadership in the enterprise.

Question 38 probes openness to the external market for scarce skill and experience sets.

Questions 39 and 40 probe the methods used to select and develop employees, in particular high-potential employees (HIPOs). The special danger for HIPO management is that the incentive of the organization to select "more of the same," and to groom them in the skill sets that have traditionally led to success, can exacerbate the problems of groupthink and isolation that can plague senior teams.

Questions 41 and 42 focus on the degree of dependence on today's high performers. Employee engagement and climate surveys are valuable leading indicators of commitment and intent to remain with the organization, and emerging challenges should be diagnosed, and corrective measures applied, at the function or work group level.

The remaining questions in this section go directly to the groupthink issue. Questions 43 and 44 probe the cohesiveness and insularity of the company's leadership, question 45 tests the organization's success at integrating new skill profiles and backgrounds into leadership positions, and question 46 explores whether a diversity of opinion is heard in strategy debates (whether a diversity of backgrounds is represented by those at the table).

Board of Directors and Governance (Questions 47 to 50)

Board success at grappling with recent governance reforms has come at a twin cost to their engagement with, and challenge of, company strategy. Not only has the time for this activity been crowded out, but the emphasis on recruitment of nonexecutive directors has reduced the intimacy of board members with industry and competitor issues. The questions here probe board dynamics, as well as the board's focus on strategy goals in managing performance and setting compensation.

The first couple of questions probe board engagement in pressure-testing strategy. Although full boards have limited time for this activity, board committees can and should push management to test the assumptions on which strategy is based (question 47). The board should also set specific strategy goals and milestones in its performance management and compensation schemes for management, in addition to the more commonly articulated financial objectives (question 48).

Question 49 is not about capacity, but capability: do board members have the specific knowledge of the industry and the company to effectively challenge the chief executive officer and other key executives?

Last, question 50 tests the organization's active diagnosis and management of stakeholder interests and expectations. This issue of corporate governance may not always be worthy of the board's time and attention; however, it is a critical red flag if no one in the organization owns and executes this important set of responsibilities.

Notes

CHAPTER 1: WHAT ARE THE LIMITS TO GROWTH?

1. Chandler, *The Visible Hand;* Penrose, *The Theory of the Growth of the Firm;* Christensen, *The Innovator's Dilemma.*
2. Bryan and Zanini, "Strategy in an Era of Global Giants."
3. We present a fuller set of results from this analysis on our Web site: www.stall points.executiveboard.com.
4. The interplay between revenue growth and income growth has been a staple of business press publishing and academic discussion (and no doubt, executive team arguments over the trade-offs involved in managing the two.) A well-constructed discussion that favors revenue growth in terms of leverage on market capitalization is presented in Mass, "Relative Value of Growth."
5. Marshall, *Principles of Economics.*
6. Osenton, *The Death of Demand.*
7. A balanced collection of this (admittedly dreary) literature is to be found in Cameron, Sutton, and Whetten, eds., *Readings in Organizational Decline.* Additionally, Pankaj Ghemawat articulates a common sentiment on the limiting relation of size to sustainable growth rate as the "law of less than proportional growth" in Ghemawat, "The Growth Boosters."
8. Mintzberg, "Power and Organization Life Cycles," 222.
9. Huyett and Viguerie, "Extreme Competition."

CHAPTER 2: STALL POINTS IN COMPANIES' GROWTH RUNS

1. Continuous Growth Companies: Abbott Laboratories; ABN Amro Holdings NV; Aegon NV; American International Group; AmerisourceBergen Corporation; Ameritech Corporation; Australia & New Zealand Bank; Banco Bilbao Vizcaya; Bank of America Corporation; Berkshire Hathaway; Best Buy Company; BorgWarner Inc.; C&S Sovran Corporation; Cardinal Health Inc.; Caremark Rx Inc.; China Mobile Hong Kong; Coles Myer Ltd.; Collins & Aikman Corporation; Comcast Corporation; Compaq Computer Corporation; Corus Group plc; Costco Wholesale Corporation; Countrywide Financial Corporation; Creole Petroleum Corporation; Dell Inc.; Deutsche Bank AG; Deutsche Telecom AG; E.on AG; Endesa SA; Eni SPA; FedEx Corporation; France Telecom; Hartford Financial Services; Hewlett-Packard Company; Home Depot Inc.; Korea Electric Power Company; Kraft General Foods; Lehman Brothers Holdings Inc.; Lowe's Inc.; Lyondell Chemical Company; McDonald's Corporation; MCI Communications; Microsoft Corporation; Millea Holdings Inc.; Morgan Stanley; Nabisco Brands Inc.; Nokia Corporation; Plains All-American Pipeline; Posco; Price Company; Publix Supermarkets Inc.; Repsol YPF SA; Rio Tinto Ltd.; Royal Dutch Shell plc; Siemens AG; St. Paul Travelers Companies Inc.; Swiss Reinsurance Company; Sysco Corporation; Target Corporation; Telefonica SA; TXU U.S. Holdings Company; United Health Group Inc.; Vodafone Group plc; Wachovia Corporation; Wal-Mart Stores; Wellpoint Health Networks Inc.; Westpac Banking Corporation.

2. George Stalk has been the most continuous, probative explorer of the relationship between time and corporate strategy. See his foundational work, Stalk and Hout, *Competing against Time*. See also Stalk and Lachenauer, *Hardball*.

CHAPTER 3: THE COSTS OF A STALL

1. Interview with authors.

CHAPTER 4: WHY COMPANIES STALL

1. Kim, "The Link between Individual and Organizational Learning."
2. Markides, "Strategic Innovation," 13.
3. Janis, *Groupthink*, 9.

CHAPTER 5: EXTERNAL (UNCONTROLLABLE) FACTORS

1. Studies of concentration in U.S. industry generally show little, if any, meaningful change across the last four decades. A fairly comprehensive study on data through 2000 shows concentration ratios declining between 1960 and 1980, and then increasing back to approximately their 1960 ranges in the latter two decades. See Pryor, "New Trends in U.S. Industrial Concentration."
2. See Communications Executive Council, *Refocusing Reputation Management*.
3. Krisher, "Komatsu on the Track of Cat."
4. Loomis, "High Stakes in the Cat Fight."

5. An unusually detailed timeline of the history of the Volvo Group can be found on the company's Web site: www.volvo.com.

CHAPTER 6: PREMIUM POSITION CAPTIVITY

1. Knudsen, Randel, and Rugholm, "The Vanishing Middle Market."
2. "Why Things are So Sour at Borden."
3. "Taking Flak."
4. "Levi's Blues."
5. Taylor, "BMW and Mercedes." Katz, *The Big Store,* 32. Krisher, "Komatsu on the Track of Cat." Uttal Bro, "Eastman Kodak's Orderly Two-Front War," *Fortune,* September 1976, 124.

CHAPTER 7: INNOVATION MANAGEMENT BREAKDOWN

1. McKinsey's Global Survey of Business Executives for the past several years has consistently shown the reliance top executives place on innovation of products and services in their current businesses to generate new revenue growth. Innovation of current products and development of new products rank significantly ahead of all other organizational capabilities. See Carden, Mendonca, and Shavers, "What Global Executives Think about Growth and Risk."
2. The distance between Xerox PARC and headquarters was more than geographic. The psychic distance between the two was well captured in Smith and Alexander, *Fumbling the Future.*
3. Booz Allen Hamilton has surveyed R&D spending trends at a thousand global companies with the highest proportion of R&D spending to sales for the past several years. They document a 5.8 percent median increase in R&D spending among their sample companies for their latest year of data, 2005. See Jaruzelski, Dehoff, and Bordia, "Smart Spenders."
4. Creswell, "Bottled Profits Aren't Flowing Like They Used to at Packaged Goods Companies."
5. Quoted in HP Growth Initiative 3M stall case dossier.
6. See Crockett, "How Motorola Got Its Groove Back."
7. The Japanese Facsimile Industry in 1990 (Harvard Business School Case 9-391-209).
8. Smith, "Rubbermaid Goes Thump."

CHAPTER 8: PREMATURE CORE ABANDONMENT

1. See Zook and Allen, *Profit from the Core,* and Corporate Strategy Board, *Growth Restarts.*
2. The private equity formula is not inaccurately summarized as: first, prune the portfolio down to businesses and segments with higher growth prospects; second, raise the quality of the management team and enfranchise them in valuation growth; third, crack legacy labor costs; and fourth, manage to an eventual "exit strategy" rather than quarterly earnings. Some of these tactics are reproducible in a public company; some are not. See

Beroutsos, Freeman, and Kehoe, "What Public Companies Can Learn from Private Equity."

3. The most recent iteration of this research that we have seen is in Ferris, Juliano, and Kapure, *The Growth Triathlon*.

4. "Philips Has Its Eyes on Tomorrow."

5. Demaree, "RCA after the Bath."

6. Smit, Thompson, and Viguerie, "The Do-or-Die Struggle for Growth."

7. A summary of Alcoa's micro-segmentation strategy can be found on our Web site: www.stallpoints.executiveboard.com.

CHAPTER 9: OTHER STRATEGIC FACTORS

1. Best practices in choosing and cultivating "strategic accounts" are analyzed in Sales Executive Council, *Reigniting Key Account Program Growth*.

2. "His Aggressive Merger-Making Has Reshaped United Technologies," *Business Week,* 10 December 1979.

3. The most thoughtful articulation of this insight is found in Zook, *Beyond the Core*.

4. Symonds, "Can Gillette Regain Its Voltage?"

CHAPTER 10: TALENT SHORTFALL

1. We have reproduced survey findings related to chief human resource officers' priorities from our Corporate Leadership Council's membership on our Web site: www.stall points.executiveboard.com.

2. Smith, "The Lures and Limits of Innovation," 84.

3. Ibid.

4. The invention of Post-it notes has created a mini-industry of commentary on the Web; in particular, see "The Rake Features Twenty-Five Years of Post-it Notes."

5. Hector, *Breaking the Bank*.

6. An intriguing account of Disney through this period is found in Dunlop, *Building a Dream*.

7. Figures from 2004 survey by Right Management Consultants, quoted in Simmons, "Teamwork Starts at the Top."

8. Off-the-record interview with the authors.

9. GE's "Senior Entry Track" practice for mix management of its senior management ranks is available only to members of our Corporate Leadership Council program for heads of HR.

10. See GE's "Senior Entry Track" practice, above.

CHAPTER 11: OTHER ORGANIZATIONAL FACTORS

1. Carter and Lorsch, *Back to the Drawing Board*.

2. Moltzen and Damore, "The Quiet Lion."

3. "Uniting the Feudal Lords of Citicorp."

4. "The Philips Group" (Harvard Business School Case 9-388-050).
5. Mohr and Littman, "What's Happening at Ralston?" 24.
6. McGough, "Changing Course."
7. Carlton, *Apple.*

CHAPTER 12: PRACTICES FOR ARTICULATING AND STRESS-TESTING STRATEGY ASSUMPTIONS

1. Kim, "The Link between Individual and Organizational Learning."
2. Burgelman and Grove, "Strategy and Action," 18.
3. Data from our most recent survey of heads of strategy on perceived performance of their organizations can be found on our Web site: www.stallpoints.executiveboard.com.
4. This process is well articulated in Hamel, "Turning Your Business Upside Down."
5. Cognitive psychologist Gary Klein and his firm, Klein Associates, developed the notion of "pre-mortem" analytical sessions for project teams to help them identify sources of potential failure.
6. One caveat on this practice: although we tend to favor processes that can be run for very low resource investment, this is an area where retaining an external facilitator might well be worth the cost. A number of consultancies have developed playbooks for conducting these workshops, and the insertion of an objective process manager can minimize internal politics. We provide references on our Web site to several consultancies our members have recommended to us.
7. Readers of Gary Hamel's work across the years are familiar with his growing impatience with the strategy conservatism of incumbent firms and their occasional misuse of "democratic" processes for strategic change. His core position on incorporation of employee input from deep inside the organization is still best captured in "Strategy as Revolution."
8. Kirby and Stewart, "The Institutional Yes," 77.

CHAPTER 13: PRACTICES FOR MAPPING THE FUTURE

1. A full portrait of these activities at IBM is presented in Harreld, "Dynamic Capabilities."

CHAPTER 14: LOCATING RESPONSIBILITY FOR GROWTH LEADERSHIP

1. Clayton Christensen's observations on declining managerial competence in strategy frame his description of "driving forces analysis," a methodology management teams can employ to conceive and implement creative, coherent strategy. Christensen, "Making Strategy."
2. Beinhocker and Kaplan, "Tired of Strategic Planning?"
3. All data on strategy activities, staffing and tenure in this chapter are taken from the Corporate Strategy Board's periodic survey of strategy departments at its membership of large, global firms. Data for the most recent survey is available on our Web site.
4. See Corporate Strategy Board, *Strategy at the Frontier.*
5. Carey and Patsalos-Fox, "Shaping Strategy from the Boardroom."
6. Ibid., 91.

CHAPTER 15: POSTSCRIPT

1. A full description of research methodology and findings is presented in Corporate Strategy Board, *Growth Restarts.*
2. Hammer, "Deep Change."
3. Zook, *Unstoppable,* 70.
4. "Brazil Special: Brazil Hits a New High," *Flight International,* 17 April 2007.
5. Zook, *Unstoppable.*
6. Quoted in Denise Pelham, "Is It Time to Outsource HR?" *Training,* 1 April 2002, 50.

Bibliography

Allio, Robert. "Russell L. Ackoff, Iconoclastic Management Authority, Advocates a 'Systemic' Approach to Innovation." *Strategy and Leadership* 31, no. 3 (2003): 19–26.

"Banks Shift Gears in Drive for Top-line Growth: Focus Turns to Consumers in the Financial Services Industry." A.T. Kearney business issue paper. 2004.

Beer, Michael, and Russell A. Eisenstat. "How to Have an Honest Conversation about Your Business Strategy." *Harvard Business Review* 82 (February 2004): 82–89.

Beinhocker, Eric D., and Sarah Kaplan. "Tired of Strategic Planning?" *McKinsey Quarterly* Special Edition: Risk and Resilience (2002): 48–57.

Beroutsos, Andreas, Andrew Freeman, and Conor F. Kehoe. "What Public Companies Can Learn from Private Equity." *McKinsey on Finance* no. 22 (Winter 2007): 1–6.

Berss, Marcia. "The Master Builder." *Forbes,* 19 November 1984.

Brandt, E. N. *Growth Company: Dow Chemical's First Century.* East Lansing: Michigan State University Press, 1997.

Bro, Uttal. "Eastman Kodak's Orderly Two-Front War." *Fortune,* September 1976.

Bryan, Lowell L., and Claudia I. Joyce. "Better Strategy through Organizational Design." *McKinsey Quarterly* no. 2 (2007): 20–27.

Bryan, Lowell L., and Michele Zanini. "Strategy in an Era of Global Giants." *McKinsey Quarterly* no. 4 (2005): 46–59.

Burgelman, Robert A., and Andrew S. Grove. "Let Chaos Reign, Then Rein in Chaos—Repeatedly: Managing Strategic Dynamics for Corporate Longevity." Research Paper Series, Stanford Graduate School of Business, January 2007.

———. "Strategic Dissonance." *California Management Review* 38 (Winter 1996): 8.

———. "The Strategy and Action in the Information Processing Industry Course (S370) at Stanford Business School: Themes, Conceptual Frameworks, Related Tools." Stanford Graduate School of Business Research Papers Series. January 2004: 18.

Burgelman, Robert A., and Yves L. Doz. "The Power of Strategic Integration." *MIT Sloan Management Review* 42 (Spring 2001): 28–38.

Byrns, Nanette, and Jane Sasseen. "Board of Hard Knocks." *Business Week,* 22 January 2007.

Cameron, Kim S., Robert I. Sutton, and David A. Whetten, eds. *Readings in Organizational Decline.* Cambridge, MA: Ballinger, 1998.

Carden, Steven D., Lenny T. Mendonca, and Tim Shavers. "What Global Executives Think about Growth and Risk." *McKinsey Quarterly* no. 2 (2005): 16–25.

Carey, Dennis C., and Michael Patsalos-Fox. "Shaping Strategy from the Boardroom." *McKinsey Quarterly* no. 3 (2006): 90–94.

Carlton, Jim. *Apple: The Inside Story of Intrigue, Egomania, and Business Blunders.* New York: Random House, 1997.

Carter, Colin B., and Jay W. Lorsch. *Back to the Drawing Board: Designing Corporate Boards for a Complex World.* Boston: Harvard Business School Press, 2004.

Chandler, Alfred D., Jr. *The Visible Hand: The Managerial Revolution in American Business.* Cambridge, MA: Harvard University Press, 1977.

Chandler, Alfred D., Jr., and Burice Mazlish, eds. *Leviathans: Multinational Corporations and the New Global Strategy.* Cambridge: Cambridge University Press, 2005.

Christensen, Clayton M. "Making Strategy: Learning by Doing." *Harvard Business Review* 75 (November–December 1997): 141–156.

Christensen, Clayton M. *The Innovator's Dilemma: When New Technologies Cause Great Firms to Fail.* Boston: Harvard Business School Press, 1997.

Christensen, Clayton M., and Michael E. Raynor. *The Innovator's Solution: Creating and Sustaining Successful Growth.* Boston: Harvard Business School Press, 2003.

Colin, Carter B., and Jay W. Lorsch. *Back to the Drawing Board: Designing Corporate Boards for a Complex World.* Boston: Harvard Business School Press, 2004.

Communications Executive Council. *Refocusing Reputation Management: Building an Enterprise-Wide Reputation Management Capability.* Washington, DC: Corporate Executive Board, 2005.

Conger, Jay A., David Finegold, and Edward E. Lawler III. "Appraising Boardroom Performance." 76 *Harvard Business Review* (January–February 1998): 136–148.

Corporate Strategy Board. *Growth Restarts: Reinvigorating Principled Revenue Growth in Mature Companies.* Washington, DC: Corporate Executive Board, 2003.

———. *Strategy at the Frontier: Calibrating Strategic Responses to Market Pace.* Washington, DC: Corporate Executive Board, 2000.

Creswell, Julie. "Bottled Profits Aren't Flowing Like They Used to at Packaged Goods Companies: Can Green Ketchup and Tuna in a Pouch Save Heinz?" *Fortune,* 18 September 2000.

Crockett, Roger O. "How Motorola Got Its Groove Back: Inside the Creation of a Hit New Phone as CEO Zander Tries to Remake the Company into a Master of Innovation." *Business Week,* 8 August 2005.

Darlin, Damon. "Design Helps H.P. Profit More on PCs." *New York Times,* 17 May 2007.

Davis, Ian. "How to Escape the Short-Term Trap." *McKinsey Quarterly* (April 2005).

———. "Learning to Grow Again." *McKinsey Quarterly* no. 1 (2004): 125–127.

Day, George S. "Continuous Learning about Markets." *California Management Review* 36 (Summer 1994): 9.

Demaree, Alan T. "RCA after the Bath." *Fortune,* September 1972.

Devan, Janamitra, Anna Kristina Millan, and Pranav Shirke. "Balancing Short- and Long-Term Performance." *McKinsey Quarterly* no. 1 (2005): 31–33.

Dewar, James, et al. *Assumption-Based Planning: A Planning Tool for Very Uncertain Times.* Santa Monica, CA: RAND, 1973.

Drucker, Peter, and Gary Hamel. "Innovate!" *BRW,* 16 June 2005.

Dunlop, Beth. *Building a Dream: The Art of Disney Architecture.* New York: Henry N. Abrams, 1996.

"Dupont Investment of 25 Millions in 1918 has Grown to 2.6 Billions." *New York Times,* 4 June 1957.

"Extroverts or Introverts II: A Litmus Test for Strategic Planners." Futures Group, 1998.

"Fast-Growth CEOs Expect Increased Growth and Hiring—But Fewer New Investments, PricewaterhouseCoopers Finds." PricewaterhouseCoopers, 3 May 2005.

Felton, Robert F., and Pamela Keenan Fritz. "The View from the Boardroom." *McKinsey Quarterly* special ed. (2005): 48–61.

Ferris, Jeffere, John Juliano, and Vivek Kapure. *The Growth Triathlon.* IBM Consulting Services, executive brief, 2005.

Gary, Loren. "Dow Corning's Big Pricing Gamble." *Harvard Business School Working Knowledge,* 7 March 2005.

Ghemawat, Pankaj. "The Growth Boosters." *Harvard Business Review* 82 (July–August 2004): 98–108.

Grove, Andrew S. *Only the Paranoid Survive: How to Exploit the Crisis Points That Challenge Every Company and Career.* New York: Doubleday, 1996.

"Growing to New Heights," *Executive Agenda.* A.T. Kearney, 2004.

"The Growth Triathlon." IBM Business Consulting Services, December 2004.

Gunther McGrath, Rita, and Ian C. MacMillan. "Market Busting: Strategies for Exceptional Business Growth." *Harvard Business Review* 83 (March 2005): 80–89.

Hamel, Gary. "Strategy as Revolution." *Harvard Business Review* 74 (July–August 1996): 69–82.

———. "Turning Your Business Upside Down." *Fortune,* 23 June 1997.

———. "Why Dinosaurs Mate." *Wall Street Journal,* 22 January 2004.

Hamel, Gary, and Gary Getz. "Funding Growth in an Age of Austerity." *Harvard Business Review* 82 (July–August 2004): 76–84.

Hamel, Gary, and C. K. Prahalad. *Competing for the Future.* Boston: Harvard Business School Press, 1994.

———. "Strategic Intent." *Harvard Business Review* 83 (July–August 2005): 148–161.

Hamel, Gary, and Lloyd Switzer. "The Old Guard vs. the Vanguard." *Wall Street Journal,* 23 February 2004.

Hammer, Michael. "Deep Change." *Harvard Business Review* 82 (April 2004): 84–93.

Hannah, Leslie. "Visible Hand of Management Laid Bare." *Financial Times,* 17 May 2007.

Hansell, Saul. "Uniting the Feudal Lords of Citicorp." *New York Times,* 16 January 1993.

Harreld, Bruce J., Charles A. O'Reilly III, and Michael L. Tushman. "Dynamic Capabilities at IBM: Driving Strategy into Action." *California Management Review* 49 (Summer 2007): 21–43.

Hector, Gary. *Breaking the Bank: The Decline of BankAmerica.* London: Little, Brown, 1989.

Hemp, Paul. "A Time for Growth." *Harvard Business Review* 82 (July–August 2004): 66–74.

Hounshell, David A., and John Kenly Smith, Jr. *Science and Corporate Strategy: DuPont R&D, 1902–1980.* Cambridge: Cambridge University Press, 1988.

"How to Grow Your Business." *MWorld* (Winter 2004).

Huston, Larry, and Nabil Sakkab. "Connect and Develop." *Harvard Business Review* 84 (March 2006): 58–66.

Huyett, William I., and S. Patrick Viguerie. "Extreme Competition." *McKinsey Quarterly* no. 1 (2005): 46–57.

"Improving Strategic Planning: A McKinsey Survey." *McKinsey Quarterly* (September 2006).

Janis, Irving L. *Groupthink: A Psychological Study of Policy Decisions and Fiascoes.* Boston: Houghton Mifflin, 1982.

———. *Victims of Groupthink: A Psychological Study of Foreign Policy Decisions and Fiascoes.* Boston: Houghton Mifflin, 1972.

Jaruzelski, Barry, Kevin Dehoff, and Rakesh Bordia. "Smart Spenders: The Global Innovation 1000." *Strategy+Business* (Winter 2006): 47–60.

Jenkins, Michael, and David Meer. "Organic Growth: Profiting from the Union of Finance and Marketing." *Financial Executive,* Marakon Associates, October 2005.

Johnson-Laird, Philip N. *Mental Models.* Cambridge, MA: Harvard University Press, 1983.

Katz, Donald R. *The Big Store: Inside the Crisis and Revolution at Sears.* New York: Viking Press, 1987.

Kennedy, Carol. "I Think Therefore I Can." *Director* (August 2000).

Kim, Daniel H. "The Link between Individual and Organizational Learning." *Sloan Management Review* (Fall 1993): 37–50.

Kirby, Julia. "Toward a Theory of High Performance." *Harvard Business Review* 83 (July–August 2005): 30–39.

Kirby, Julia, and Thomas A. Stewart. "The Institutional Yes." *Harvard Business Review* 85 (October 2007): 74–82.

Kirkpatrick, David, and Gary Hamel. "Innovation Do's and Don'ts." *Fortune,* 6 September 2004.

Knudsen, Trond Riiber, Andreas Randel, and Jorgen Rugholm. "The Vanishing Middle Market." *McKinsey Quarterly* no. 4 (2005): 6–9.

Krisher, Bernard. "Komatsu on the Track of Cat." *Fortune,* 20 April 1981.

Lawton, Christopher. "H-P Raises Fiscal-Year Forecast." *Wall Street Journal,* 17 May 2007.

Leamer, Edward E. "The Truth about GDP Growth." *Harvard Business Review* 82 (October 2004): 24.

"Levi's Blues." *New York Times,* 21 March 1999.

Loomis, Carol J. "High Stakes in the Cat Fight." *Fortune,* 2 May 1983.

Mackey, Jim, and Liisa Välikangas. "The Myth of Unbounded Growth." *MIT Sloan Management Review* 45 (Winter 2004): 89–92.

Markides, Constantinos. "Strategic Innovation in Established Companies." *MIT Sloan Management Review* 39 (Spring 1998): 31–42.

Marshall, Alfred. *Principles of Economics.* London: Macmillan, 1890.

Mass, Nathaniel J. "The Relative Value of Growth." *Harvard Business Review* 83 (April 2005): 102–112.

McCafferty, Joseph. "Going for Growth: Finding New Sources of Growth Is Harder Than Ever." *CFO Magazine,* 1 March 2004.

McGough, Robert. "Changing Course: Bob Crandall Is Steering American Airlines in a New Direction." *Financial World,* 23 July 1991.

McKibben, Gordon. *Cutting Edge: Gillette's Journey to Global Leadership.* Boston: Harvard Business School Press, December 1997.

"Meeting Your Growth Goals in Challenging Times." *Executive Agenda,* A.T. Kearney, First Quarter 2005.

Mintzberg, Henry. "Power and Organization Life Cycles." *Academy of Management Review* 9 (April 1984): 207–224.

———. *The Rise and Fall of Strategic Planning.* New York: Free Press, 1994.

Mohan-Neill, Sumaria. "The Influence of Firm's Age and Size on Its Environmental Scanning Activities." *Journal of Small Business Management* 33 (October 1995): 10–21.

Mohr, Betty, and Margaret Littman. "What's Happening at Ralston?" *Prepared Foods,* 1 February 1993.

Moltzen, Edward F., and Kelley Damore. "The Quiet Lion: Rosen Pounces, Takes Back Control of Compaq." CRN. Available online at: http://www.crn.com/it-channel/18803879 (23 April 1999).

Moore, James F. "Strategy-Making as Continuous Design." Working paper, *GeoPartners Research,* 1991.

Murray, Alan. "A Word to Motorola: Give Us More Than Bafflegab." *Wall Street Journal,* 9 May 2007.

Ohmae, Kenichi. *The Mind of the Strategist: The Art of Japanese Business.* New York: McGraw-Hill, 1982.

Oldfield, Stewart. "Slowdown Sees Brokers Rerate HSBC." *South China Morning Post,* 17 September 1998.

Olsen, Thomas A., Monica Pinto, and Shalina Virji. "Navigating Growth in Emerging Markets: Six Rules for Improving Decision-Making between Corporate and Local Leadership." Marakon Associates, 2004.

Osenton, Tom. *The Death of Demand: Finding Growth in a Saturated Global Economy.* Upper Saddle River, NJ: Financial Times Prentice Hall.

Penrose, Edith. *The Theory of the Growth of the Firm.* Oxford: Oxford University Press, 1959.

"Philips Has Its Eye on Tomorrow." *Business Week,* 12 December 1964.

Pistorius, Carl W. I., and James M. Utterback. "The Death Knells of Mature Technologies." *Technologies Forecasting and Social Change* 50 (1995): 133–151.

Pozen, Robert C. "If Private Equity Sized Up Your Business." *Harvard Business Review* 85 (November 2007): 78–87.

Pryor, Frederic L. "New Trends in U.S. Industrial Concentration." *Review of Industrial Organization* (May 2001): 301–326.

"The Rake Features Twenty-Five Years of Post-It Notes." http://www.rakemag.com/stories/printable.aspx?itemID=5383&SelectCatID=46 (June 2007).

"Realizing the Potential of Multibusiness Companies for Organic Growth." Boston Consulting Group, July 2005.

"Rising to the Growth Challenge." A.T. Kearney, 2005.

Rosenzweig, Phil. "By Invitation: The Halo Effect, and Other Managerial Delusions." *McKinsey Quarterly* no. 1 (2007): 76–85.

Samuelson, Robert J. "Ghosts That Still Haunt GM." *Washington Post,* 30 November 2005.

Sales Executive Council. *Reigniting Key Account Program Growth: Actively Managing the Customer Portfolio for Strategic Fit.* Washington, DC: Corporate Executive Board, 2006.

Schlange, Lutz E., and Uta Juttner. "Helping Managers to Identify the Key Strategic Issues." *Long Range Planning* 3 (October 1997): 777–786.

Simmons, Kathy. "Teamwork Starts at the Top." *Contract Management* 45 (September 2005): 4–6.

Slywotsky, Adrian, Richard Wise, and Karl Weber. *How to Grow When Markets Don't.* New York: Warner Business Books, 2003.

Smit, Sven, Caroline M. Thompson, and S. Patrick Viguerie. "The Do-or-Die Struggle for Growth." *McKinsey Quarterly* no. 3 (2005): 34–45.

Smith, Douglas K., and Robert C. Alexander. *Fumbling the Future: How Xerox Invented, Then Ignored the First Personal Computer.* New York: William Morrow, 1988.

Smith, Lee. "The Lures and Limits of Innovation." *Fortune,* 20 October 20, 1980.

———. "Rubbermaid Goes Thump." *Fortune,* 2 October 1995.

Sparks, Whitney. "Gary Hamel's Idea Hatchery." *BusinessWeek Online,* 11 August 2005.

Stalk, George, Jr., and Thomas M. Hout, *Competing against Time: How Time-Based Competition Is Re-Shaping Global Markets.* New York: Free Press, 1990.

Stalk, George, and Rob Lachenauer. *Hardball: Are You Playing to Play or Playing to Win?* Boston: Harvard Business School Press, 2004.

Stewart, G. Bennett, III. "Champions of Profitable Growth." *Harvard Business Review* 82 (July–August 2004): 59–63.

Sweeny, Douglas M. "Global Market Trends in the Networked Era." *Long Range Planning* 31 (1998): 672–683.

Symonds, William C. "Can Gillette Regain Its Voltage?" *Business Week,* 16 October 2000.

"Taking Flak: At Procter & Gamble Brands Face Pressure and So Do Executives." *Wall Street Journal,* 10 May 1993.

Taylor, Alex. "BMW and Mercedes." *Fortune,* 12 August 1991.

Toevs, Alden L. "Excellence in Planning and Budgeting: Creating an Effective Means to an End." *Bank Accounting and Finance,* Summer 1998.

Treacy, Michael, and Jim Sims. "Take Command of Your Growth." *Harvard Business Review* 82 (April 2004): 127–133.

"Uniting the Feudal Lords of Citicorp," *New York Times,* 16 January 1994.

"U.S. Multinationals See Strong 2005 Revenue Growth, PricewaterhouseCoopers' Management Barometer Finds." *PricewaterhouseCoopers Management Barometer,* 7 March 2005.

Whitehead, Don. *The Dow Story.* New York: McGraw Hill, 1968.

"Why Things are So Sour at Borden." *Business Week,* 22 November 1993.

Zook, Chris. *Beyond the Core: Expand Your Market without Abandoning Your Roots.* Boston: Harvard Business School Press, 2004.

———. *Unstoppable: Finding Hidden Assets to Renew the Core and Fuel Profitable Growth.* Boston: Harvard Business School Press, 2007.

Zook, Chris, and James Allen. "Growth outside the Core." *Harvard Business Review* 81 (December 2003): 66–73.

———. *Profit from the Core: Growth Strategy in an Era of Turbulence.* Boston: Harvard Business School Press, 2001.

Acknowledgments

It is difficult to convey how inadequate the cover of this book is to the task of recognizing all of those whose work and insight the book itself contains. *Stall Points* has been, at all stages, a team effort marked by extraordinary contribution and singleness of purpose. The book is also the product of the Corporate Executive Board and its global membership of executives. Our thanks go to the Executive Committee of the firm, which funded and patiently supported the work at every step, and to our past and present chairmen, Jay McGonigle and Tom Monahan.

The founder of the Corporate Executive Board, David Bradley, animated this enterprise with two core values that have endured intact across twenty-five years and that we consider pillars of our work: the Force of Ideas and the Spirit of Generosity. Both of these values were on stunning display in the Stall Points Initiative that it was our privilege to document in this book.

In fact, both were clearly present in the individual to whom we dedicate this book, George Bodway, former manager of Corporate Planning for Hewlett-Packard and a founding member of our Corporate

Strategy Board. In an early meeting of the Board, George shared his analysis of HP's unprecedented growth challenge in an earnest series of overhead foils and pen plots that charted the unknown waters into which his firm was then heading. He then invited our team to join the interdisciplinary group of academics, consultants, and practitioners that he convened in Palo Alto under the banner of The HP Growth Initiative. Characteristically, he agreed to allow us to share our findings with the Corporate Strategy Board membership at large, a generous gesture that immediately benefited hundreds of his peers around the world and made the present book possible. Among the staff we worked with at HP over the course of the Initiative, Jim Mackey deserves special mention for his deep engagement with the topic and support of the work.

On our side, we assembled what at the time and in retrospect amounted to a dream team. The team was led by two extraordinary individuals: Jerome Sorkin and Seth Verry. In his role as leader of the Corporate Strategy Board, Jerry was the architect of our approach to the work as well as our representative at round-table meetings of Initiative participants. While he has risen now to lead the Corporate Executive Board's development of a new growth platform, his formative influence on this work remains obvious, and his spirit and intelligence continue to form the heart of this enterprise.

Seth Verry was the day-to-day manager of the study team, which included such rising stars as Mark Little, Pat Spenner, and Joel Whitaker. In addition to his roles as manager and researcher, Seth was also the lead insight generator on the team. We well remember Seth chasing us down excitedly at the elevator bank at our Watergate offices in Washington, D.C., one late evening to share what would emerge as the core insight of this work. No one has engaged longer or been more absorbed by challenges to large corporate growth over the years than has Seth, who has presented and discussed this work with executive teams around the world. His knowledge of modern corporate history is encyclopedic, and his interest is insatiable.

When we resolved to publish this book, we made the decision to expand the research base from the original sample we drew for HP to include the entire historical roster of Fortune 100 companies, some six hundred companies since the index was created. We also expanded our coverage period to extend a full half-century, from 1956 through 2006. This of course requires good data tools, and we are indebted to Compustat for the quality of its database and the service provided by its staff. Even more than the tools, of course, an undertaking such as this requires analysts with equal gifts of quantitative acumen and business judgment. Here we were blessed by the presence on staff of Bernard Fallon and

Leslie Altizer. Bernard's centrality to this project can be summarized as follows: no number is final until Bernard says it's final, and any number that he says is final, is. Full stop. His rectitude in matters of methodology and data integrity is invaluable to the Corporate Executive Board, and his work for us introduced on too many late nights and weekends. Leslie extended his stay with our firm to see this project through, for which we give special thanks.

The team that reviewed stall case studies included the authors, Seth, Bernard, and two Executive Board veterans: Martha Piper, beloved of generations of our members and her fellow colleagues and now a partner with New Profit Inc., and Mark Little, now the senior director of operations and strategic business systems for Tessera North America. Martha and Mark also read drafts of the manuscript and offered thoughtful perspective. Karen Potter and Donna Stroka prepared and reviewed stall case studies and managed the flow of the project. Peter Buer read the entire manuscript twice through (a labor approaching love), offering guidance at the line-edit and managerial levels. To the invaluable Christina Borg fell the task of managing the authors, carving out (and protecting) blocks of time for us to write from the otherwise busy schedules of our day jobs in the enterprise. She also prepared the bibliography. But for her dedication, you would not be holding this book in your hands. Thank you, CEB.

Rounding out our internal roster, we must give prominence to the contributions of two extremely talented professionals. Thaddeus Verhoff designed and created the graphics in this book and patiently worked with us under deadlines that typically had no slack by the time we handed the baton to him. He told us at one point that "the work is its own reward." When you get to know Thad, you realize that he really believes this.

The other commendation here goes to Anita Feidler in our Information Resources Center. We can attest that she is literally un-stumpable: she can take the barest fragment of a quotation and return with a formal citation, no matter how obscure the journal or subject. She would be an asset to any organization, and we're grateful that she's on our team.

Finally, our thanks to those professional colleagues who offered us help and encouragement along the way. George Stalk of the Boston Consulting Group has been a true friend to us across this process, helping to lift out the insights contained in the work and sharing a veteran author's perspective on the publishing process. Clay Christensen of Harvard Business School invited us to present this work to his second-year MBA students in the "Managing Innovation" course and has been a constant source of inspiration to us.

Three founding members of our Corporate Strategy Board read the manuscript and offered thoughtful guidance. Jim Haymaker, vice president of strategy and business development at Cargill Corporation, brought deep historical perspective on the strategy function and on the increasing danger of stalls arising from accelerating rates of business model change. Dan Simpson, a vice president in the office of the chairman and CEO of The Clorox Company, helped us to see the work through the eyes of a first-time reader considering whether life was long enough to read yet another book on strategy. Dan Leemon, a charter member of the Corporate Strategy Board during his time as head of strategy for Schwab and now a member of our firm's board of directors, helped us to understand the very human reasons that executives have difficulty articulating, and challenging, the assumptions underlying their strategies.

The staff at Yale University Press have been very patient with this team of first-time authors. We are indebted to Michael O'Malley, whose back arched over lunch several years ago when we described the work we had done in this area. Alex Larson, an editorial assistant with the press, has handled his intermediary role with skill and grace. And Laura Jones Dooley, our manuscript editor, kindly endured our minor prevarications around deadlines and "finished copy" even as she polished the language and flow of the manuscript. Ericka Perry of our firm proofread the book.

As must be clear from our recounting of the expertise and dedication of all of those who have contributed to the work, any errors that remain in the final product were acts of omission or commission by the authors.

Index